to Canada, Britain, China, Denmark, Australia, and Germany. The impact of his teachings was registered on such intellects as Shaw, Tolstoy, Sun Yat-sen, and Woodrow Wilson. The power of his personality was so great that all men and women with whom he came into personal contact became devotees and disciples. His death, at the height of his second campaign for mayor of New York, brought to a dramatic close a career which had been devoted to changing the conditions which make for human misery and poverty.

This biography by his daughter is the story not only of the economic crusader and dazzling personality, but also of the Henry George who once spent a whole afternoon in a London cab going about trying to find someone to mend his small daughter's favorite doll; who would become so engrossed in making a speech that he would absently remove the cuffs from his shirt sleeves; who once went fearlessly into San Francisco's Chinatown and knocked down a huge Chinese laundryman who had insulted Mrs. George; who counted among his enthusiasms bicycling, ice cream, and a pet monkey.

This was the man who in 1880 set out with nothing in his carpetbag but his book of gospel, *Progress and Poverty*, and ended by shaking the world's economic thought. As one of his intimate friends wrote of him, "[His] was the courage which makes one a majority."

Anna George de Mille, author of this book, was Henry George's younger daughter. The introduction was written by his granddaughter, Agnes de Mille.

HENRY GEORGE

CITIZEN OF THE WORLD

Portrait of Henry George by George de Forest Brush.

(Courtesy of the Metropolitan Museum of Art)

HENRY GEORGE

CITIZEN OF THE WORLD

by

ANNA GEORGE de MILLE

Edited by

DON C. SHOEMAKER

With an Introduction by

AGNES de MILLE

THE UNIVERSITY OF NORTH CAROLINA PRESS

CHAPEL HILL

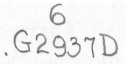

EDITOR'S FOREWORD

NNA GEORGE de MILLE was intensely proud of her
authorship of this biography of her father—as indeed she
had a right to be. She literally suffered through the slightest
changes made upon suggestion in the original manuscript and
she stood in dread and contempt of what she called "ghost
writers." Consequently, the form and spirit of her biography
have been preserved, for the editor was well aware of Mrs. de
Mille's wishes. He is indebted, and the author would also have
expressed that indebtedness, to many persons too numerous to
mention here for their assistance in at last bringing this account
of the life of Henry George into print. Among those to whom
special acknowledgement should be made are: Mrs. Louis F.
Post; Mr. Lawson Purdy (one of Henry George's few surviving
intimates, whose memory of some events has been checked
against the manuscript); the late Lord Josiah Wedgewood;
Mr. Will Lissner of the *New York Times;* Mr. Robert Clancy,
executive director of the Henry George School; the *Henry
George News; The American Journal of Economics and Sociology,* in which portions of the biography have appeared; the
Robert Schalkenbach Foundation; and the faithful keepers of
the Henry George Collection in the New York Public Library.
The kind help of these persons and institutions from time to
time has made possible the publication of this book.

DON C. SHOEMAKER

v

INTRODUCTION

ANNA GEORGE de MILLE

A NOTE ABOUT THE AUTHOR

by AGNES de MILLE

THE MOST astonishing aspect of the Henry George legend was his effect on all people with whom he came into personal contact. Without exception everyone, man or woman, was overwhelmed. He seemed to command a power, particularly in his later years, that was almost mystic. Men did not merely admire, they worshipped. I have met people who differed from his theories; I have yet to meet anyone who heard him speak or who knew him and was not dazzled. They became disciples, followers, and heralds, or in the case of his avowed political enemies, reluctant admirers. Today, fifty years after his death, old men's eyes fill with tears at the mention of his name, and I, the granddaughter, have been asked to take off my hat so that the shape of my head could be studied. If strangers could be moved to such immoderation, how should a daughter born and reared in the aura of this blazing personality set herself to tell the story with historical coolness?

She was aware of the hazard. With humbleness, with industry, with watchfulness lest she betray her purpose by any weakening exuberance, she tried to tell the facts. She was afraid that her relationship would discredit the argument. She did not realize that her relationship was her contribution, and that the overtone of faith that rings through every sentence gives the work its fervor and true meaning. She thought to safeguard her impersonal approach with little subterfuges and masquerades like the enchantingly naive paragraph on page 198 in which she says it was an accident that all of George's children adopted his ideas; indeed, a son of Gandhi would have had as fair a chance of turning militarist as a young George of embracing high tariff protectionism.

In her effort at discipline she all but obliterated herself from the tale. She neglected, for instance, to note the fact of her birth, and the date had to be inserted by her editors. More remarkably, she very nearly eliminated her own mother in a kind of biographical suttee. Mrs. George was by all indications a woman of unusual strength and nobility, but, although she was my mother's constant companion, a real paucity of incident illustrates her memory. One gathers what she was by reflection in her husband's life and through his letters. It is in the family traditions, however, and in my mother's character that one must look for the fantasy and liveliness of spirit that I believe were hers. Henry George had heartiness, but his wife had drollery, caprice, and the delicate conceits to make all family occurrences festivals of charming invention. It was she who danced like a sprite and loved music for its own sake; he believed all art should serve a moral purpose. It was she who thought the graces of life worth time and energy, as it was only she, of course, who had the time to foster them. The decorated chair and crown of wild flowers at a birthday breakfast; the crèche at Christmas time; the puddings and black fruitcake started weeks before with all the household and neighbor girls sitting around the dining table cutting fruit, and later, when the mixing got too heavy for a woman all the neighbor boys commandeered to help; the jam and preserves in the summer; the bag of crushed grapes hanging by the kitchen door dripping purple juice into the pan below while the late bees buzzed; the fine sewing and embroidery with silks; the incredible doll's clothes made as exactly as her own reception gowns; the chic and wit of the hats with holes for Teddy-bear ears; the frock coats with holes for tails; the tiny picture books one inch square, fashioned for very little hands; and the wisdom to establish and insist on daily ritualistic courtesies so that reconciliation would have easy patterns to follow after times of anger—these were my mother's household magics. I presume they were Annie Fox's.

I imagine also that my mother's zany humor, a kind of wild impertinence, stems from her mother. When quite exhausted with respectfulness and high moral tone mother's childish candor would rip through proceedings and shock her strongly-schooled conscience with its vitality and arbitrary freshness. The women's humor was the balance wheel to George's indefatigable ardor. This was the background of starch and needles and teakettles and family jokes that made it possible for him to take on the large and thankless job of persuading mankind to live differently from the way it had grown accustomed to.

The women's basic characteristic was, of course, their courage. They could not be beaten down or disheartened. In this they matched George himself, and in their passion for doing what was right, and in their ebullient enthusiasm for all sincere projects, great or trivial. Avowed high-mindedness has gone out of style these days. People are reluctant to speak of moral purpose lest they be considered smug. But my mother came of a stock that believed with the heart and acted accordingly and cared not a fig for opinion. This becomes apparent throughout the book. What is less emphasized is the enchanting sweetness and sprightliness of manner which was also part of the background. Perhaps she was not aware of it. Its first expression being the lovely evanescence of daily practices and an essential of her own nature, she may very likely have taken it for granted. Furthermore, I think she would have considered it disrespectful to her father's importance. But I believe any just picture of Henry George's life must take into account the room next to his study where women's laughter came low over their sewing and the sound of the Irish maids singing as they dusted.

George always acknowledged his women's role in his life. But they with devout feminine adoration lowered their faces, and drew their skirts about them and tried not to obtrude.

Born when George was thirty-eight, ten years younger than the next oldest child, my mother, Anna Angela George, was the petted baby in a family which revolved entirely around the father, a man who had become already a world figure. From birth she saw great men hat in hand in their modest parlor. When she was barely three the family made a trip to the British Isles that shook the economic structure of that country. When she was in her teens she watched him grapple with every powerful political figure in his country. When she was twenty he died, a martyr to his cause, and was given by the citizens of New York a hero's funeral. Her life was stamped with this sacrifice.

Like all George women she believed her activities valid only in service to others, but above all in service to her father's cause. She formed clubs, went on lecture tours, served as trustee for the Henry George schools, laid wreaths on public monuments, attended conferences and banquets all over Europe and the United States, did all manner of exhausting and wearying services, and talked and talked to whomever would listen, the plumber, the cook, the distinguished foreign visitor, the traffic cop who had thought simply to give her a parking-ticket, customs officials certainly, tax advisors above all, and most wonderfully certain Shubert chorus girls who found themselves in my employ and therefore inadvertently within the orbit of her attack. Every handbag contained a pamphlet, and every pocket. Desks and cupboards and suitcases bulged with them. Her correspondence was enormous, carried on without a secretary, mostly in longhand and embracing hundreds of people from Mahatma Gandhi, Einstein, and Lord Wedgewood to the daughter of a secretary who had worked for George's newspaper in San Francisco. Was she a crank? Of course she was. Great ideas are borne forward by just such. The apostles were not exactly half-convinced. She believed her father was the greatest man she had ever met, and he probably was. She believed the world would go to ruin if it did not pay heed, and it all but has, exactly as he said it would.

She commenced writing the life of her father about eighteen years ago. Not being a trained writer, she found the work laborious; not being a scholar with a technique for collecting and annotating facts, she found the research slow. Furthermore she was discouraged by the continuing indifference of publishers. George's memory had dimmed, and he who had once been far better known than Karl Marx was no longer considered a burning political issue. But she persisted in spite of dreadful setbacks. Discouragement was not in the family tradition. Had not her father been beaten down again and again? Had he not ultimately died fighting?

Her health failed. She continued her researches staggering up to the Public Library and back with a heart that stitched her ribs together with pain. She continued writing far into the nights though she fainted and vomited with weakness. Why did we not stop her? This was all she lived for. This was her purpose. The flame burned white-hot. We could not tamper with it.

By 1947, the book was in reality all but completed. During the last months she had been in correspondence with Don C. Shoemaker, the young editor of *The Asheville Citizen*. He offered his services to help in the final editing. She urged haste.

We begged her to pause, to spare herself. But she knew her time was measured.

Mr. Shoemaker had made his first corrections and returned the manuscript to her, and she was in agreement with all suggested changes. He knew her intimately, knew her idiom of speech and her point of view. And he had taken scrupulous care not to alter either. He also, being a distant relative, (his grandmother was George's sister Chloe) was well acquainted with the background of the story.

Her last enterprise was a tour through the Negro colleges of the South lecturing on her father's work. She stayed in residence wherever she spoke and she was one of the first white women to do so. But a week after her return she collapsed with a stroke. She was carried to the hospital with a paralyzed throat. The manuscript went with her. All but blind and barely able to hold a pen she asked to have the book propped on her chest. The feel of the paper as she turned the pages seemed to bring reassurance. The last time I heard her voice was an order on the telephone for research material. "Bring me," came the dark whisper, "the English reform laws of 1884." That afternoon five hours before she died came a letter from The University of North Carolina Press saying they would publish. She read it and understood it. It lay in the last moment under her hand on the counterpane.

When Henry George, Jr., after his father's death visited Tolstoy the ailing venerable man said, "I shall see your father before you do. What shall I tell him?"

"Tell him," said young George, "I kept the faith."

We laid Anna George by her brother's side, and this message is on the stone above them.

She was very small with piercing blue eyes, red hair, and an impertinent tongue. She would and did lay down her life for what she believed in. She talked gay nonsense. She was quite capable of embracing heroism, but casually in a household way and deprecating its importance. She considered her final crisis an inconvenience. She wished to live to finish the book; failing this, she hoped her death would be unobtrusive and no burden to the family. She left exact instructions that it should not be.

I remember her with shining eyes, her curly hair unruly beneath her hat, standing tip-toe in size-one shoes and lifting her head gaily to George Bernard Shaw in the middle of a howling group of reporters. She had always wished to meet him, and, after hearing the astonishing tribute he had paid her father's memory in the only speech of his last American trip, she faced him, shaken to the core with excitement. Tears stood in her eyes and she trembled.

"You mentioned Henry George in your speech last night. I am his daughter."

"You're better looking than he was."

"I have more hair."

"Have you also his beautiful hands?"

"Alas, no."

"Have you inherited his great gift for speaking?"

Her face transfigured with pride and devoted memory, she replied, "All I have inherited from my father is his love for ice cream."

Shaw saw the look in her eyes, heard the childish words, and was silent. He bowed, laughing, over her hand.

This book stands as testimony that on this one occasion she spoke far less than the truth.

CONTENTS

ILLUSTRATIONS

HENRY GEORGE

CITIZEN OF THE WORLD

CHAPTER I

HENRY GEORGE: AN INTRODUCTION

O N JULY 9, 1881, Alfred Russell Wallace, the British naturalist, wrote to his friend, Charles Darwin, from Godalming:

> I am just doing what I have rarely if ever done before—reading a book through a second time immediately after the first perusal. I do not think I have ever been so attracted by a book, with the exception of your *Origin of Species* and Spencer's *First Principles* and *Social Statics*. I wish therefore to call your attention to it, in case you care about books on social and political subjects, but here there is also an elaborate discussion of Malthus's "Principles of Population," to which both you and I have acknowledged ourselves indebted. The present writer, Mr. George, while admitting the main principle as self-evident and as actually operating in the case of animals and plants, denies that it ever has operated in the case of man, still less that it has any bearing whatever on the rest of social and political questions which have been supported by a reference to it. He illustrates and supports his views with a wealth of illustrative facts and a cogency of argument which I have rarely seen equalled, while his style is equal to that of Buckle, and thus his book is delightful reading. The title of the book is *Progress and Poverty*. It is the most startling, novel and original book of the last twenty years, and if I mistake not will in the future rank as making an advance in political and social science equal to that made by Adam Smith a century ago.

Darwin died less than a year later without recording whether he had read Henry George's book. But very many others read it. "Henry George," wrote John A. Hobson in 1897, "may be considered to have exercised a more directly powerful influence over English radicalism of the last fifteen years than any other man."

1

Henry George left school in his native city of Philadelphia at the age of fourteen, but he continued his education before the mast, at the printer's case, and at the editor's desk. His economic thinking was based on his belief in individualism and in the philosophy of freedom. Although he had conceded the ideal of Socialism to be "grand and noble" and "possible of realization," he believed it "evident that whatever savors of regulation and restriction is in itself bad and should not be resorted to if any other mode of accomplishing the same end present itself." In order to meet the problem of mass unemployment, he wrote, "it is not necessary to nationalize capital, as the Socialists would have us do, nor yet to coax employers to benevolently give a larger share of their earnings to their workmen."

And yet, paradoxically, it was George who gave the impetus to the British Socialist movement which grew out of the Fabian Society. Sidney Webb pointed out: "Little as Henry George intended it, there can be no doubt that it was the enormous circulation of his *Progress and Poverty* which gave the touch that caused all seething influence to crystallize into a popular Socialist movement. The optimistic and confident tone of the book, and the irresistible force of its popularization of Ricardo's Law of Rent sounded the dominant 'note' of the English Socialist party of today."

George Bernard Shaw was even more emphatic in acknowledging the debt which he felt the Fabians owed George: "My attention was first drawn to political economy as a science of social salvation by Henry George's eloquence and his *Progress and Poverty*, which had an enormous circulation in the early 'eighties, and beyond all question had more to do with the Socialist revival of that period in England than any other book."

And he added, "When I was swept into the great Socialist revival of 1883, I found that five sixths of those who were swept in with me had been converted by Henry George."

The first volume of *Das Kapital* had appeared in 1867, twelve years before the publication of *Progress and Poverty*. But evidently it did not receive much attention until the latter work began to make people curious about economics and economic theory. For George's book, said H. Russell Tiltman, "dominated the minds of the Radical wing of the Liberal party just as it galvanized into action those who had been groping toward a Socialist commonwealth. It even achieved the undoubted feat of making Karl Marx a popular author, for chapters of *Das Kapital* were published and read as sequels of *Progress and Poverty*."

Half a century later Philip Snowden, Chancellor of the Exchequer, introduced in Parliament the Finance Act of 1931, invoking the spirit, the name, and even the words of Henry George with this sentence which concluded the Budget Debate: "The principle underlying this bill is to assert the right of the community to the ownership of the land."

George's influence touched not only Great Britain. It may be traced, in varying degree, to Australasia, China, Western Canada, Denmark, Germany, and of course his own United States. The actual teaching of Georgist principles was first introduced on a wide scale in Denmark, which has adopted national land value taxation and where George's economic theories have taken deepest root.

In America the Georgist movement is largely sustained by the Henry George School in New York, founded in 1932, and its twenty-four branch schools in other large cities, and by publications in this country and abroad, including the publishing enterprises of the Robert Schalkenbach Foundation, which was endowed for the purpose of disseminating Georgist literature. The Henry George School claims students in every county of the United States and in every country of the world.

In his lifetime and afterward, George's influence on leading personalities was profound. The so-called Progressive movement of the early part of the century owed much to his writings and to the memory of his inspiriting personality. To the names which will be found in this book, many others might be added —names of men who were affected in some way by George's teachings and who acknowledged directly or indirectly their debt.

For example, Sun Yat-sen, the father of the Chinese republic, said of the American economist, "I intend to devote my future to the promotion of the welfare of the Chinese people as a people. The teachings of Henry George will be the basis of our program of reform."

The immense impact of George's teachings was registered on other great intellects. Wrote Leo Tolstoy, after reading *Progress and Poverty*, "People do not argue with the teaching of George; they simply do not know it. He who becomes acquainted with it cannot but agree."

In our own time, Aldous Huxley wrote in the foreword to *Brave New World,* "If I were now to rewrite the book, I would offer a third alternative ... the possibility of sanity.... Economics would be decentralist and Henry-Georgian."

And Woodrow Wilson, the consummate scholar of government, put it this way, "The country needs a new and sincere thought in politics, coherently, distinctly and boldly uttered by men who are sure of their ground. The power of men like Henry George seems to me to mean that."

YOUNG GEORGE

H ENRY GEORGE was born in Philadelphia in 1839. In
that year, as today, Philadelphia was the third largest
city in the United States, yielding then only to New York and
to Baltimore in population. Only thirty-nine years before, it
had conceded its place as capital to the new city of Washington on the banks of the Potomac.

A compact settlement, built on the banks of the Schuylkill
and Delaware rivers, Philadelphia had ready access to the
ocean and its port abounded in shipping from all parts of the
world. In the year of Henry George's birth, Philadelphia
boasted the United States Mint, the United States Navy Yard,
and the United States Marine Hospital, as well as the first and
most extensively used library (founded by Benjamin Franklin
in 1731) in the Western Hemisphere. Philadelphia had art
galleries and museums, three big theaters, an abundance of
churches, and the New Alms House which was "the most perfect of its kind in the country." [1]

The architecture of the town was marked with the Quaker
severity of William Penn and the houses where some 258,000
Philadelphians lived were, for the most part, monotonous red
brick, with low white marble front steps. They bordered brick
sidewalks on narrow cobblestone streets, lined with trees. In
one of these regulation Philadelphia houses—smaller than the
two flanking it—on Tenth Street south of Pine,[2] lived a publisher
of church and Sunday School books, Richard Samuel Henry
George, with his wife and tiny daughter and his sister-in-law,
Mary Vallance.

The George home was comfortable though small. It was
pleasantly furnished according to the style of the time in
mahogany upholstered in fashionable black horsehair. On the
walls hung family portraits, a few engravings and needlework

pictures of scenes from Shakespeare. The large, heavily-bound family Bible, standing on a pedestal table, occupied a prominent place in the parlor. It was a typical middle-class home of the early and middle 1800's.

Into this setting on the second day of September, 1839, arrived a boy—strong, husky, and blue-eyed—who in due course was taken to St. Paul's Protestant Episcopal Church,[3] by his father, a vestryman, and there baptized "Henry."

Henry George's father, the son of a sea captain, was born in New Brunswick, New Jersey. After one sea voyage, however, he had settled in Philadelphia. There he took a clerical post in the Customs House. He had married Miss Louisa Lewis, who bore him two sons. But wife and children had died, leaving him with a young adopted daughter whom he placed in a small private school conducted by Catherine and Mary Vallance.

John Vallance, the father of these two young schoolmistresses,[4] was born in Glasgow, Scotland, and had been brought to Philadelphia as an infant. There he later married Margaret Pratt, granddaughter of the goldsmith Henry Pratt,[5] who was a friend of Benjamin Franklin and a member of his *Junta*. Margaret Pratt's uncle, Matthew Pratt, the painter,[6] had made Franklin's first portrait. John Vallance, well known as an engraver of portraits and encyclopedia plates, was one of the founders of the Association of Artists in America.[7] When he died in 1823 two of his daughters turned to teaching. It was in their school that Richard S. H. George wooed and won Catherine Pratt Vallance.

Caroline Latimer George was the first child of this marriage; she was followed by Henry, Jane Vallance, and Catherine Pratt George. As the family grew (there were ten children, eight of whom lived) with the addition of Thomas Latimer, John Vallance, Chloe Pratt, and Morris Reid George, they moved from the small house on Tenth Street to a larger one at Third and Queen. Aunt Mary Vallance—"one of those sweet and patient souls who, in narrow circles, live radiant lives"[8]—continued to make her home with them and acted as the children's second mother.

Before he met Catherine Vallance, Mr. George had left the Customs House and had gone into the business of publishing books for the Protestant Episcopal church. For a time he maintained a bookstore at Fifth and Chestnut Streets. He was a progressive man, even to the extent of having illuminating gas installed in his house although friends and neighbors feared it meant inviting sudden death.

Richard S. H. George was a Democrat in politics, in which he took a lively interest as a spectator. Conservative in religion, he began each day with a reading of the Bible to his family. The Sabbath was dedicated to austere devotion, and the family attended service morning, afternoon, and frequently evening. Through the Philadelphia streets, the quiet broken by the intermittent beat of horses' hoofs on the cobblestones, the red-headed, blue-eyed Georges marched along the narrow brick pavements, Henry leading with Jane or Caroline; then the other brothers and sisters who were big enough to walk, followed by the adult members. The boys were clad in long trousers and pea jackets with broad white collars; the girls in wide skirts and pantalettes that reached down to their ankles; Mrs. George and Miss Vallance in close-fitting bonnets and with long, dark shawls draped over their voluminous hoops. All carried prayer books.[9]

Trim, neat, decorous, they walked two by two. This formality had proved its uses on occasion. One Sunday John Vallance, wearing the white trousers that had been made from a pair belonging to his Uncle Thomas Latimer, eluded his watchful older sisters. Just before starting time, he slid down a neighbor's cellar door wet with a fresh coat of green paint. Since nothing but tragic illness or sudden death could keep the George family from church, an accident like this called only for re-forming of ranks. On that Sunday, John Vallance hid in the cellar while the children marched to church in closer formation.[10]

Life for the Georges was pleasant and simple. All the children who were big enough helped with the housework even though the family kept a "hired girl." They depended on themselves for their amusements. As strict church members, cards, dancing, and theater-going were denied them. They lacked the luxury of a family piano and knew little of music, but there was much reading and discussion of books—history, travel, and poetry.

In a family of eight children there was always something to do together. In winter they went sledding and skating. In the summer they paid occasional visits to "Lemon Hill" and its tropical garden belonging to Henry Pratt, Grandmother Vallance's cousin.[11] One or the other of the rivers afforded boating, and, in

hot weather, swimming. (The elder George once saved Henry
from drowning; once Henry himself rescued his brother Tom.)
But the best times for Henry were the trips to the docks where
Mr. George instructed his eldest son in the lore of the sea as
it had been taught him by his father, Captain Richard George.

Henry loved to revive his father's memories of older days.
Mr. George would begin:

"Your grandfather Captain Richard George was born in York-
shire, England. He came young to this country and married
Mary Reid of Philadelphia (the Reids had been here for several
generations). He had two ships.

"I cannot remember dates but I do remember Aaron Burr.
There was such a fuss about him during his arrest that I used to
go to Market and Twelfth or Thirteenth Streets almost every
day to see the soldiers keeping guard, pacing the pavement.
Although I was a mere brat of a boy, I took a notion that if I
could not see Burr I would sit in his carriage.

"There was a good, kind old gentleman named Barkley who
had been one of our most wealthy merchants but 'ruined by the
times.' Burr used often to visit him—so I watched and one day
he drove up to Mr. Barkley's door and I saw him pass in. I
approached the coachman and asked if I could take a seat for a
few moments. To my surprise he consented; he opened the door
and I entered and sat there about ten minutes. I thought it a
great triumph. So much for my determined curiosity. I used to
brag about it to the boys and got many a bloody nose."

The boy was fascinated by his father's experiences:

"Although times were hard, I didn't feel them. I had a pleasant, happy home, let me tell you. We had four 'prentice boys
and two girls in the kitchen, all in good tune and happy.

"One time father arrived at Almond Street wharf from
France, where he'd gone with a flag of truce, carrying out pas-
sengers and bringing back a lot, including General Jean Victor
Moreau, the Republican French general who was exiled because of Napoleon's jealousy. I took on board lots of provisions
for them. It was hard work—the crowd was so dense. Going so
often to the ship, I found I was as much noticed as the General
himself. The boys crowded me hard and one fight I had built
me right up, and afterwards I was A. No. 1 among the boys and
cock of the walk. I went on the principle of 'Do nothing you are
ashamed of and let no living man impose on you.' " [12]

Henry learned his three R's from his mother and Aunt Mary

Vallance but his years of actual schooling were spent at a small private institution conducted by Mrs. Graham and at Mount Vernon Grammar before he went to the Episcopal Academy. At the Academy he had for fellow students a fine group of lads,[13] among them Bishop Alonzo Potter's two sons, Henry Codman, who later was to become bishop of New York, and Eliphalet Nott, who became president of Union College. Two other close friends were the sons of the Rector of St. Paul's—Heber [14] and Wilberforce Newton,[15] with whom Henry George often played. It was great fun, for the Newtons frequently had missionaries visit them, missionaries who brought pets, "monkeys and other beasts of the tropical clime." Then, too, the Newtons lived conveniently close to the Sunday School, and Sunday School banners could be used in the children's games. The banner with the picture of St. Paul preaching at Ephesus repeatedly figured in the game of "firemen's parade," Henry of course as leader, bearing it proudly aloft.

Because his father was a publisher of church books, young Henry George was carried through the Episcopal Academy on a reduced tuition. But when the book publishing business became unremunerative and Richard S. H. George had to return to his old job at the Customs House, the boy believed himself no longer entitled to the special tuitional reduction and begged to be taken out of school. He was so earnest about it that his father let him leave the Academy and put him under the celebrated tutor Henry T. Lauderbach, from whom the boy received sound training in methodical study. Thus, when he entered high school at the age of thirteen, he was able to make extraordinary progress.[16]

Regular attendance at church and daily reading of the Bible gave young Henry an excellent grounding in the Scriptures. But it was his mother's passion for quoting poetry and his conversations with sailors on the docks and the stories brought by missionaries to his father's house which did most to stimulate the boy's already active imagination. This education was supplemented by books constantly borrowed from the public library, though some of them—novels, for instance—had to be smuggled up to his little room and devoured in secret. But the greatest educational influence was the Franklin Institute.[17]

The prospectus of that organization read: "Without going into the history and internal arrangement of the Institute, it will be sufficient for us to say that it affords to any respectable person, who chooses to become a member, the privilege of hearing, with his family and apprentices, for a very moderate fee, excellent courses of lectures on natural history, philosophy, chemistry and other scientific and literary subjects." Through his Uncle Thomas Latimer, who was a member of the Institute, Henry had the privilege of hearing the "excellent courses of lectures."

The Customs House job paid Mr. George only eight hundred dollars a year—scant money, even in 1852, for a man with a family.[18] And Henry, sensitive to the family's straitened finances, felt that as the oldest son he should at least earn his own keep. He loved school but after five months he persuaded his parents to let him leave and go to work. He was not yet fourteen.

Henry George scoured Philadelphia for a job. At length he found one—wrapping packages and running errands for a china and glass shop. It was a trying occupation for a boy. Although for years there had been strong public sentiment for a ten-hour day, it had not yet come into effect. The hours were long; the pay was short—only two dollars a week. The job gave Henry no time for trips to the wharves unless he could manage a detour that way while on one of his errands. The love of the sea was strong within him. He managed to find time to observe the weather regularly and to keep a diary with notations of winds and temperatures.[19] At night he made model brigs, but he had small chance to sail them; during the daylight hours he was working, and of course one didn't sail toy boats on Sunday. Altogether the new job in the china shop was not very satisfactory. As soon as he could manage to leave, the boy took a new position as clerk in the office of a marine adjuster.

This was less fatiguing. Moreover, the atmosphere of the shipping business was pleasant. But the work soon became dull and the lad grew increasingly anxious to get out of this constricted life into the great world of his dreams.

Henry George's father was a wise and observant man. He noticed his son's restlessness and became apprehensive lest the lad be tempted to run away from home. So, putting aside his own parental fears and yearnings, he decided to place the boy in the charge of a young friend, Captain Sam Miller of the ship *Hindoo,*[20] and send him on a cruise. He hoped to cure Henry, once and for all, of his desire for a life at sea.

CHAPTER III

THE SAILOR AND HIS VOYAGES

THERE WAS excitement among Henry George's relatives and friends, for it was no small hazard in 1855 to circle the globe. To the George family it was the first break in their tight little circle. Now, at the age of fifteen, Henry was putting childhood abruptly behind him.

Small for his age, with disproportionately small hands and feet and a complexion delicate as a girl's he looked ill-equipped for the rough life of the sea as he stood at the corner, his red hair gleaming in the sunlight, waving his cap in a last good-by. Gripping tighter the gifts he carried, a new Bible presented by St. Paul's Sunday School [1] and James' *Anxious Enquirer*, [2] a present from Cousin George Latimer, he turned quickly and joined his chattering escort. His father was there, and so were Uncles Thomas Latimer and Joseph Van Dusen [3] and a group of young friends who carried his sea kit. All of them went with him as far as Market Street wharf [4] where they delivered him to Captain Miller. The youthful sea captain and the boy boarded a steamboat and crossed the Delaware River to New Jersey, where they took a train for New York.

It was the first great adventure for the lad who had never been more than a stone's throw from home. A few days later he wrote from New York, "I signed the shipping articles at $6 a mongth [sic] and two mongths' advance, which I got this morning...." [5]

During his eight days waiting in New York harbor he had a chance to see something of a city greater even than Philadelphia in size. He was much impressed by New York's "business and bustle," and he wrote his family, "The upper part is a beautiful place—the streets wide and clear and regular and the houses all of brown stone and standing ten or twenty feet from the pavement, with gardens in front." [6]

11

The *Hindoo* was delayed in getting to sea because of the scarcity of sailors. Some who applied were so inefficient that Henry had to be sent aloft to do the slushing down of the masts. On April 7, the ship was towed downstream by a steamboat. Off the Battery she dropped anchor. Henry wrote home to Philadelphia:

The view from this spot is beautiful—the North river and New York bay covered with sailing vessels and steamers of every class and size, while back, the hills, are covered with country seats. I saw at one time four of the largest class ocean steamers going down the bay at once, while ships, barques, brigs and schooners are all the time going in and out. . . . I ate my first meal sailor style today and did not dislike it at all. Working around in the open gives one such an appetite that he can eat almost anything.[7]

Three days later the *Hindoo,* a 586-ton, full-rigged ship—large for her day—laden with lumber and carrying a crew of twenty, set sail for Australia.

It had been agreed between Mr. George and Captain Miller that Henry was to be treated like any other seaman. The boy soon learned how others lived and he appreciated the comfortable home he had left. To the end of his life he was to remember "how sweet hard-tack, munched in the middle watch while the sails slept in the tradewind had tasted; what a dish for a prince was seapie on the rare occasions when a pig had been killed or a porpoise harpooned; and how good was the plum-duff that came to the forecastle only on Sundays and great holidays." [8]

Once he said to a sailor, "I wish I were home to get a piece of pie." His companion, a Yorkshireman, asked quietly, "Are you sure you would find a piece of pie there?" His expression and the note of reproof in his voice so shamed the boy that long years later he wrote of the incident: " 'Home' was associated in my mind with pie of some sort—apple or peach or sweet potato or cranberry or mince—to be had for the taking, and I did not for the moment realize that in many homes pie was as rare a luxury as plums in our sea-duff." [9]

The trip also introduced him to the tyrannical powers that the navigation laws conferred on a master of a ship. For although Sam Miller was a good man, he, like every other captain, had command of and absolute control over the poorly fed, ill-paid men sailing under him. For he was at once employer and judge.[10] This experience made Henry George a lifelong advocate of sailors' rights.

It was August 24, 1855, when the crew of the *Hindoo* first sighted Australia. They were 137 days out of New York. The ship hove to in Hobson's Bay, near Melbourne, and spent a month unloading and reloading cargo, taking in ballast and changing crew members. From Melbourne it sailed to India and up the Hooghly branch of the Ganges to Calcutta in less than ten weeks, arriving there on December 4. Henry George had seen a little of Australia during a period when times were hard and thousands were out of work. Now he had a chance to see a little of India—its extremes of riches and poverty,[11] its beauty and squalor, its negligence of its people. "The very carrion birds," he remembered years later, "are more sacred than human life."

It was not until December 10, eight months after he had sailed from New York, that he received the first letters from home.[12] His sister Jennie wrote from Philadelphia, "Hearing that a ship was going to sail in a few days we thought we would write the first opportunity. The flowers are coming up beautifully. Your rose bush has got any quantity of buds and they are quite large."[13] One of his young friends known as "Dicky Doubter" addressed him as "Dear Mackerel" and wrote him gossip of their cronies (nicknamed "Soda Ash" and "Sea Dog," respectively), and closed his letter a trifle lugubriously with, "I hope God will protect you through all the dangers of the sea. Good-bye. It may not be in this world that we meet but I hope it will be above."[14]

Henry's parents evidently took the separation cheerfully though not without some qualms. The elder George wrote:

The parting with you was much harder for your mother and myself than I at first supposed it would be. . . . You have our prayers, morning and evening, for your safety, health and prosperous voyage, which may God in His goodness vouchsafe to hear and answer, returning you in health and safety to your home. . . . Your little brig [15] is safely moored on the mantelpiece. First thing when we wake, our eyes rest on her, and she reminds us of our dear sailor boy. When you get home no doubt she will look as rusty as your own ship, and will want a thorough overhauling.[16]

The voyager's letters home were written with care but the spelling was abominable. And they were little more than sea logs. This must have disappointed the family back home in Philadelphia, waiting anxiously for personal news.

We crossed the line November 5 when 42 days out. Here we were fortunate as not to experience much of that wet calm and squally weather so peculiar to the line. From this place until we arrived at about 10° North we had the same fair airs as on the other side of the line, with every prospect of a short passage. Then the wind became stronger and more variable, but dead ahead. She [the *Hindoo*] would often head on one tack E.S.E. and on tacking ship, instead of heading N.N.W. as she ought to do, she would not lay higher than W. Progress under the circumstances was impossible, and for over a week we did not gain a single inch to the northward.[17]

But the boy, now sixteen years old, penciled some notes—badly punctuated and poorly spelled—on the back pages of his sea journal recording his impressions of Calcutta and the Ganges. They foreshadowed a literary style which was to come into flower later:

The river, at times very broad and again contracting its stream into a channel hardly large enough for a ship of average size to turn in, was bordered by small native villages, surrounded by large fruit trees, through which the little bamboo huts peeped. As we advanced the mists which had hitherto hung over the river cleared away, affording a more extensive prospect. The water was covered with boats of all sizes, very queer to the eye of an American. They were most of them bound to Calcutta with the produce and rude manufacture of the country—bricks, tiles, earths, pots, etc. They were pulled by from four to ten men, and steered by an old fellow wrapped up in a sort of cloth, seated on a high platform at the stern. Some had sails to help them along, in which there were more holes than threads. On the banks the natives began to go to their daily toil, some driving cattle along, others loading boats with grain, while the women seemed busy with their domestic tasks. As we approached the city, the banks on both sides were lined with handsome country residences of wealthy English. At about 10 A.M. we came to Garden Reach. The river which here takes a sudden bend, was crowded with ships of all nations, and above nothing could be seen but a forest of masts.[18]

On January 15, the *Hindoo* started down the Hooghly with a cargo of some twelve hundred tons of rice, seeds, etc., and with a new crew. Henry George was provoked by the fact that it took "over two weeks getting down a river eighty miles long." [19]

The cook became ill and died on the trip home. Henry had to do a turn in the galley for about a week. He hated it. The days seemed long and monotonous. However, a pet monkey he had bought in Calcutta did much to relieve the boredom of the voyage. The animal was also of great service in keeping roaches off his face as he slept and off his food as he ate. [20]

On June 14, 1856, after an absence of one year and sixty-five days, the *Hindoo* again anchored in New York harbor. With fourteen months' pay (about fifty dollars) in his pocket, Henry George took a train to Philadelphia.

The boy who returned home was very different from the boy who had sailed away to see the world. He was broader of shoulder and more self-reliant. Though he was only seventeen years old he seemed much older. His white skin, burned by wind and sun, made his eyes seem bluer. His red hair had grown darker. On his shoulder, sailor-fashion, perched his little pet monkey. The creature seemed to resent the affectionate greeting given her master. Her intense jealousy was focused principally on his small brother Morris, and to Henry's regret the monkey had to be given to a friend who had no young children.

The homecoming had its rich rewards. Henry could regale his family and his former playmates with tales of foreign places, with descriptions of storms at sea and of strange and different peoples, and with his knowledge of every kind of boat afloat— barks and brigs and barkentines and brigantines and ships and schooners and sloops. He knew every part of the rigging on each of them. The children delighted in giving him a piece of string and watching his small, skilled, but now calloused, hands tie difficult sailor's knots. He could box the compass with a speed that made his words nearly indistinguishable. And above all else the children loved to hear him sing chanties, learned at sea, in his high, off-pitch voice.

To the children's regret, however, Henry's older friends and acquaintances demanded much of his time—Jo Jeffreys in particular.

The boys made their headquarters in Henry's little room with the narrow bed in the corner, the small case of books on the bureau, and the sea chest on the floor against the wall. [21] In the dim gas light that could be coaxed into brightness only on occasion, they would sit and smoke and discuss all things in heaven and earth.

But these were the leisure hours. Mr. George had found Henry a place in a printing house in an effort to keep him ashore. There the boy first learned to set type. Working at the case helped to broaden his education. He learned to spell correctly and he absorbed much general information from the material he set in type and from association and discussion with others in the print shop. He made it a practice to appeal to the men around him for accurate information about historical and political dates and facts.[22]

One day, while setting type as an apprentice, the first puzzling question of political economy came to the boy. An old printer pointed out that wages were low in the old countries and higher in the new ones. It seems strangely contradictory that where population and progress were centered and where industrialization was heaviest, wages should be lower than in new, sparsely settled places.[23] He gave long thought to this anomaly.

But the topical affairs of the nation also absorbed Henry George's interest. He became an ardent abolitionist and frequently argued the matter with his parents. His father, being a loyal Democrat, supported Buchanan. His mother reminded him that the Scriptures seemed to sanction slavery. She was convinced that the tales of cruelty to slaves were exaggerated and that the majority of slaveowners were the same sort of "humanely disposed people" as herself.

However, the boy was already beginning to understand some of the connotations of the word "property." He contended hotly against what the owners "could do" since "if slaves were property, their masters, having the right to do what they please with their own property, could ill-treat and even kill them if so disposed." [24]

With his friends, he formed "The Lawrence Literary Society," which met in a small building that had once been a church. The object of the association was "educational"; it focused on the writing of essays. The name of "Hen" George appeared on two of these essays, one on Mormonism, toward which he took a belligerent attitude, and the other on "The Poetry of Life." [25] But the literary ambitions of the club soon waned in favor of social activities. The boys developed a fondness for telling lurid ghost stories, for boxing and fencing, and for singing raucous songs. They smoked "long black segars" and indulged in a drink labeled "Red Eye." [26] Perhaps this was a reaction to the austere home life which most of the boys experienced. For card-playing was forbidden and Sunday in Philadelphia was a day of such puritanical observance that even riding in a public conveyance was considered desecration of the Sabbath.

In the meantime Henry had become so proficient at the case that he could set an average of 5,000 ems a day, including distributing and correcting. For this, however, he was earning only two dollars a week. Even that meager wage ceased when, remembering his grandfather's injunction, "Do nothing that you are ashamed of and let no living man impose on you," he refused to submit to a domineering foreman and quit his job.

There was little other work in Philadelphia at the time. During a lull in his search for permanent employment, Henry George embarked on a topsail schooner carrying coal to Boston. He applied as a seaman, but the Captain, noting his youth (he was barely eighteen) wanted to turn him down.

"I had told him," George related long afterward, "that I could handle the sails and steer. He seemed to doubt it and said: 'You can't steer this schooner.' But I did steer her. The sea was very rough and the schooner rolled and pitched, the waves often dashing over the wheel." [27] By the end of the voyage he had made himself so useful that he was paid off at the full rate of an able seaman. "It was the highest compliment ever paid me," he boasted later.

When he returned to Philadelphia the outlook for work seemed darker still. Henry had been corresponding with friends who had gone to Oregon, and soon he developed a longing to go West where he believed he could earn a living. A cousin, Uncle Dunkin George's son Jim, was in California. The Philadelphia boy wrote to a friend in September, 1857:

There are thousands of hard-working mechanics now out of employment in this city. If you hear of any business men or rich corporations in your part of the country who are in want of a nice young man of my well known talents and capabilities, recommend me without loss of time as I am pretty damn hard up at present and haven't as much money as you could shake a stick at. Indeed, I would not have any hesitation in taking a situation on board a good canal boat for a short time, provided that it would pay. I have been trying for some time to secure a berth on board the United States Lighthouse

steamer *Shubrick*, now fitting out at the Navy Yard for California;
but she will not sail for two weeks at least and even then it is very
doubtful whether I can succeed and go out in her.[28]

Although he may not have sensed all its implications at the
time, Henry George had become a victim of the Panic of 1857.
There had been a business recession in 1855, then a flurry of
prosperity, and then: "In August (1857) the storm broke in all
its fury. Banks and corporations crashed; railroads became bank-
rupt; land values dropped sharply; building operations came to
a sudden end." [29]

There was widespread unemployment in the cities, including
Philadelphia. The panic lasted until the summer of 1858.[30] In
spite of good crops, city workers were faced with starvation
through the latter part of the preceding year. The jobless in
cities from Chicago to the East held protest meetings and even
threatened violence. Mobs threatened to raid banks, calling
them "plundering shops," and in New York a procession
marched on Wall Street.[31]

Doubtless this feeling of insecurity affected young George,
for like other youths he turned toward the promise of the West.
As will be seen, hard times followed him there. But in the meantime he was only too glad to leave the East and try for a place on
a ship sailing for California.

The *Shubrick* was only 140 feet in length and 371 tons burden.
She was a side-wheeler and had two masts, the foremast square
rigged. She looked as trim as a pleasure yacht but she was
armed with six cannon and also "a novel contrivance for squirt-
ing scalding water," since her duty was not only to supply
lighthouses and maintain buoyage but also to protect government property against Indian tribes along the Pacific coast.[32]

After writing a letter to the congressman from his district
seeking support, Henry George was accepted, greatly to his
delight, for the *Shubrick*'s crew as steward or storekeeper at
forty dollars a month. He planned, when he should reach
California, to work his way to Oregon where friends had promised him help in getting a job.

On December 22, 1857, a year and a half after his return on
the *Hindoo*, Henry received his order to sail. He hurriedly said
good-by to his family, and, embarking on the little craft at the
Navy Yard, steamed down the Delaware toward the long passage around the Horn to the Golden Gate.

Christmas Day, spent at sea, was one he would never forget. At home the family was deep in holiday festivities. At sea, the day started sunny and calm. But suddenly, without warning, a squall blew up and steadily mounted to the fury of a hurricane. Seas broke over the little ship, stove in part of the superstructure, ripped off the port shutters, and washed overboard everything movable on deck, including harness casks, deck engines, and spare spars and lumber. There was nothing to do but lighten the vessel. Henry and a Negro deck hand heaved overboard bags of coal while "the sailing master hung on the bridge shouting to us through the speaking trumpet and barely able to make himself heard as he told us that the work we were doing was for life or death." [33]

The lightening of the cargo saved the ship. By morning, when the storm had abated, she was able to proceed. The shipboard routine was resumed. A few items from a penciled list in the writing of the storekeeper give an idea of his responsibilities:

> *Shubrick* voyage. Clothes served out. Dec. 27, 1857.
> De Camp—Suit oil clothes, Sou'wester.
> Simmons—Monkey jacket
> Wilson—Sou'wester, Guernsey
> George—Oil jacket, 1 pair Socks
> John Lee—Jacket & Sou'wester, 2 Shirts, 2 Shirts
> 2 Pr. Drawers, ½ doz. Socks, 1 pr. Boots.
> Sylvester—Monkey jacket, Oil suit & Sou'wester.[34]

Six days after the storm the vessel reached the West Indies and recoaled. On her journey down the coast of South America the *Shubrick* stopped for five days at Rio de Janeiro. Henry had a chance to wander along the rocks, catching crabs and toadfish, and to paddle about in a canoe made of one solid piece of wood, the counterpart of the one used by Robinson Crusoe. He visited the city once but saw little of it, "as it was too infernally hot to walk the narrow streets." [35]

Out of this voyage came an experience which Henry George set down eight years later in the *Philadelphia Saturday Night*, a prosperous weekly newspaper owned by his friend Edmund Wallazz. It was called "Dust to Dust," and in its way it is one of the strangest of all the strange stories which have come from the sea.

Yellow fever had broken out aboard the *Shubrick* soon after the ship had left Rio. Several of the crew were stricken and all recovered save the popular second assistant engineer, S. W. Martin. The story continues:

The crisis seemed past, and if his strength would only last until he neared the Cape, all would be well. . . . Only one port remained to be passed before we should hail the rain and fog, and strength-giving winds—Monte Video. But when we entered that great stream, more sea than river, the mighty La Plata, on which the city is situated, Martin was dying. . . .

For some time in intervals of consciousness, Martin had been aware of his approaching end, and the only thing that seemed to trouble him was the idea of dying so far from those he loved, and of being buried where affection might never mark his resting place. It was his last and earnest request that his grave might be made on shore, where his body could be recognized by his friends, and not committed to the waves; and though it was very doubtful if the privilege could be granted, yet the captain resolved to take the corpse into the harbor, and try to obtain permission to bury it ashore.

And when night came, sadly we talked in little groups upon the deck, while the sound of hammer and plane from the gangway, told that the "last house" of one of us was being built. Though no star shed its light, still it was not all blackness. The "river of silver" beamed with a luster of its own. Not alone the furrows our prow threw aside, or the broad wake we left behind, but the whole surface of the water glowed with phosphorescent brightness, and we seemed to force our way through a sheet of molten silver.

All night long we steamed up the river, and when the sun again arose—it showed us the harbor of Monte Video. Out beyond all the other shipping lay a stately frigate, the Stars and Stripes of the great republic streaming from her peak in the morning breeze—the old *St. Lawrence*, flagship of the squadron. . . . We were bringing them news and letters from home, and every port of the great ship thronged with faces eager to see the comer from the land they loved. Running up under her quarter, we were hailed and answered, and after the usual inquiries, our captain mentioned the death of young Martin, and his wish to have him buried on shore; but was told that it was impossible, that we would infringe the quarantine rules by even entering the port with the corpse; and was directed to steam back some miles and commit the body to the waves, before entering the harbor.

The shrill whistle of the boatswain sounded; a boat dropped from the frigate's davits, reached our side, took letters and papers, and our little steamer turned slowly round to retrace her path. We had felt sad while coming up, but a darker gloom hung over all while going down the river. It seemed so hard that the last and only request of the poor boy could not be complied with.

But swiftly down the current in the bright, fresh morning dashed our little boat, and when the lofty frigate was hull-down behind us, we turned and stopped for the last sad rites.

Upon the quarter deck, in reverential silence, all hands were gathered. The large box-like coffin, in which we had hoped to commit our dead to mother earth, bored full of holes and filled up with heavy materials, was placed by the side, covered with the flag. The beautiful burial service was commenced, its solemn sentences sounding doubly solemn under such mournful circumstances—there was a pause—then came the words, "We therefore commit his body to the deep!" and with a surge the waves closed above the dead.

Hardly a word was spoken as the wheels again took up their task, and we began to ascend the river, but every eye was fixed on the spot we were leaving, and at the same instant an exclamation sprang from every lip as the coffin was seen to rise! The engine was quickly stopped, a boat lowered, and taking a small anchor and a heavy chain, they tried to secure and sink the box. But it was no easy task in the fresh breeze and short, chopping sea, and the coffin seemed almost instinct with life and striving to elude their efforts. Again and again they were foiled in their attempt to fasten the weights, but were at last successful, and once more the water closed above the corpse.

After waiting some time, to make sure that it could not float again, we started once more up the river, and this time awe was mingled with our grief. Most men who follow the sea have a touch of superstition. There is something of the vastness with which nature presents herself upon the great waters which influences in this direction even minds otherwise sceptical. And as we steamed up the river, it was more than hinted among many of us that the strong desire of the dying man had something to do with the difficulty of sinking his body.

This time we passed the frigate, saluting, but not stopping, and entered the port. It was war time; on the Pampas some phase of the interminable quarrels of the Southern federation was being fought out, and the harbor was crowded with men-of-war. Nearly all of the Brazilian navy was there, watching the progress of events; and besides these, and the numerous merchantmen, the ensign of almost every nation was displayed above some armed vessel. By direction of the officer who boarded us, we proceeded past them all, to the farther side of the harbor, where we were ordered to lie in quarantine seven days before being allowed to coal.

The new scene, the various objects of interest around and the duties of clearing up, conspired to make us forget the events of the morning, but the sun was yet some distance above the western horizon when a startling circumstance occurred to recall them to our minds.

Nearly all hands were busily engaged below, only two or three loitering around the deck, when the quartermaster, sweeping the harbor with his glass, noticed something floating in, which riveted his attention. Again and again he looked at it; then, with surprize and dismay in his face, called the officer of the deck. The whisper spread through the ship, and in a few minutes all were watching in silence the object that seemed drifting towards us. Onward it came, through all the vessels that lay beyond us—now lost to our view, now coming in sight again—turning and tacking as though piloted by life, and steadily holding its course for our steamer. It passed the last steamer, and came straight for us. It came closer, and every doubt was dispelled—it was, indeed, the coffin! A thrill of awe passed through every heart as the fact became assured.

Right under our bow came the box; it touched our side; halted a moment, as if claiming recognition, and then drifted slowly past us toward the shore.

There was an excited murmur forward, a whispered consultation in the knot of officers aft; then one advanced—"Man the quarter boat, boys; take pick and spades; tow the coffin ashore, and bury the body!"

It was the work of a moment—the boat shot like an arrow from our side, the ashen oars bending with the energy of the stroke. Reverently and gently they secured the box, and with slow, solemn strokes towed it to the foot of the desolate looking hill that skirts the bay. There, breaking it open, they bore the corpse, covered with the flag, a little distance up the hillside, and making in the twilight a grave among the chaparral, laid it to rest, marking the spot with a rude cross, which concealed from observation by the bushes, would yet serve as a mark of recognition, and secure the grave, should it be noticed, from the intrusion of vandal hands.

And so, in spite of all, that dying wish was gratified, and the body which the waters refused to receive was laid to rest in its mother earth.

Instead of going around the Horn, the course taken by sailing vessels, the sidewheeler went through the Straits of Magellan. But the weather was so severe that the coal supply ran out and the crew had to moor the *Shubrick* to a bank and cut wood ashore for fuel. The scenery in the western part of the Strait "was a most impressive sight," wrote Henry George years later. "We ran upon a schooner which belonged to English missionaries who were praying and working with the natives. We saw a number of Terre del Fuegans [*sic*], and they were not altogether attractive. I heard afterward that the Patagonians killed and ate those very missionaries who were trying to convert them." [36]

The *Shubrick* stopped at several ports along the west coast of South America, and then, 155 days after her departure from Philadelphia, on May 27, 1858, finally passed through the Golden Gate.

CHAPTER IV

BEGINNINGS IN CALIFORNIA

SAN FRANCISCO, situated on flower-carpeted hills that creep down to one of the most beautiful harbors in the world, was hardly a handsome city when Henry George reached it in 1858. But it was indisputably picturesque, with the greater part of the population of fifty thousand living either in tents or little clumsily built wooden houses, lined up along poorly paved or dirt streets. Some of the new buildings were substantial, and the old adobe ones, including the garden-surrounded Mission, were quaint and charming. Flowers grew everywhere on trees and vines and roadsides. The hills were abloom with color. The air was velvet soft and the blue sky was cloudless when the *Shubrick* steamed into San Francisco harbor.

Although the great gold rush had started nine years earlier, San Francisco retained the air of a boom town. The highways about the city teemed with men attracted by the lure of sudden fortune—or at least a comfortable living. Few women or children were to be seen on the busy streets. The hordes of husky, roughly clad men—prospectors, miners, lumberjacks, seamen, and cowboys—who far outnumbered the businessmen were, for the most part, surprisingly young-looking despite their bearded faces.

It was a very different world from the one Henry George had left in the placid East. He wrote a friend that it was "a dashing place, rather faster than Philadelphia." [1]

His plan had been to push on to Oregon, but the summons he had expected did not come. So, managing to get discharged from the *Shubrick* and freed of the shipping articles which he had been compelled to sign, he remained in San Francisco.*

* There is some confusion over the status of George's "discharge." It may be that he "jumped ship." His son relates in the *Life* that when the youth came

Making his temporary home with Cousin Jim George and Jim's wife Ellen, the boy had time to look around.

Letters from home arrived frequently. His father reassured him, "Don't think I regret the step you have taken. On the contrary, the more I think of it, the more I see the hand of Providence in it." [2] His mother wrote how the children missed him and added her counsel of hope and courage, "I want you to do something or be somebody in the world. I do not think you will disappoint me. Have less confidence in self and more in a higher power." [3]

Henry looked around San Francisco for work but the search was futile. When his little store of money was used up, he decided to join Jim George and an acquaintance, George Wilbur, in the gold rush along the Frazer River just across the Canadian border. At the first opportunity he worked his way as a seaman on a topsail schooner to Victoria. It was during this voyage that he had a conversation with some miners, also traveling to the gold fields, which left an indelible impression on him.

One of the older miners remarked that "wages will not always be as high as they are today in California. As the country grows, as people come in, wages will go down." [4]

This simple observation of a poor miner coincided with the statement made by the Philadelphia printer. Yet it puzzled the boy. Why, if the country develops, should the condition of those who had to work for a living become worse instead of better? This question, planted in the mind of a youth who was not yet nineteen, seemed to demand an answer.

When he reached Victoria, Henry George found that floods on the Frazer River had interrupted mining operations. He took a job in a miner's supply store which Jim George had opened. It must have been an austere life. Henry had written to his sister Caroline that "California is sadly in need of missionaries and I think it would be a good notion for the Sunday

---

ashore he sought the seclusion of Jim George's home and that Jim George's wife, Ellen, agreed to "confer with Commander De Camp (of the *Shubrick*), which she did. The Commander, as a consequence, failed to notice the absence of the boy, who, after a short season of this retirement, regarded himself as free of the *Shubrick*." This was in May. His enlistment did not expire until Nov. 11, 1858. In a footnote Henry George, Jr., writes: "Though the *Shubrick's* record shows that later on there were a number of desertions among the officers and crew of the vessel, there is no indication whatever as to when Henry George left, or that he did not remain until the expiration of his term of service."— Editor

School to send a few out, provided they were gold-fever proof. The great want of the country in my opinion, is women. Imagine, if you can, a place entirely destitute of them, and you can form some idea of the mining districts and even of some of the large towns." [5]

His pay in the mining town of Victoria was irregular and poor. To save room rent he slept rolled up in a blanket on the counter of Jim George's store or on piled bags of flour on the floor. Living in the shop had its advantages; Henry was always on hand for after-hour customers. When he wanted to sleep he placed a sign on the outside door: "Please give this door a kick." [6]

A falling out with Jim George caused him to leave his cousin's employ, and he went to live in a tent with young Wilbur. For some months the two friends scratched out an existence. Meager as were their rations, Henry, not always to Wilbur's liking, insisted on sharing them with half-starved Indians who visited the mining camp. One day, while Wilbur was off trying to find food, his partner invited three of them to the tent. The only edible thing he found to offer them was a bag of sugar. The Indians ate it, every grain. [7]

But finding gold—or a job—proved impossible. Henry borrowed money from Wilbur and others to buy steerage passage back to San Francisco. He had no coat, so Wilbur lent him his own. Food on shipboard was notoriously scarce, so six friends clubbed together and bought Henry six pies from an old man who peddled them to dwellers in the mining camp. Fearing their bon voyage gift might be eaten by other hungry travelers, they hid the pies under the blanket on Henry's berth. When night fell he had forgotten about the present. He wearily flung himself into his bunk without undressing. Next morning he discovered the sad fate of the pies. [8]

Back in San Francisco, jobs were still scarce. He was ready to turn back to the sea when he found a position in a printing house at sixteen dollars a week and was able to pay nine dollars a week for "a beautiful little room and first rate living" in one of the best hotels in San Francisco, the What Cheer House. It had a splendid little library where he spent many of his evenings. But there was little else to do for recreation. He wrote his sister Jennie, "I have few acquaintances either here or in Victoria—I mean boys or men. Don't on any consideration think I have thought of girls, for I haven't seen one to speak to, save those I told you about, since I left Philadelphia, but I suppose in some respect it is much better; I spend less money. . . . I suppose you have all grown somewhat since I left. I have not changed much, except that I have grown even uglier and rougher looking. You thought I looked hard when I came from Calcutta, but you should have seen me in Victoria!" [9]

He had grown a beard, of course, as soon as he could entice one to grow—a small red affair it was—to make him look older than his nineteen years.

The printing house job did not last long in these times of uncertain business conditions. Unable to follow his trade, he obtained a position as weigher in a rice mill. Shortly after this, George Wilbur returned from Victoria and the two boys took a room together on Pine Street, eating their meals at the What Cheer House.

"It would please Ma," Henry wrote to Jennie, "if she knew how regular and quiet I am in my habits. However, I suppose it is as much from necessity as from choice, for if I had money I suppose I would be the same as most others." [10]

His routine was Spartan in its simplicity. He arose at six and had an early breakfast at the hotel before going to the mill. He returned in the evening at six-thirty for supper and, afterward, quiet reading in the What Cheer library until nine o'clock, his usual bedtime. But George Wilbur would often wake up in the middle of the night and find his roommate reading or writing. [11] "Good heavens, Harry, what's the matter?" he would ask. "Are you sick?" The reply would either be an order to go back to sleep or a request to get up and dress and go for a walk. A quick turn in the night air seemed to quiet the young student —for now he was reading seriously—and make him ready for sleep.

Wilbur's forbearance was tried by more than restlessness, however. On those mornings when he awakened to find that Henry had left unusually early for work, absent-mindedly wearing his roommate's much longer trousers and in their place leaving his own too short ones, Wilbur was, naturally, quite exasperated. [12]

Friends in the East were perturbed by Henry's frequent change of jobs. "You are not competent to succeed at a dozen employments," wrote Jo Jeffreys, "nor can you hope to amass a fortune by laboring at them alternately." [13] But however much the boy tried to follow his friend's advice, he was forced to change employment again. The rice mill shut down. This time Henry decided to try the mines in the interior of the state. He had no money for transportation so he started out to walk. To save his little cash he slept in barns and did chores to pay for his food. It was a rough experience. At length sheer want of living necessities forced him to turn back, although he had managed to go some distance toward the mines. Suffering real privations he worked his weary way back to San Francisco.

Henry had been gone two months. When he returned he found the long awaited offer of work in Oregon—only he was too late and the offer had expired. The opportunity he had missed proved a bitter disappointment. And hardest of all to bear was word of the death of his friend and counselor, Cousin Ellen George, who had helped to brighten his first days in California.

CHAPTER V

ANNIE CORSINA FOX

WHAT A TIME we live in, when great events follow one another so quickly that we have no space for wonder," Henry George wrote to his sister Jennie in 1860.[1]

There was much indeed to challenge the sobering youth. California felt the agitation of the oncoming Civil War in the fatal duel between Chief Justice David S. Terry of the California Supreme Court and David C. Broderick, the most outspoken anti-slavery man in the West. Broderick's death quickened the great debate on slavery and secession. And when John Brown was hanged after the Harper's Ferry raid a few months later, Henry was made conscious of the events across the continent by a letter from his father which concluded, ominously enough, "The end is not yet."

But California was growing amidst the turmoil and debate. In letters home, Henry noted the progress of the Pony Express and remarked that "next year we will in all probability have a telegraph across the plains and our evening journals will contain New York news of the opening."

It was during this period that the youth, who had pulled far away from the strict orthodoxy of his Philadelphia religious training, was drawn back "to the church" by two friends who introduced him to the preaching of the liberal and broadminded Reverend S. D. Simonds, a Methodist. In 1860, Henry George became a member of the Methodist church. While his family had for generations been Episcopalians, the fact that the youth had joined any church caused great rejoicing in the home circle. "Oh, my Son," wrote his father, "what a thrill of joy your letter sent through us all, when we read that you had given your heart to Christ." [2]

On September 2, he became of age. Now he could join the typographical union and qualify as a journeyman printer. At journeyman's wages, he held a printing job for a short time and was able to send money back to Philadelphia. Then came a long spell of intermittent work.

"All my society is of the rougher sex," he had written to Jennie some months earlier. "In fact I don't care much about making the acquaintance of any ladies, at least such as are found here."

But not long after his twenty-first birthday George Wilbur persuaded him to go to a party. Henry went reluctantly, for he danced poorly, disliked small talk, and took no stock of flirting.

The night was clear and fragrant with heliotrope and citrus blossoms. When the two youths arrived at the party—at the McCloskey home—the entertainment was in full swing. A tenor was bleating a sentimental ballad. The two youths waited on the porch and looked in through the windows.

The large living room was handsomely furnished and decked lavishly with flowers—but flowers all of one type, begonias—plants of differing sizes, colors, and varieties, blooming wherever a pot could be perched. The place was crowded with people. Young George's glance roamed from person to person but always came back to a small woman in her early fifties who was sitting sedately in a high-backed chair. Severely dressed in plain dark silk, she wore a rare lace shawl around her shoulders. Her only jewels were five small diamond stars, glistening against the velvet ribbon which banded her blue-black hair.[3]

"Who is that old lady?" whispered Henry.

"That's the grandmother, that's Mrs. McCloskey," answered Wilbur.

"Well, it's getting pretty late," said Henry after peering again through the window. "You know we have to get up early."

Wilbur laid an affectionate but detaining hand on his shy friend. The song burbled on. Almost at the end of his endurance, Henry was about to bolt for home when the painful solo finished and a young girl glided into the scene.

Her widely hooped skirts of ecru piña cloth [4] floated about her like a cloud. Her brown hair was parted and drawn satin-smooth to a knot at the back of her head. Her beautifully modeled shoulders and arms were white as marble.

"Who is she?" Henry demanded.

"Oh, that's Mrs. McCloskey's granddaughter," Wilbur re-

Annie C. Fox (Mrs. George) at seventeen. From a daguerreotype taken in San Francisco, 1860.

Henry George with
Henry George, Jr., 1864.

George's three oldest children in 1870, *upper right*, Henry, Jr., *lower left*, Dick, and *lower right*, Jennie.

sponded. "That's Miss Fox. The party's for her. This is her birthday."

"Let's go in," said Henry George.

Annie Corsina Fox, who because of her sedate and dignified demeanor had, from her thirteenth year, been addressed as "Miss Fox," was not what one might call a really pretty girl. Her features were too large and not sufficiently regular for prettiness. Her large, grave eyes dominated her thoughtful face. Her skin was so delicately fair that her nickname was "Peaches-and-Cream." She was small, barely five feet in height and tiny boned. Beautifully formed,* she had exquisite shoulders and arms and little patrician hands. Water could be run under her instep and she wore a size one shoe.† Her voice was soft and well modulated; she sang naturally and melodically. She danced like a fairy. Indeed her passion for dancing was so great that at times it led her into foolishness. Once, at a ball, she made a wager with her partner that she could tire him out. She did— and three more partners, and the orchestra; and it was not until the arrival of her guardian-uncle, after two solid hours of waltzing, that she was peremptorily stopped from what might have developed in our day into a "dance marathon."

She was born in Sydney, Australia,[5] where her father, Major John Fox of the British Army, was stationed. There, when Fox was thirty-six, he had met and married the sixteen-year-old Elizabeth McCloskey, daughter of a prosperous Irish iron-monger and government contractor who had come with his family from Limerick. There the two daughters Teresa and Anna Corsina Fox were born.

But life did not run smoothly for the high-spirited British, Church-of-England soldier and his somewhat strait-laced Irish-Catholic wife—or rather between the husband and the mother-in-law. Elizabeth McCloskey sided with her mother; her marriage to Major Fox ended tragically in a separation.

* At the birth of Henry George's second son, Richard, a neighbor woman who was a photographer and painter, and who was that night assisting as midwife, was so struck by the great beauty of Annie George's body that she asked the young husband for permission to photograph his wife nude. Her request was indignantly refused. It is characteristic of my mother that she considered this anecdote of too intimate a nature for inclusion in the present work.—Agnes de Mille

† This was a family trait. My mother also wore a size one street shoe. For dancing and bedroom slippers she had to go to the children's department.—Agnes de Mille

Anna—"Annie," as she was called—was five years old when
Grandfather Henry McCloskey gathered up his family and
again migrated,[6] this time to California.* After establishing
them in ample comfort in San Francisco, he returned to Australia to build a railroad. But he never completed this work; he
contracted a fever and died. His daughter, Annie's mother,
died soon after her separation from Major Fox. The cause of
her death was given as consumption; her family believed it
was a malady infinitely more complex—a broken heart in grief
at the irrevocable parting with her soldier husband.

Mrs. McCloskey, now the matriarch of the family, reared the
two children in comfort in San Francisco. She had three hob-
bies, or fads—fine china, fine shawls, and fine begonias. Once in
the flower market for which the city was famous, she spotted
an unusual begonia. "How much is that?" she asked. She was
dressed simply, except for one of her rare shawls, and the merchant appraised her quickly and answered, "Oh, you couldn't
afford to buy that plant."

Mrs. McCloskey was incensed. She replied instantly, and
with an imperious gesture, "Send the begonia to my home!"

When it arrived she found to her dismay that the little
flower had cost her eighteen dollars.

The McCloskeys lived in a house which had been brought in
sections from Australia. The family in San Francisco also included a son, Matthew McCloskey, and Joseph Flintoff and
his wife, a second daughter of Mrs. McCloskey. The two men
affected the manners of the wealthy Spanish ranchers in the
California of the 1850's and 1860's, sporting high, shiny riding
boots, silver spurs, and large sombreros of the finest felt. Matthew McCloskey owned and developed real estate in the section of San Francisco known as "Happy Valley."

* There is a family tale, told me by my mother, to the effect that on this trip
the vessel ran into a hurricane. The crew believed themselves lost and worked
in an agony of terror to save their lives. The captain, learning somehow that
Annie Fox had been born with a caul over her face, lashed the child to a mast
in the open weather. There she stood, a five-year-old baby, on the heaving deck,
drenched with sea water and haggard with the wind, while the crew filed past
and gently laid their hands on her. No person born with a caul could be drowned
at sea.

She never forgot this episode. I believe in some way it may have given her
a sense of strength and protective force. Time and again her husband and her
husband's friends turned to her in moments of extreme crises for reassurance,
for the talisman touch that would prevent their being swept away.—Agnes de
Mille

When her granddaughters were old enough to go to school,
Mrs. McCloskey sent them to the Sisters of the Order of St.
Vincent de Paul, usually known as the Sisters of Charity, in
Southern California. Most of their schoolmates were Spanish,
and the atmosphere of the peaceful convent [7] in the beautiful
mountain-encircled Pueblo de Nuestra Senora la Reina de Los
Angeles reflected the old California before the coming of the
"Gringos." *

The bond between Tessie and Annie was peculiarly close. It
was a cruel blow to Annie when the older girl left her to take
the veil at the age of seventeen. As Sister Teresa, wearing the
wide white cornet of the Sisters of Charity, she was sent to
Vicksburg to nurse wounded Confederate soldiers. After the
Civil War she became a teacher and rose to a high rank in her
order.

Annie remained in Los Angeles for a time as a student-
teacher after she finished her regular course at the convent
school. She was a fragile girl and the Sisters watched over her
tenderly. She taught English to some of the Spanish girls and,
in order to gain the benefit of the California air and sunshine,
busied herself with picking flowers for the convent altars. When
her grandmother's health began to fail she returned to San Francisco.

At the time of her seventeenth birthday party, when she met
Henry George, Annie Fox was engaged to be married to an
exemplary and charming young man of ample means. But before she had known the Philadelphia boy many months, Annie
broke her engagement.

Henry George pressed his suit with many attentions and with
as many gifts, mostly books, as he could afford to buy. When
Mrs. McCloskey died, Annie went to make her home with the

* The religious rituals were, as always in a primitive community, intensely
dramatic. Annie Fox told my mother that Holy Week was awesome in its in-
tensity. The statues were of course shrouded in purple, but the high altar was
also veiled and shut away from view. At Easter dawn, with a burst of triumphant singing, the curtains were pulled back, and the altar, blazing with lights
and banked with orange blossoms, acacias, and lilies from the mission garden,
burst on the view of the congregation and gave forth such overpowering per-
fume and incense as to cause young girls to swoon as they fell on their knees.

It is wonderful that a sensitive child reared in this atmosphere could rid herself of all religious domination, and, although Annie Fox always devoutly believed in God and an afterlife, she disassociated herself from any specific church.
Her children were baptized as Catholics only in deference to the older sister,
Teresa Fox.—Agnes de Mille

Flintoffs and Uncle Matthew McCloskey became her guardian. The uncle liked young George but he was hardly enthusiastic about the court paid his niece by the delicate looking and shabbily dressed youth. It was plain that the youth's attentions were anything but platonic.

MARRIAGE

N EWS REACHED California in mid-April of 1861 that the
United States flag had been fired upon at Fort Sumter.

Back in Philadelphia, Mrs. George wrote to her son expressing her grief at this "horrible, calamitous and most sorrowful
of all wars. . . . When and what will be the end?" she asked.[1]

But the impact of this event was slow in reaching California
with all the force which it had exerted in the East. It was in
September that Henry George wrote, in the midst of a long
letter to his sister Jennie, "If I were home I would go. Not that
I like the idea of fighting my countrymen, but in this life or
death struggle I should like to have a hand. . . . I have felt a
great deal like enlisting. I should like to place my willingness
on record. . . . It may be my duty yet." [2]

The youth of twenty-one was now passing through a period
of hard times. With one hundred dollars he had managed to
save he had bought, along with five other young printers, a
small paper which they renamed the *Evening Journal*. However, the project proved a failure. Henry George seemed to
despair, but there was hope mingled with desperation when he
wrote again to Jennie, "Sometimes I feel sick of the fierce
struggle of our high civilized life, and I think I would like to
get away from cities and business, with their jostlings and
strainings and cares altogether, and find some place on one of
the hillsides, which look so blue and dim in the distance, where
I could gather those I love and live content with what Nature
and our own resources would furnish; but alas, money, money,
money, is wanted even for that. It is our fate—we must struggle,
and so here's for the strife!" [3]

The six *Evening Journal* partners some weeks made as much
as six dollars each—but not always. Henry got behind with his
room rent, and, running into debt thirty dollars, had to sleep

in the office. His clothes became shabbier and the toes of his shoes wore out. Try as he would, he could not hide his poverty. At length he sold his share of the paper, receiving in payment some mining stock which later proved to be worthless.

He saw Annie Fox frequently at the Flintoff home. One night, when her Uncle Matt McCloskey called and found the impecunious young George there, he intimated to the youth that he might better appear less frequently. Matthew McCloskey was a hot-headed Irishman. Henry was young and deeply in love. An angry and demonstrative quarrel began. It was the terrified little Annie who kept the two from coming to blows.

The uncle ordered the young man from the house. The greater part of that night Annie spent in prayer. When Henry ignored Matthew McCloskey and came to see her the next morning, she told him that she could not live any longer with either of her uncles and that she was determined to go back to Los Angeles, where she could take a position as teacher in her old school with the Sisters of Charity.

Henry George was out of work at the time. He had no intention of suggesting matrimony. But he could not bear to part with Annie Fox. He drew a fifty-cent piece from his pocket and said solemnly, "Annie, this is all the money I have in the world. Will you marry me?"

The girl thought a moment, and then answered with great feeling, "If you are willing to undertake the responsibilities of marriage, I will marry you."

They made their arrangements quickly. At nightfall, Isaac Trump, one of Henry's friends from the *Shubrick* days, came to the door of the Flintoff home and inquired for "Mrs. Brown." This was the prearranged signal for which Annie, sitting nervously in the parlor, had been waiting. She hastily put on a bonnet and shawl, and, giving Isaac Trump a small but heavy cloth-covered package, followed him out through the garden to a waiting carriage. The package contained the books, mostly poetry, Henry had given Annie, and not jewels as Trump had suspected.[4] Scarcely another thing did the girl take to equip herself for her new life, for she had disdained everything provided by her uncles save the clothes on her back, a fine Spanish shawl, a Bohemian glass bottle, and a recipe for black fruitcake.

Isaac Trump's own fiancée was waiting in the carriage. After they had driven a short distance, Henry George, in his neatly brushed (and borrowed) clothes, joined them. The two couples went to a restaurant and had dinner (a really good dinner could be had for twenty-five cents) and then walked through the moonlit streets. The young man carefully carried his bride-to-be over places left wet by the December rain.

Other friends awaited them at Bethel Methodist Church. There, the Reverend Mr. Simonds performed the wedding ceremony, using the Episcopal service and a ring which had belonged to Annie's grandmother. Later a priest gave the Catholic sanction.

Lacking funds for a honeymoon trip, the young couple went quietly to the house of a friend. The bridegroom had not only borrowed the clothes in which he had been married but also the money to pay for the expense of the wedding.

On the morning after the ceremony Henry George arose at five o'clock to hunt for a job. He found work as a substitute typesetter remaining on the job all that day and most of the night. By continuing to "sub" this way for several weeks he managed to pay their board bills until a position on *The Union* drew them to Sacramento.

He had written Jennie George of his love for Annie Fox long before the other members of the family knew of her existence. His sister had replied, "I felt a sudden choking, a sudden loneliness and jealousy, when I first read your letter. I have got over that now. Come home and bring her with you. I will love her; so will they all, I know. In the meantime do not forget me; do not cease to love me as much as ever, will you? There can be two places in your heart—one for Annie and one for me." [5]

As soon as news of the marriage reached Philadelphia, Annie was mentioned with Henry in the daily family prayers. A succession of welcoming letters went back to the little bride in California. Jennie wrote, "Henry always had one particular place at the foot of the table (ask him if he remembers it) and I used to sit beside him, but I will let you sit there when you come." [6] Although the bride's family forgave the runaways, the young couple's pride prevented them from going even to Annie's guardians for help in time of need.

Yet no one could live in peace of heart while the Civil War raged. Henry wrote again to Jennie:

Every day the telegraph is in working order brings us news of the success of the Republic. I cannot help feeling regret that the contest will be over and the victories won without my having taken the slightest part in it. If I am East after the war is ended I will feel abashed among its heroes. If I had been home, I would have gone if I possibly could, but here there was no chance unless one could pay his passage to New York, for those [regiments] which were raised here were merely to garrison posts and fight Indians.[7]

Work on *The Union*, sporadic as it was, still kept Henry George and his bride in Sacramento. They lived close to the State Capitol in a part of the city that abounded in beautiful trees and flowers. They had the loan of a small boat which they frequently sailed, and Henry kept himself physically fit by rowing and swimming. He spent much of his spare time, of which there seems to have been an unwelcome abundance, in reading. Six months after his marriage he wrote to Jennie:

The Overland Mail stage has not yet commenced running. This is disheartening, for to its regular intervals we are looking for the revival of our business, which just now is unprecedentedly dull. The proprietors of *The Union* state their determination to run two double sheets a week as soon as the Overland Mail resumes, which will give me all the work I care to do. I am not one of those who love work for its own sake, but feeling what it brings, I am happiest when hard at it. It is no wonder that wealth is sought by all means, good or bad. . . . It is but the want of a few dollars that keeps us separate, that forces us to struggle on so painfully, that crushes down all the noblest yearnings of the heart and mind. I do not complain that no special miracle is worked in my behalf, that by none of those lucky windfalls which sometimes come to fools I am enriched; but it really seems that strive as hard in whatever direction I may, the current still turns against me. At any rate I will do the best I can, make the most of my opportunities, and for the rest trust in God.[8]

CHAPTER VII

FROM HAND TO MOUTH

UNBEKNOWNST TO Henry George, his beloved sister Jennie had fallen ill a continent away. She had been his confidante from boyhood into maturity. Once she wrote him in California, "What would I give if I could fly on the new telegraph to you and have a talk, if it were only for an hour. I wish we could send letters on it, don't you? Just to think a month's space between us. When you are reading this, what I say is a month old." [1]

It was not until weeks after her short illness that Henry learned the shocking news of Jennie's death. As late as the summer of 1862, the United States mail was slow and almost indescribably inefficient. Travelers who went to California by the Salt Lake route bore tales of broken mail bags, seen at stations, where letters lay "scattered knee deep," [2] and of mail bags that had been lying on the plains all winter. Thus a letter from Uncle Thomas George was weeks in reaching Henry, and the shock of Jennie's death was all the more profound for the time it had taken to relay the news.

The letter from Philadelphia reached Henry at *The Union* plant. He bore his sorrow alone until after his work was done. When he returned home in the early morning, Annie could see from his white, drawn face that something was deeply wrong. No longer able to contain himself, Henry broke into a flood of tears and handed her the letter from Thomas George and another from his mother. After a time he began pacing the floor, muttering over and over to himself, "There is another life! There *is* another life after this! I shall see my sister again!" [3]

Jennie's death seems to have opened the way for a deep and abiding conviction of a life beyond this one. That faith grew stronger with the passing of time. A message of condolence to his mother some years later, when her own sister died, bears this out: "The older I grow and the more I think, the more fully I realized the wisdom and benefice that pervades the universe and that is impressed on all its laws. . . . As we were born so we die. As there were others here to receive us, so must there be others there to meet us, and the Christian faith promises that the wise and good in all ages have believed that death is but a new birth. . . . Our little life, what is it, our little globe, what is it, to the infinity that lies beyond?" [4]

But now the youth of twenty-three had little time for philosophy. The days bore down upon him with heavy responsibilities.

A son, Henry, Jr., had arrived in the tiny George home. Out of sheer economic necessity the young father was compelled to turn his hand to things other than typesetting. Once he was hired to collect tickets at the door of the hall when a young newspaperman whose nom de plume was Mark Twain came to Sacramento to give a lecture. There is no record of a meeting between the two or of George's impressions of the rising American humorist.

Although he managed to pay his debts and send money home to Philadelphia, accumulating any savings proved impossible. Some slight investment in mining stocks, which were subject to frequent assessments, proved almost worthless. And then Henry lost his job at *The Union* because of a disagreement with the foreman, John Timmins.

There was nothing to do but return to San Francisco, which Henry George did at the end of January, 1864, after more than a year at the Sacramento newspaper. He spent five days attempting to sell clothes wringers but did not make a single sale. Finally obtaining a job as a substitute typesetter, he sent for his wife and baby son to come to San Francisco.

An opportunity suddenly opened in December when George and Isaac Trump were able to purchase part of the equipment of the *Evening Journal,* which had died after a starving existence. They opened a modest printing shop, but Henry's elation at owning a business of this sort was short lived. Alas for ambition, sudden drought brought on hard times in California. Cattle died in droves. Furthermore, the gold supply lessened and the losses of farmers, ranchers, and miners deepened into a general depression. Work became scarce. The partners in the little printing business were desperate. When they could, they took out of their receipts as much as twenty-five cents a day each,

which they spent for food. Mrs. Trump was living with her
mother so Isaac took his dinner with the Georges.

At the time of her marriage, Annie Fox's sole accomplish-
ment as a cook was the baking of rich, black English fruit
cake. She always kept a supply of this delicacy so that when
her husband came home from work between two and four
o'clock in the morning he might appease his hunger before
going to sleep. She also had served it for the collation when the
George Wilburs [5] and the A. A. Stickneys [6] came for their
frequent and hilarious card games. But now there was no money
to buy the ingredients for even homemade cake. The little
family subsisted on milk, corn meal, potatoes, bread, and the
cheapest fish that could be bought. Usually the husband went
to work without breakfast on the plea that he would get it
downtown. His wife suspected, and she was right, that he went
without it. And she was brave and self-sacrificing in her own
way.

Although fragile and delicately reared, Annie George never
complained of hardships. One by one she secretly pawned her
few pieces of jewelry, saving only her wedding ring. She
turned to needlework to supplement the family income, but
with one small child to care for and another coming, she had
not the strength to do regular sewing. At length family finances
reached such a state that she could not afford to buy anything
more. She refused to run up bills. But she did not lack for
initiative. Although Henry failed at six different lumber yards
to exchange printing for wood, Annie successfully arranged
with the grocer and milkman for her husband to print advertising cards in return for a little cornmeal and milk.

In this time of bitter want a second child, Richard Fox
George, was born.[7]

"Don't stop to wash the child!" ordered the doctor. "The
mother is starving. Feed her!"

The only food in the house for Annie George was the loaf of
freshly baked bread which a neighbor, the photographer, had
just brought.

Henry George went in search of food—or money. He stopped
first at his little printing office in the hope that some of the
debt owing him and Isaac Trump had been paid. But no
money had come in. There was no friend to whom he might
turn for a loan, for all were as poor as he.

Frantically, he paced the streets. Annie *must* have food.

There had been a light but dismal rain, and the day was gray and damp. Everyone he passed looked cold and poor. Henry was growing desperate when a well-dressed man appeared. The shivering youth walked straight up to the stranger and demanded five dollars.

"What for?" the man asked as he studied the gaunt young face with its burning eyes.

"My wife has just been confined and I have nothing to give her to eat," said Henry.

Whether it was because of pity or fear of bodily assault, the man gave him the money without further question.

"If he had not," said Henry George long afterward, "I think I was desperate enough to have killed him." [8]

The struggle for mere subsistence continued. However, on some days fifty cents was paid on a bill at the office and on a few fortunate days there was as much as several dollars as the partner's share of the receipts. When the new baby was less than three weeks old the little family moved from the upper flat of the small wooden house on Russ Street, which had rented for eighteen dollars a month, to a smaller place on Perry Street where the rent was nine dollars. Mrs. George sewed for her landlady and earned the second month's rent. Her ambition of a comfortable home life was for her husband to make twenty dollars a week!

Henry George had kept diaries irregularly since his days at sea.[9] In the entries for February, 1865, there appeared hints of his own black mood. Once he wrote: "I have been unsuccessful in everything." [10] At another time: "Am in very desperate plight, Courage." [11] And again: "Don't know what to do." [12]

But on March 3, the sole entry consisted of two words: "At work." And on March 4: "At work. Got $5 in the evening." He was setting type sporadically. He also tried to interest carriage builders in a new wagon brake—for he was seeking every way he knew to make money.

However, the lean period carried its lesson. The desire and resolution to equip himself more completely made Henry George use his spare hours for study and for practicing composition. One of his essays, "On the Profitable Employment of Time," which he mailed to his mother, shows not only his own longing for ease and wealth but his consciousness of wasted opportunity and his promised efforts of reformation.

"I am constantly longing for wealth," he wrote. And further,

"It would bring me comfort and luxury which I cannot now obtain; it would give me more congenial employment and associates; it would enable me to cultivate my mind and exert to a fuller extent my powers; it would give me the ability to minister to the comfort and enjoyment of those I love most. And therefore it is my principal object in life to obtain wealth, or at least, more of it than I have at present. . . ."

This was precious little. But Henry's first formal essay of his manhood indicated firm resolve. He went on: "To secure any given result it is only necessary to supply sufficient force. . . . It is evident to me that I have not employed the time and means at my command faithfully and advantageously as I might have done, and consequently that I have myself to blame for at least a part of my non-success. And this being true of the past, in the future like results will flow from like causes." [13]

As his style improved, Henry resolved to send letters to the newspapers. To his delight one letter discussing laws relating to sailors and another letter urging working men to think about political and social questions were printed. This success gave him courage to write a fanciful sketch, "A Plea for the Supernatural," which he sent to the magazine *Californian*, a weekly publication to which Mark Twain and Bret Harte were contributors.[14] The story was accepted [15] and was later reprinted in *The Boston Evening Gazette*.

This was a period of dark despair. But Henry George had learned that he could write.

CHAPTER VIII

NEWSPAPERMAN

NEWS OF the assassination of Abraham Lincoln reached California when Henry George was working part time as a typesetter for the *Alta California*. It stirred him profoundly. And, not incidentally, it gave him his first opportunity to catch the public eye with the vigor and clarity of style which he had developed in his writing.

Vitally interested in public affairs, the young printer had watched admiringly the course taken by the Civil War president. He had come to revere this man for whom he had cast his first vote. While anger and grief over the tragedy surged through him, he raged with Isaac Trump and others against the "copperhead" newspapers which had attacked Lincoln so recklessly. He determined to join with his friend in leading an attack on the *News Letter*, a particularly virulent anti-Lincoln newspaper. But when he reached the *News Letter's* office, he found Trump already in command of a mob which was sacking the plant and flinging its contents into the street.

Merely witnessing the scene acted as a safety valve for George. His anger somewhat softened, he went home and wrote an article of some five hundred words which further relieved his feelings. This he slipped, unsigned, into the editorial box of the *Alta California*. The next day it appeared in print.[1] A few lines reveal its tenor:

A man rushed to the front of the President's box, waving a long dagger in his right hand, exclaiming: "Sic semper tyrannis!"
—*Alta* despatches, April 15, 1865.

What a scene these few words bring—vivid as the lightning flash that bore them! The glitter and glare, curving circle and crowded pit, flash of jewels and glinting of silks—and the blanched sea of upturned faces, the fixed and staring eyes, the awful hush—silence of death! ... They came to laugh at a comedy, and a tragedy is before them which will make a nation weep. ...

While the world lasts will this scene be remembered. As a martyr of freedom—as the representative of justice in a great nation, the name of the victim will live forever; and the Proclamation of Emancipation, signed with the name and sealed with the blood of *Abraham Lincoln* will remain a landmark in the progress of the race.[2]

The editor of the *Alta California* sought out the author in the composing room and engaged him at once to write a description of the Lincoln mourning decorations in San Francisco.

This proved to be the first newspaper writing for which Henry George received pay. But reporting was not enough for him. He must express his emotions in a less impersonal form. In the little parlor of his home he wrote a eulogy of the dead President which was given the leading place on the editorial page the following day. He wrote of Lincoln:

He personified the best, the most general character of the people who twice called him to the highest place they could bestow, and the strength and the virtue of a nation, enriched by the best blood of all races, were his.

He was not of those whom God lifts to the mountain tops and who tell of his truth to ears that will not hear and show His light to eyes that cannot see—whom their own generation stone and future ones worship; but he was of the leaders who march close before the advancing ranks of the people, who direct their steps and speak with their voice. ...

His was not the eloquence which sways men at will ... yet in all he said there was the power, eloquent in its plainness and honesty, of a man truer than his pledge, better than his word. ... And as in our times of need, the man that was needed came forth, let us know that it will always be so, and that under our institutions, when the rights of the people are endangered, from their ranks will spring the men for the times. ...[3]

With peace restored in the nation, eyes in California turned abroad. The state had many sentimental ties with Mexico, the immediate source of much of her culture and of some of her population, and now the neighbor to the South was engaged in a struggle that claimed the allegiance of liberals everywhere. Napoleon III of France, in an attempt to get control of the rich lands of Mexico, had persuaded the Archduke Maximilian of

Austria, who was being importuned by Mexican exiles, to go to that country in 1864 and set himself up as emperor. The peons and all freedom-loving Mexicans weary of generations of foreign domination united themselves behind Benito Juarez and revolted against the Spanish pretender and his French mercenaries.

The resistance of the Mexican patriots strongly appealed to Henry George. He joined an expedition in San Francisco which was being organized to aid the fight for Mexican liberation. The editor of the *Alta California* was prepared to give George a contract for news letters about the expedition, and the fact that he would receive pay for this work was the final persuasion which he needed.

Although this meant separation for a time—and, if he did not return, perhaps widowhood and poverty for her—the wife, now twenty-one years old, consented to his going. When the time came for parting, Henry and Annie George knelt beside their sleeping babies and prayed together. Then the young husband and father joined the other members of the band of Mexican liberators at Platt's Hall.

He was to be first lieutenant of his company and John Hungerford (subsequently father-in-law of John Mackay), was to be the colonel. After much delay the expedition boarded the old barque *Brontes*. To their dismay, the adventurers found that the boat was ill provisioned and equipped with 10,000 condemned rifles, half a dozen saddles and a few casks of water. Some of the men were little less than pirates, and they were hatching a secret plan to seize a French transport. Luckily the Federal authorities got wind of the matter, arrested these plotters (the rest of the expedition was freed), and nipped the whole project in the bud.[4] Years later during a political campaign this experience was to lead to the charge in some newspapers that Henry George had once engaged in a piratical expedition.

This was the nearest George ever came to war. At the time he was bitterly disappointed that his campaign for Mexican freedom began and ended in San Francisco harbor. Later he was grateful when he realized that this particular expedition would have come to no good. But he did not let the matter rest there. He helped to establish the Monroe League (of which Annie George became the only woman member), which

Henry George in 1886.   Mrs. Henry George, c. 1885.

Henry George with his two daughters, Jennie and Anna, 1886.

was to send another expedition to aid the Mexican patriots. But this, too, failed.

Soon after the *Brontes* affair a typesetting position opened in Sacramento for official California state printing on a contract basis. George moved his family back to the city which they had left the year before. His small salary was sufficient for a modest living and the Georges remained in Sacramento this time for nearly a year. Henry became a member of a literary society known as the Sacramento Lyceum. At one of the meetings, after listening to a speech in favor of protection which was delivered by a land agent of the Central Pacific Railroad, George's economic beliefs were sharply reversed. "I was a protectionist when he [the speaker] began," he wrote later, "but when he got through I was a free-trader. If what he said was true, it seemed to me that the country that was hardest to get at must be the best country to live in; and that, instead of merely putting duties on things brought from abroad, we ought to put them on things brought from anywhere, and that fires and wars and impediments to trade were the very best things to levy on commerce." [5] This of course was ridiculous.

Although George was becoming more and more interested in public affairs, he found time after the day's work at the case to write and get published the account of the *Shubrick* sea burial, previously cited,[6] and a fanciful sketch entitled "The Prayer of Kohonah." [7]

In September of 1866, the new *San Francisco Times* offered George a job in its composing room and the family left Sacramento a second time. Henry had thought of writing a novel, but encouragement from James McClatchy, the *Times'* editor, led the young compositor to try his hand at editorial writing. When McClatchy left the paper after a brief stay, George's latest editorial was shown to the new editor, Noah Brooks, who later said, "The article was written in a neat, regular and small hand, with lines far apart, on sheets of buff paper such as was used for wrapping. It showed a largeness of thought that made me suspect that the young man had been borrowing." But, searching through current periodicals, Brooks found no sign of appropriation, so he printed the article. Then he looked up the author and saw "a slight young man, rather undersized, who stood on a board to raise him to the proper height to work at his case." [8] Though "not prepossessed with him," [9] Brooks later invited George to write at the regular editorial column rates, and eventually engaged him as a full-time editorial writer.

Despite his height and slight build, Henry George had broad shoulders and a carriage of head and expression which were to command attention everywhere. His dark auburn hair had been heavy but now it was showing signs of thinning. His approaching baldness concerned Annie George, who frequently interspersed in her letters, when the two were separated, such admonitions as, "Do you take care of your hair? Don't neglect it on any account. . . . Have you had anything done for your hair? If you would rub it with glycerine, it would do you good." [10]

Evidently he neglected to use glycerine, for he grew steadily balder and his rapidly thinning hair became darker. His beard was several shades lighter and was what the Scots call "sandy." The grey-blue eyes, with their far gaze, were keener than ever. His small hands, with their tapering fingers and pink palms, clumsy with hammer or saw, were dexterous with ropes and boats and quick at the case. His feet were small in proportion to his height.

One day the husband and wife with their son, Henry, Jr., went together to buy shoes for the family. As they were leaving the store Mrs. George heard the man who had waited on them remark to another clerk, "Sure, not much to be made outer that crowd! Himself has a bye's fut, herself has a gurrl's fut, and as fur the child, he has no fut at all!" [11]

After seven months as typesetter, reporter, and editorial writer for the *San Francisco Times*, Henry George became managing editor at a salary of fifty dollars a week. He retained the position for more than a year. During this time he improved his writing style. He studied deeply the questions of the day which he discussed in his editorials: free trade, paper money, personal and proportional representation, public franchises, privileges in the Army, the Australian ballot, "women's rights," and many other topics.

This study equipped him to write an article for the celebrated new magazine, *The Overland Monthly*, whose chief contributors were Mark Twain, Bret Harte, and Joaquin Miller. A seven-thousand-word article, "What the Railroads Will Bring Us," appeared in the October, 1868, issue and brought him forty dollars. It shows sharp traces of the trend in economic thought which he was to develop later. The new railroads, which had received vast land grants and cash subsidies from the Federal government, and which seemed capable of extensive graft and corruption because of their involvement in politics, gave him pause. "Let us see whither we are tending," the article begins, continuing:

The completion of the railroad and the consequent great increase of business and population, will not be a benefit to all of us, but only to a portion. As a general rule (liable of course to exception) those who have, it will make wealthier; for those who *have not* it will make it more difficult to get. Those who have lands, mines, established business, special abilities of certain kinds, will become richer for it and find increased opportunities; those who have only their own labor will become poorer, and find it harder to get ahead.[12]

In spite of study and hard work, life had its lighter moments for Henry George. These included another and more direct contact with Mark Twain.

The author, hard up and in debt, came to Platt's Hall to deliver a lecture, the proceeds of which he hoped would pay his way East. But one of his creditors sent the sheriff to collect the money taken in at the gate, together with a gold watch with which Mark Twain had been presented at a testimonial dinner. Before the sheriff could seize the money, the author's friends "vamoosed" with the box office receipts while others, including Alec Bell and Henry George, passed the watch from one to another just a jump ahead of the sheriff. All of his confederates contrived to meet Mark Twain and give him his belongings when he was out of the county, on the ferry, bound for the railroad train in Oakland.[13]

Another child, Jane Teresa, named in honor of Henry's sister Jennie and Annie's sister Teresa, was born into the George household during the period of steady work on the *San Francisco Times*. When little Jane was one year old, Henry George decided to send his family on the long-dreamed-of journey to Philadelphia, for by that time he had saved enough money for the trip. They were put in charge of his brother Val who had, some months earlier, joined them in California.

The overland journey was not an easy one. The Pullman Company had started to build sleeping cars the year before (1867) but they were not yet to be found on all trains—even if one had money to pay for the luxury of using them. Sometimes, on the long jumps, Mrs. George had to make a bed for the three children by putting the valises between two seats, with folded shawls for a mattress. One night, in a small country station, two tough-looking, tobacco-chewing miners boarded the train. Every seat was taken, and nearly every occupant, including Val George, was asleep. Realizing that her children were using more space than was their right, Mrs. George hurriedly began to shift them to make room for the newcomers. One of the miners quickly restrained her with his blackened hand. Doffing his rumpled hat, he said in a squeaky whisper,

"Why, Ma'am, leave 'em lay! Don't disturb 'em. They're the purtiest things we seen since we left home over a year ago."

The two men feasted their eyes on the sleeping children: Harry, now five years old, with red hair and a sensitive face; merry little Dick with long blonde curls; and the tiny sister "Jen," her small head covered with ringlets of sun-yellow. After impressing the picture on their minds the men clumped down the aisle as lightly as their big boots would permit and stood until they reached their destination.[14]

Upon her arrival in Philadelphia, Mrs. George received a warm welcome from her husband's family. She wrote back to California that "Father sent Tom to New York to meet us.... In Philadelphia they all met us at the door, but Father took me out of the carriage and was the first to embrace me.... Harry darling, all is happiness around me, but I am not happy for 'my heart is over the sea.'"[15] Annie George wrote him of her embarrassment over the expenses of the journey, some of which she did not anticipate, and added, "The folks home here have no idea of our situation. I spoke of getting a new cloak when I first came and Mother wanted to know which I would get, 'cloth or velvet.' I said cloth by all means. It amused me more than a little. They were astonished when they saw my wardrobe. They all dress nicely, have all got silk dresses too, and none of them have any idea of the troubles we have been through."[16]

It must have been a comfort to Henry, who through the years had been straining to send money home to Philadelphia, to be told that "their poor times are nearly as good as our prosperous ones, so don't worry about them."[17]

A beautiful devotion grew up between Annie and her husband's father, but difference in religious creed seemed to raise a barrier between her and his mother. "If I was an Episcopalian," Annie wrote Henry, "I think I would be all she would wish. . . . That I cannot be. I would not change my liberal opinion for any creed much as I respect it. I go to church with Mother or Aunt Mary every Sunday but being a Catholic in name is as bad as being practically a Catholic." [18]

With tact Annie managed to widen the horizon of the conservative household. Discovering that the boys secretly played cards outside of the home, she got permission to teach the game in the house and soon had the family indulging in "Old Maid" and "Casino" and even "Big Bonanza." In the same way she taught her young brothers and sisters-in-law to dance, first with pillows for partners, then with one another. But none of them had been "caught" early enough, for these pupils were not much credit to their teacher. With the help of Tom she bought a small melodeon on which all the younger members of the family practiced. (Mrs. George wrote a trifle naively to her son in California, "When they all become good players I will enjoy it more." [19])

With her clever needle, Annie made a wedding dress of soft muslin, hemmed by hand with dozens of tiny ruffles, for her sister-in-law Kate. The girl was married to a young actor, Jared B. Chapman, whose father, William Chapman, had been for years the "low comedian" of the Walnut Street Theater in the time of Mrs. Drew and James Wallack. Jared Chapman was acting small parts in the same company when he met and fell in love with Catherine George, who was teaching school—"Kate" with the merry tongue and knee-length braids of red-gold hair. But so great was the consternation in the George household at the thought of the properly brought up girl marrying an actor that the very good actor (for that he was) gave up his profession to settle down to a sandy farm in New Jersey and become a very poor farmer. However, Jerry Chapman sometimes yearned so much for his lost art that he would steal off for a session with his makeup box and wigs and appear again at his own front door as an apparent stranger to accost his unsuspecting wife. On occasion she threatened to call her husband in from the fields to oust the obnoxious interloper before she discovered who he really was!

Meanwhile, in California, Henry George had left the *San Francisco Times* when a raise in pay he sought was not granted. He became managing editor of Charles De Young's new morning paper, *The Chronicle*. As soon as he was installed he contrived to have John Timmins, who four years earlier had discharged him from the *Sacramento Union,* made foreman of the composing room at *The Chronicle*.

But this connection lasted only a few weeks. George disapproved of De Young's policy. When an opportunity to go East was offered him, he seized it.

After eleven years' absence, Henry was going home to Philadelphia.

CHAPTER IX

RIDDLE AND ANSWER

IN DECEMBER, 1868, Henry George left for the East to seek membership in the Associated Press for The *San Francisco Herald,* a newly revived Democratic newspaper which had hired him for this mission.[1] It was agreed that if he could not wangle an Associated Press contract he was to establish a special Eastern news service for the *Herald.*

From his seat of vantage on the four-horse "mud wagon" crossing the plains (the transcontinental railroad was not yet finished, although thousands of Chinese coolies had been imported to work on it),[2] George had a fine opportunity to see the vast expanse of countryside and to ask many questions of the experienced driver.

Were these vast tracts of virgin land, stretching to the far horizon, part of the "alternate sections" that had been deeded to the railroad, along with the mile-wide strips that would border the tracks on either side? Were they some of the twelve million acres presented the Union Pacific by Congress? [3] Were they some of the lands that had been bought from the Indians by wily white men for two cents an acre, and sometimes paid for, not in money but in merchandise? [4]

There was much to ponder over during that bumpy, jerky ride in the springless, lumbering stage—enough, indeed, to make Henry George forget his physical discomfort. However, when he reached the railroad and boarded a sleeping car it seemed like the height of luxury even though he had to share his berth with a stranger.

He went straight to Philadelphia to join his wife and children and to be reunited with his parents and his brothers and sisters, whom he had not seen for eleven years. It was a joyous meeting but his time at home was short. Engaging a boyhood

friend, John Hasson, as his assistant, he went to New York to
lay the *Herald's* appeal before the Associated Press.

New York had changed as he remembered it from boyhood.
Its population numbered nearly one million. Castle Garden,
the old concert hall at the Battery, had been turned into an im-
migration depot to accommodate the many thousands of newcomers.[5] In this expanding metropolis, in contrast with the
palaces of the rich (a two-million-dollar home was being built
for a newly wealthy merchant)[6] were ten thousand tenements
which the immigrants helped to crowd to overflowing. The
poverty was reflected in the death rate, which was double
that of London.

Henry George waged a stubborn but hopeless fight with the
Associated Press. While he was in New York he contributed
a letter to the *New York Tribune* attacking some of the problems
of the West.[7] He criticized the Wells-Fargo Express for its reck-
lessness in handling mail and the Central Pacific Railroad for
its excessive freight charges. As to the railroad, he wrote, there
would be some excuse for its policies if it had been constructed
by private means—

But it has been, and is being, built literally and absolutely by
the money of the people, receiving liberal aid from cities, counties
and State of California, as well as the immense gratuity of the
general government. . . . The Central Pacific can dictate to California, Nevada and Utah, and the Union Pacific to the States through
which it passes more completely than the Camden and Amboy dictated to New Jersey, and each or both will be able to exert an almost
irresistible pressure upon Congress in any manner in which their
interests are involved. The Central already influences conventions,
manages Legislatures, and has its representatives in both Houses
at Washington. . . .[8]

Failing to get the Associated Press franchise for the *San Francisco Herald,* George returned to Philadelphia and began collecting all the news he could, wiring it in cipher to his paper.
His small and independent service proved to be so good that the
other San Francisco papers, which were members of the Associated Press, brought pressure on the Western Union Telegraph
Company. As a consequence, George was denied the use of
Western Union wires from Philadelphia. He promptly moved
back to New York and continued to send news from there. But
Western Union countered by posting a new schedule of rates

which proved to be an increase in charges for the *Herald* and a reduction for the Associated Press.

Strangely enough, George's employer did not protest, and the young newspaperman fought the dragon of monopoly alone in New York. "Let no man living impose on you," he remembered. He managed to reach high officers of Western Union, to whom he protested that the discrimination in service meant the crushing of his newspaper, but his protests were in vain.

His failure prompted him to write a report to Eastern newspapers. Only one, the *New York Herald,* published it. This exposure of monopoly again failed to sway Western Union, and the San Francisco paper's telegraph news service had to be curtailed so much that competition with its Associated Press rivals became impossible.[9] At this juncture Henry George said good-by to his family in the East and at the end of May returned to San Francisco.

The six months on the Atlantic coast had meant failure and defeat. Yet they shaped the course of his life. His bitter experience at earning a living in bountiful California was bad enough, but he had found conditions even worse in the East. In these crowded cities where material development was far advanced and where, closer to the culture of Europe, there had been fifty years more of "civilization" than there had been on the Pacific frontier, Henry George felt that wealth should be more abundant. Yet men begged and sweatshops flourished in the very shadow of magnificent churches and luxurious homes.

Indeed, the contrast was inescapable. While in the West a few controlled vast tracts of rich soil and affected the lives of a minority who toiled on those wide lands, in the East a similarly privileged group owned less acreage but wielded unbelievable power over a majority crowded into the great cities. Prominent in this New York City group were the Astors, Goelets, Livingstons, and Rhinelanders; the Trinity Church Corporation, mulcting the very people to whom it doled charity; and the Sailor's Snug Harbor Foundation, financing its benevolences to a few old seamen by extracting high rents from landsmen.

If in the West sudden fortunes were made and lost in mining adventures, in the East fortunes were made and lost in Wall Street. Henry George saw in this a form of gambling more pernicious in its effect than that which centered around the digging for metals, and lacking its virtues. In California were the "Big

Four," dishonestly acquiring land titles, subsidies, and franchises through corruption of politicians and law courts.[10] But New York also had its privileged few who, through flagrant bribing of the conscienceless State Senator William Marcy ("Boss")Tweed and his famous ring, contrived at criminally low cost to get title to the highly valuable waterfront of Manhattan Island as well as to franchises and public utilities and rights-of-way.*

In California was the ubiquitous railroad with far-reaching powers that seemed to take toll of every enterprise in the state. But in the East was a chain of railroads extracting subsidies from a much greater public, making appallingly heavy levies on industry, and through the knavery of their chief manipulators (Cornelius Vanderbilt, Jay Gould, and their cohorts) corrupting the courts and city and state governments.[11]

East and West, George thought, the unscrupulous few were able to prey upon the weak many—the few becoming richer; the many, more impoverished. And side by side with wealth stalked want. Human beings seemed to be starving in the midst of plenty. Certainly no beneficent Creator could have willed it so! There must be some natural law that was being broken, else why this unequal distribution?

Which should he do: attack the political dishonesty or seek out the cause of privilege?

It seemed hopeless that any one man could make an impression in the fight against these monster wrongs—let alone a man who had just failed to vanquish a comparatively small monopoly. And why should he, Henry George, who wanted to live quietly and provide a life of ease for those he loved, who wanted to study and travel and read history and poetry and to write a novel—why should he even attempt this apparently unequal struggle?

Not yet thirty, small, slender, shabbily dressed, the type of man who would pass unnoticed in a crowd, he had roamed the great metropolis, through its public squares and past its mansions and its tenements, seeking out the answer to the gnawing question. The shocking contrast between immense wealth and debasing poverty allowed him no peace. And putting aside the dream he once had cherished of acquiring wealth for himself,

* Henry George, Jr., *The Menace of Privilege* (New York: Macmillan, 1905); Gustavus Myers, *History of the Great American Fortunes* (New York: Modern Library, 1938).

he asked only to be shown the way to relieve this suffering—
and the strength to do it.

And then: "Once in daylight, and in a city street, there came
to me a thought, a vision, a call—give it what name you please.
But every nerve quivered and there and then I made a vow." [12]

And from this vow—to seek out and remedy, if he could, the
cause that condemned people to lives of squalor and misery—
he never faltered.

The remedy, the answer to the riddle of progress and poverty,
was to come sooner than George knew. But in the meantime,
back in California, he plunged into new work. Severing his
editorial connection with the *San Francisco Herald,* for which,
however, he set type for a time, he wrote editorials for *The
Evening Bulletin* and made his first attempt to enter the political arena. He tried to get a nomination on the Democratic
ticket for the State Legislature, where he hoped to fight the
telegraph, express, and railroad monopolies. This effort failed
when he refused to pay the assessment asked by the party managers. Disappointment seemed to follow disappointment.

But then a door opened in what had seemed a blank wall.
Henry George received his first offer of an editorship.

He had become acquainted with Governor Henry H. Haight[13]
of California at a meeting of the American Free Trade League.
Haight, like George, had been a Republican and had turned
Jeffersonian Democrat. The two men found that they had much
in common. When the owners of a little Democratic paper,
the Oakland *Transcript,* were looking for a capable man as
editor, Haight influenced them to select George.

While in New York he had written an article in which he
discussed in general the relation of capital and labor and in
particular the wage question as it concerned the hordes of
Chinese coolies migrating to the Pacific coast and toiling uncom-
plainingly for forty dollars a month.[14] Taking note of the rising feeling among white laborers against these immigrants,
George noted:

Our manufacturers have talked of the pauper labor of Manchester,
Leeds and Sheffield. Here is cheaper labor at their own doors. Labor
which will deem itself well remunerated by wages upon which English operators could not keep themselves out of the poor house—
which will not agitate for its own rights, form trade unions, or get
up strikes: which will not clamor for eight hour laws, but will labor

without murmur twelve or fourteen hours a day, not even asking Sundays; which is patient, submissive, enduring, with the patience, submissiveness, and endurance which countless ages of tyranny have ground into the character of the down-trodden peoples of the East.[15]

Although the author pointed out that this problem on the Pacific coast was at bottom a labor problem, he contended also that since there was such a thing as family, nation, race—and the right of association—there is the "corelative right of exclusion."

The article had been printed on the front and second pages of the May 1, 1869 edition of the New York Tribune, occupying four and three-quarters columns. While writing it, "wishing to know what political economy had to say about the cause of wages,"[16] he had read, and had been deeply impressed by, John Stuart Mill. This, in spite of the fact that Mill was both a Malthusian and a materialist while George was neither one.

He sent a copy of the Tribune article to the Englishman and, to his surprise and delight, a letter of commendation arrived. This letter, together with a long editorial, George now printed in the Oakland Transcript. The fact that the celebrated British economist should write at such length to a young, almost unknown editor, and on a subject so important to California, caused much comment. "Concerning the purely economic view of the subject," Mill had written, "I entirely agree with you; and it could be hardly better stated and argued than it is in your article in the New York Tribune." But he suggested that the "character and habits" of the immigrant Chinese might be improved. "If every Chinese child were compulsorily brought under your school system, or under a still more effective one if possible, and kept under it for a sufficient number of years," the British economist asked the young California editor, "would not the Chinese population be in time raised to the level of the American?"

It was soon after this that the answer to the riddle of the problem of poverty came to Henry George while on one of the long horseback rides which were his principal recreation.

He had ridden his mustang into the hills around Oakland and had stopped to let it rest. Absorbed in thought, he gazed over the vast stretches of unused land on every side. A teamster passed and the two men exchanged greetings. For want of something better to say, George asked casually what this land was worth.

"I don't know exactly," said the teamster. And, pointing in the direction of some grazing cows, small in the distance, he added, "But there is a man over there who will sell some land for a thousand dollars an acre." [17]

A thousand dollars an acre! Why, it was worth only a small fraction of that! This soil had no greater fertility than thousands of acres further away. Further away . . . not so near to the growing colonies of men.

And quick as a flash came the answer to the riddle that had troubled him.

When settlers came, when population increased, land would grow in value. Without a stroke of work on the part of the owner (who could go live in Siam if he wished), these idle stretches would become, with the expansion of the cities of Oakland and Berkeley and San Francisco, worth a fortune to him. In anticipation of this rise in value, the owner was now holding his land for one thousand dollars an acre. Soon he would be able to collect the value that he had had no part in creating.

Suddenly it was clear to George that land value is not the result of a man's labor but of the growth of the community and the development of its activities. Morally, he reasoned, this unearned gain "belongs in usufruct to all." To permit a few individuals to take for their aggrandizement this wealth that is created by the community thereby forces the community to levy exactions upon labor and thrift for the maintenance of its services. The very process, while thus penalizing labor and thrift, offers rewards to the few for withholding land from use to the many—rewards that accrue to the speculator, the profiteer in that which is absolutely necessary to human life. . . . Here were fundamental reasons for the increase of poverty along with increase of wealth.

"I then and there recognized," he wrote long after, "the natural order—one of those experiences that make those who have them feel thereafter that they can vaguely appreciate what mystics and poets have called the 'ecstatic vision.'" [18]

THE ANSWER

EIGHTEEN MONTHS later the "ecstatic vision" in the California hills took substance in Henry George's first considered and extended writing on the subject which was to spread his name around the world. In the meantime his friend, Governor Haight, was deep in his fight against the subsidy policy of the Central Pacific Railroad and had called upon George for help.

"The Great Absorber," as the railroad was known, had been acquiring vast tracts of land and demanding more and more of the people's money while the four Sacramento former shop-keepers and traders who were at the helm, manipulating the corporation, were gathering to themselves the power of feudal lords.

In 1862, these men, the "Big Four"—Leland Stanford, Charles Crocker, Mark Hopkins, and Colis P. Huntington—had managed to make Stanford the governor of California for a two-year term at the same time that he had been chosen president of the Central Pacific.[1] Their strategy had helped materially in the passage by Congress, in July of that year, of the Pacific Railroad Act.

This act and its later amendment had deeded to the railroad vast tracts of public domain. The Central Pacific deeds included a wide strip of land for rights-of-way as well as "alternate sections" of one square mile on both sides of the entire line thus making the company one of the biggest land owners of the West.[2] The act had further provided a government loan in the form of thirty-six-year bonds at 6 per cent interest in amounts ranging from $16,000 per mile of track on flat land to $18,000 per mile on mountain land. (In one place the four promoters contrived to have 150 miles of flat land considered as mountain land, thereby netting themselves nearly half a million dollars.) "Indeed they had the entire road constructed with scarcely the expenditure of a single dollar of their own," said Gustavus Myers.

The power of this combine was becoming a national scandal. The "Big Four" openly purchased votes, flagrantly corrupted legislators as well as congressmen, and bought legal decisions. They underbid competing ship and stage transportation until it was destroyed, and then jacked up freight rates, thereby crushing the life out of trade. California wondered whether the coming of the "iron horse" was such a blessing after all.

Governor Haight was determined to check this evil power. Believing in the ability of Henry George, he asked the young journalist to leave the Oakland *Transcript* and take the editor's chair on the chief Democratic party paper, the *Sacramento Reporter*. The proposal delighted George. In February, 1870, he moved to the state capital with his family, recently returned from their long visit in Philadelphia.

The new arrangement kept George and Haight in close contact. One evening the young editor took the Governor home with him. It was late, the meal was over, and Mrs. George had gone to bed. Great was her perturbation when she heard the cheery voice of her husband announcing that he had brought the Governor of California home to dinner! She dressed hastily and gave a gracious welcome and warmed-over Irish stew and rice pudding to the distinguished visitor, whom, by the way, she had never met. And Governor Haight, assuring her that Irish stew and rice pudding were among his favorite dishes, consumed them with great relish.[3]

George remained with the *Reporter* only nine months. He had used his pen to resume the fight against the Western Union Telegraph Company and the Associated Press monopolies, but he spent much of his energy attacking the Central Pacific Railroad's plea for further subsidies. Since this giant monopoly commanded money as well as politics and press, it was able quietly to buy control of the *Reporter*, and then to force on George a policy with which he could not agree. To remain would mean a higher salary and relief from financial worry. But the editor resigned and moved with his family back to San Francisco.

His ouster from the paper which he had turned into a weapon against graft and corruption did not silence his attacks on the "Octopus." [4] In San Francisco he wrote a sixteen page pamphlet which he called "The Subsidy Question and the Democratic Party." Governor Haight considered this such a valuable contribution that he had a large edition of the pamphlet printed and circulated in his campaign for re-election. In the brochure George pointed out that railroad subsidies are to be condemned "by the economic principle that the development of industry should be left free to take its natural course . . . by the political principle that government should be reduced to its minimum—that it becomes more corrupt and more tyrannical, and less under the control of the people, with every extension of its powers. . . ." [5]

The pamphlet did much to make Henry George's name known throughout the state. It also made him all the more the target for the powerful railroads. When he obtained the Democratic nomination for the Assembly, he received proportionately an even smaller vote than Haight or the others on the ticket. He returned home late, after the ballots were counted, and laughingly told his wife, "Why, we haven't elected a constable!"

Although he appeared to take his defeat lightly, in reality it was a disappointment.[6] A seat in the Assembly might have meant an opportunity to write into the California land laws his principles of equity and justice.

In spite of the interruptions of the Haight campaign he had been working during the period from March to July, 1871, on a concrete answer to the economic riddle which possessed him. His labors resulted in the long brochure, "Our Land and Land Policy."

The pamphlet of forty-eight pages of closely printed type was the equivalent of 130 pages of ordinary book size. It was a careful study of Federal and California state lands and land grants. It was a plea that these reckless land grants should cease, and it cited case after case in California of private estates amounting to one, two, and three hundred thousand acres—several of over four hundred thousand acres.

In the first section, for instance, George pointed out that a single railroad, the Northern Pacific, had received 25,600 acres for the building of each mile of track. And were the company land of the Central-Southern Pacific Railroad Corporation divided, he wrote, "it would give them something like two million acres apiece." [7]

The brochure dealt with George's theories on the relation between labor and land and indicated what our land policy should be. It was in fact the kernel of what has since been called the Single Tax theory. Wages are high in new countries where the land is free, he pointed out, but in the old countries where land is monopolized, wages are low and poverty is great. He asserted that economic rent, or the return for the use of the land, should be collected and employed for social needs and that no taxes at all should be levied on the products of labor:

The value of land is something which belongs to all, and in taxing land values we are merely taking for the use of the community something which belongs to the community.... In speaking of the value of land, I mean the value of the land itself, not the value of any improvement which has been raised upon it....[8] The mere holder of the land would be called on to pay just as much taxes as the user of the land. The owner of a vacant city lot would have to pay as much for the privilege of keeping other people off it till he wanted to use it, as a neighbor who has a fine house upon his lot, and is either using it or deriving rent from it. The monopolizer of agricultural land would be taxed as much as though his land were covered with improvements, with crops and with stock.

Therefore:

Land prices would fall; land speculation would receive its death blow; land monopolization would no longer pay....[9]

The whole weight of taxation would be lifted from productive industry. The million dollar manufactory, and the needle of the seamstress, the mechanic's cottage and the grand hotel, the farmer's plow, and the ocean steamship, would be alike untaxed.

Imagine this country with all taxes removed from production and exchange! * How demand would spring up; how trade would increase; what a powerful stimulus would be applied to every branch of industry; what an enormous development of wealth would take place.... Would there be many industrious men walking our streets, or tramping over our roads in the vain search for employment? [10]

"Our Land and Land Policy," coming from the pen of a man not yet thirty-two years old, suggested a new[11] and startling solution to the economic crisis. But it did not meet with the recognition for which the author had hoped. While approxi-

---

* George pointed out, with evident horror, that "40,000,000 of our people have to raise $800,000,000 per year for public purposes." The population now is between three and four times that figure but the amount raised from Federal taxes alone is nearly fifty times the figure he mentioned in 1871.—Editor.

mately one thousand copies of his brochure were sold, George realized that if he really wished to command attention he would someday have to cover the field more thoroughly and in a much larger book.

Yet here was an economic classic—one of the few native to America—in its embryo form.[12]

CHAPTER XI

THE EVENING POST

DURING 1871, Henry George also tried his hand at fiction, with "How Jack Breeze Missed Being a Pasha," [1] which he published in *The Overland Monthly* together with an article "Bribery in Elections." [2] The latter was the first article to be published in the United States advocating the Australian ballot. [3]

Aside from this writing, George found nothing to anchor him in California and thought seriously of going to New York or Philadelphia to try to establish himself. And then, again, as if by magic, opportunity opened. A printer friend, William Hinton, came to him with the suggestion that they start a daily newspaper. The two men managed to get together $1,800; and this plus the sale of delivery routes in advance, enabled them to launch the *San Francisco Evening Post.* [4]

There were no pennies in circulation on the Pacific coast; the nickel was the smallest coin in use. However, the proprietors of the *Post* were determined to publish a penny paper, following the example of successful dailies in the East. They persuaded the Bank of California to import one thousand dollars' worth of shiny new coppers from the Philadelphia Mint. When four of these pretty coins were handed back in change to the amazed citizens of San Francisco who had offered nickels for the new paper, the novelty served as an excellent advertisement.

The *Post* was free of political affiliations and was bold and fearless from the start. It caught on and won a respectful following. When the four-page paper was four months old an offer was made to buy it. The business manager, A. H. Rapp, who owned an interest, wanted to sell. George and Hinton consented and each received $2,700 as his share. But under the new management, and without Henry George's pen to give it vigor, the little *Post* soon declined. After sixty days' struggle the new purchaser offered it to George and Hinton for a nominal sum. They bought it back and it promptly recovered its strength.[5] Less than nine months from its birth the paper had to be increased in size and its price advanced to two cents, then to five cents, as further expansion became necessary.

The *Post* was nearly two years old when John P. Jones, United States Senator from Nevada and a warm advocate of President Grant, approached the owners and offered to furnish them on their own notes enough money to buy the best press that could be obtained. Improved facilities for more rapid press work seemed a necessity. The *Post's* owners accepted the proposition and Hinton went East where, for $30,000, he bought a Bullock perfecting press of the type George had seen in the plant of the *New York Sun*. The machinery was set up in the new office at 402 Montgomery Street, where the *Post* could boast the first perfecting press on the Pacific coast.

A party was held to celebrate the occasion. The new press was demonstrated to the guests, and for those who didn't mind climbing three flights of stairs, there was not only delectable food but plenty of California champagne and California tobacco.

The editorial office was on the top floor. There, in a small room containing the paper-cluttered desk, a crowded bookcase and a green baize covered sofa, worked the editor.[6] Often smoking a cigar, George would dictate to his secretary, Stephen Potter, and while Potter transcribed his shorthand notes the editor would continue the article at his own desk, writing in longhand. This system enabled him to get through a vast amount of work in a short time.

The typewriter was just then coming into general use. George wanted one but the business department ruled against the investment. Since the typewriter company would not give one of its machines in exchange for advertising, the daily drudgery with the pen had to be continued. But George had the last word. One day, when the last news form crashed from the third-floor composing room to the press room in the basement and was reduced to printer's pi because the dumbwaiter rope broke (the weakness of this rope having been noted far in advance of the accident), the business department came in for a few pithy and well-chosen editorial remarks on "spigot-bunghole economy."

George was inclined to absent-mindedness. Several times

young Potter, his secretary, met him on the street, standing on the edge of the sidewalk buried in thought and oblivious of his surroundings. On such occasions it was necessary to speak to him repeatedly before he heard.

In money matters he was not only liberal but careless. As the banking methods of both himself and his secretary were somewhat crude, the two hit upon the happy arrangement of using one of Potter's pockets for George's money to take care of petty cash transactions. If money, the origin of which could not be recalled, was found in this pocket, then it was tacitly assumed to be the editor's.

All through its existence the *Post's* editorials frequently advocated taxation of land values in lieu of all other taxes. This editorial policy was ridiculed by rival papers as "George's Fad." One of the critics printed a cartoon of the *Post* editor as a boy astride a stick, with whip in hand, galloping across a newspaper page in pursuit of airy phantoms. The cartoon was labeled "Harry George Riding His Hobby."

The policy of the *Post* was opposed to Grant and Reconstruction, advocating the nomination of Horace Greeley. George went as a delegate from California to the Democratic convention that met in Baltimore in June, 1872. After a visit to Greeley at his Chappaqua estate in West Chester County, New York, George rushed home to San Francisco to take up the fight for his candidate. "Grant," he wrote in an editorial on November 2, "represents the hatreds growing out of the war. . . . Greeley represents the spirit of reconciliation and magnanimity." [7]

But his candidate was beaten. George, sorely disappointed, turned again to a relentless hammering at the California "Octopus." He wrote much in this vein: "The interests of individuals, towns, cities, counties and the State and Federal governments have all been trampled upon and sacrificed to swell the gains of Stanford, Huntington, the Crockers, and some half dozen others belonging to the ring." [8]

Although his editorials were chiefly focused on municipal and state affairs, he was thoroughly aware of what was happening in the East. For instance, when attacking local corruption, he remarked, "Can the records of Tammany, or any other thieving ring, show a more outrageous case of jobbery! Boss Tweed and even the cormorants of Grant's Washington Ring might come out here to take a lesson!" [9]

Rumors that Vanderbilt might buy the Central Pacific Railroad provoked this editorial reaction:

Vanderbilt is even more grasping and tyrannical than Stanford ever was. . . . Has it [*The Call,* a rival] never heard of the wars of Vanderbilt with Fisk and Drew and with rival corporations, in which conventions were systematically packed, legislatures bought by wholesale, companies of bullies hired and even the bench retained? Does it not know that the great State of Pennsylvania is Tom Scott's pocket borough and that its legislature is so notoriously owned by the railroad king, that a member once got up and said: "If Tom Scott has no further business with this House, I move that it now adjourn"? If we do get Vanderbilt instead of Stanford, we are afraid that we shall look back to the latter as the frogs in the fable looked back to their King Log, after Jupiter, in answer to their prayer, had sent them a stork.[10]

And his alarm over the wanton manner in which public lands were being deeded away caused him to report: "Tom Scott and his railroad crowd are likely to get eight million acres of land in Texas under decision of the U. S. Supreme Court confirming the grants of the Memphis, El Paso and Transcontinental Railroad." [11]

But the editorials in the *Post* were not concerned entirely with the railroad trust. George urged self-improvement for laborers, fought for shorter working days and reported the success of the eight-hour law in Australia, urging its adoption in the United States. "It is to political action," he explained, "that working men must look for the remedy for all their real grievances, for those are grievances which spring from bad laws." [12]

On another occasion he took up the cudgels for misused seamen. The *Post* became a champion of sailor's rights. It exposed the unbelievable cruelty of the captain and mate of the ship *Crusader* and later the officers of the *Sunrise*.

The latter ship arrived in San Francisco minus three seamen who had been aboard. These three, two men and a boy of seventeen, were foreigners who had been shanghaied. Goaded and tortured by the first mate and the captain, they had jumped overboard rather than remain on the hell-ship. The remaining members of the *Sunrise's* crew were able to talk. But for three days, in spite of long news accounts in the *Post,* in spite of George's appeals to the authorities and his flaming editorials,

no legal action was taken. "Then Editor George of the *Post*
went before District Attorney Latimer and made affidavit upon
information and belief, charging Captain Clarke and his two
mates with maliciously beating and wounding Charles B. Brown,
on the high seas." [13] During the three days delay the first mate
had disappeared. Now the *Post* offered $400 for his arrest.
Eventually he was caught and punished with the other officers
of the *Sunrise* after an exciting though revolting trial.

The public was at last made aware of the hideous injustice
done to sailors: their scurvy-producing food, their wretched
pay, their slavery to commanding officers. As long as he held an
editorial pen, Henry George fought for their rights.

He fought for women's rights, too. On July 2, 1872, he wrote:

We have long been a warm sympathizer with female school
teachers in their contest to secure an equality of rights and compensation in pursuit of their noble calling. No arguments have yet been
presented sufficient to convince us that women have not the capacity
to fill the very highest positions in educational institutions, nor
have we been able to see by what rule of right or principle of
justice women should receive less pay than men for performing the
same duties equally well.... The true rule is to open the ranks of
competition without regard to sex. Let those who are best qualified
be chosen, whether male or female.[14]

His strong belief in feminism was proved in behavior as well
as in word. One day as he went home he saw his wife approaching from another direction. Catching sight of him she hurried up
and explained, "I was delayed shopping. I'm sorry—I always
like to be home waiting for you."

"Annie," he responded almost severely, "don't you ever talk
that way again. Just why must you get home at a certain time?
I don't possess you! Never put me in the position, even in your
thought, of being your master, to whom you need give an
accounting of your actions! I'm free to come and go as I see fit—
and so must you be!"[15]

San Francisco was bitterly divided over the issue of women's
rights. Women who solicited votes at local option elections
were treated disrespectfully. The *Post* attacked their ungallant
assailants, and this provoked the wrath of the saloons where
much of the antifeminist agitation had its center. Henry George
was quick to retaliate. He inspired an investigation of the liquor
interests, and it was proved on analysis of samples of the liquor

sold in San Francisco that it contained large quantities of fusel oil. This was chronicled in the *Post* and made every saloon George's enemy.

As champion of the unfortunate and oppressed, the editor's position demanded physical as well as moral courage. George kept up his strength by swimming, rowing, and horseback riding. "When the George family was living out in the Mission, a suburban part of town, he concluded to buy a horse and ride to the *Post* office daily," recounts William Cleveland McCloskey.[16] "It was the most extraordinary piece of horseflesh imaginable. Small, bony, angular, a veritable old plug. Henry George certainly was a picture astride that beast, and many a jibe and joke was held at his expense over the old nag."

He had always been strong and fearless. One night, years before, when as a printer he had come home late at night, he found his wife quivering with fright. On that afternoon when the Chinese laundryman came for his pay he had tried to kiss her. He was the biggest Chinese she had ever seen, but somehow she had succeeded in shutting the door. Her husband quieted her fears. Not until long afterward did he tell her that alone he had gone to Chinatown and had sought out the laundryman. Delivering a blow powerful enough to knock the surprised giant flat, and flinging the pay on the sidewalk beside the prostrate figure, the enraged husband then stalked out of the Chinese quarter unmolested.[17]

Now as editor of the *Post* this same courage was needed as he campaigned against the powers of graft and corruption—"the ring." Month after month he fought for prison reform, for better food in prison, city hospital, and almshouse. He pled the cause of two small boys sent to the "Industrial School." They had stolen a valuable watch and sold it for two dollars, with which they bought candy. "It is a sin and a shame," wrote George, "that we have no public institution to which children who fall into crime from want of parental control can be sent with any hope of reforming them."[18]

Repeatedly he exposed the wicked methods used in this so-called reform school where the boys were underfed, inhumanly punished, and herded together in a way which turned those who were potentially good citizens into hardened criminals. He attacked the cruelty of the superintendent, George F. Harris, and expressed his humiliation that San Francisco should permit "the ring to re-elect their friend, the boy-torturer."[19]

Finally an investigation took place. The ferocious-looking Harris, his hand on his pistol, stood at the gate but according to Judge Robert Ferral, George, without the least hesitation, "walked right up to him, looked the burly ruffian straight in the eyes and passed into the yard without a word. All through that investigation Harris avoided the steady, indignant gaze of the brave little man who pressed his charges of brutality and drove him from his position and out of the city." [20]

On another occasion George became indignant at the harsh way alcoholics were treated in San Francisco prisons and directed the attention of the Society for the Prevention of Cruelty to Animals to these unfortunates! Once, when he remonstrated with a policeman who was treating a drunkard brutally, the patrolman threatened to arrest him. Whereupon George said he would save him the trouble, and, exercising a citizen's prerogative, arrested the officer. Leaving the intoxicated man to his own devices the editor and the policeman marched to the station house and entered charges against each other. [21]

While working at his desk one day, George was disturbed by a turmoil in the street below. From his window he saw that the cause of the commotion was a drunken sailor, clad only in the scantiest of garments, who was hanging perilously by one hand from the bottom of a small iron balcony outside his lodging house window. His balcony and the editor's own balcony were fairly close together in adjacent buildings and almost on the same level. George rushed to the aid of the unfortunate man. Bending over his own balcony, he managed to clutch the sailor's wrists and to draw him up. The feat required strength and balance. Then one of the *Post's* printers, coming to George's assistance, grasped one of the drunkard's waving legs and helped lift him over the railing to safety.[22]

The *San Francisco Evening Post* had been started in November, 1871. Because of its editorial policy, it had a grim financial struggle during the first two years. But installation of the new perfecting press lowered the cost of production and the *Post* grew in circulation despite the depression of 1873. Expansion seemed desirable. On August 20, 1875, the publishers launched the *Morning Ledger*[23] with "a mammoth eight-page Sunday edition"[24] which, beginning with the September 19 issue, carried news, editorials, theatrical criticism, book reviews, and illustrations.

Here, for the first time in journalism, was an illustrated

Sunday paper.[25] The editors refrained from soliciting advertisements, preferring to wait until advertisers should seek the paper.

Editing a morning as well as an evening daily meant so much work that on many nights George could not go home. Instead he slept—when he could spare the time to sleep—on the little green couch in his office. Sometimes, to keep himself going, he sent his secretary to the saloon at the corner for a bottle of "Cutter whiskey."[26] Not being an habitual drinker, a little liquor quickly affected him. One night when he had promised to speak for Father Matthew on "Temperance" and had braced himself for the ordeal he arrived at the meeting in definitely inappropriate spirits. His speech began with a discussion of temperance but somehow veered off to the subject of economics and became an eloquent appeal for the abolition of one tax after another until there should be only one thing left to tax—land values. The speech was an instant success; even Father Matthew was pleased.[27] Eventually the editor obtained a more dependable tonic from his doctor.

Shortly after the launching of the *Morning Ledger* there was a great fire in Virginia City, Nevada, the mining center. Many San Franciscans were heavily involved, and a severe decline in mining stock and the suspension of payment by the Bank of California followed the fire. This resulted in a financial panic in San Francisco. Early in November, when it was impossible to collect money, George had to suspend the *Ledger*. At this point Senator Jones demanded the return of the money lent for the purchase of the new press or the surrender to him of the *Post*. George felt like fighting, for he knew that a statement of the situation from his pen, published in the paper, could kill its future with another editor, but considering the employees who would thereby lose their jobs, he refrained from writing the statement. And so, without a cent of compensation, on November 27, 1875, he and William Hinton gave over the paper to the representatives of Jones.[28]

Henry George had loved the *Post*. It was the fruit of his labor. It had been an instrument for waging the fight against injustice, corruption, and privilege. It had been the source of a comfortable living after years of struggle. Now it was gone. And once again he was flat broke.

CHAPTER XII

INSPECTOR OF METERS

IT IS ALL in a lifetime, and I have seen too much to think
I can certainly tell what is good and what is evil fortune,"
Henry George wrote to his friend John Swinton of the *New
York Sun* the day following his loss of the *Post*.[1]

Thus he took another defeat philosophically. Analyzing the
event a few days later in another letter to Swinton, he explained
his situation in San Francisco in these words:

> They look on me as a pestilential agrarian and communist and
> will avoid what they call my hobbies. But though they do not know
> it, the very aggressiveness and radicalism of the *Post* was its strength.
> In making a paper that will not affect gunny bags, they will kill it as
> you will in time see. . . . I ran the *Post* for four years lacking a week,
> and successfully. If I never did anything more I have the satisfaction
> of knowing that I have perceptibly affected public thought and
> planted ideas which will some day bloom into action. As for being
> depressed I am not—twenty-four hours are enough for me to cry
> over spilt milk.[2]

Now his sponsorship of William S. Irwin, newly elected Governor of California, fortunately stood him in good stead. Governor Irwin appointed the erstwhile editor as State Inspector of
Gas Meters, monotonous work for a man of his intellect but
welcome because it paid (in fees) a modest salary and provided
some leisure. Four months after he took up this work George
wrote to his father that "I have done writing enough and now
I propose to do a little speaking." He had had his fill of the
newspaper business for the time, he wrote, and had started the
study of law "to employ my leisure in that way as much as I
can, and before my term is out get admitted to the bar."

He wrote of his home life:

There has been no period when I felt so contented.[3] In all this
Pacific coast, yes in all the United States, there is no happier home
than mine. It is now nearly fifteen years since Annie and I were
married, and we are more lovers today than we were then, while
our three children are nothing but pleasure and pride.

The boys in school nickname Harry (Henry, Jr.) "The Orator."
They are always glad to hear him speak. His last piece is Mark
Anthony's address over the dead body of Caesar.* Dick recited for
me the other night almost the whole of "Horatius," and that is a very
long poem; while little Jen, not to be outdone, recited "The Night
Before Christmas"... the boys know more of Shakespeare than I
did at twenty-five and are fast picking up, without any strain, a
knowledge of history, etc.... If it were not for the embarrassed way
in which I got out of the *Post* there would be no difficulty about our
coming to the Centennial exposition in Philadelphia in style.[4] But
I can see my way clear now and don't propose to go in debt again.
... Now I want to concentrate, and study and think, and then when
I get ready I will come permanently before the public again in
some way or other.[5]

As inspector of gas meters he was obliged to travel about
the state, where he made interesting contacts and was able to
study local conditions. It not only gave him time to read law
but also to do some writing. He wrote articles for the *Sacramento Bee,* took an active interest in the doings of the Legislature, and entered vigorously into the Tilden-Hayes presidential campaign.

On the night of August 15, 1876, he made his first political
speech in behalf of Tilden, whom he believed to be a free
trader. Delivered at Dashaway Hall under the auspices of the
Tilden and Hendricks Club of San Francisco, the speech was
not a political harangue but a carefully prepared study of
economic conditions. He considered the Presidential contest
to be "a solemn, momentous inquiry, demanding from each
voter a conscientious judgment."[6] Reading his manuscript
slowly and deliberately, he warned, "The Federal tax-gatherer
is everywhere. In each exchange by which labor is converted
into commodities, there he is, standing between buyer and
seller to take his toll."[7] At one point he sketched vividly the
social conditions of the period:

* He won only second prize, however; his classmate, David Warfield, who in
time was to become a great dramatic star, won first.—Editor.

See seventy thousand men out of work in the Pennsylvania coal fields; fifty thousand laborers asking for bread in the City of New York; the almshouses of Massachusetts crowded to repletion in the summertime; unemployed men roving over the West in great bands, stealing what they cannot earn. . . . It is an ominous thing that in this centennial year, states that a century ago were covered by the primeval forest should be holding conventions to consider the "tramp nuisance"—the pure symptoms of that leprosy of nations, chronic pauperism. . . . What can any change of men avail so long as the policy which is the primary cause of these evils is unchanged? [8]

This address was so successful that it was printed and used as a campaign pamphlet. In spite of George's lack of oratorical training he was invited to "stump" the state for the Democrats. This gave him a reputation as a speaker and he was asked to deliver the final address of the campaign.

"Whether I go into politics, into the law or into the newspaper business," he wrote his mother, "I do not intend to rest here; but to go ahead step by step. . . . I propose to read and study; to write some things which will extend my reputation, and perhaps to deliver some lectures with the same view. And if I live, I shall make myself known even in Philadelphia. I aim high." [9]

There had been no chair of political economy at the University of California, and when plans were made to establish one, Henry George, who had proved his threefold power as original thinker, writer, and speaker, was suggested for the place. His familiarity with economics as evinced in "Our Land and Land Policy" and his long record of thoughtful editorials won him an invitation to deliver several lectures at Berkeley before the students and faculty.

A college professorship, as George confided to his wife, was one of his ambitions. And so he took much care in the preparation of the first lecture, "The Study of Political Economy." He made no attempt to expound his own theories on how the unequal distribution of wealth might be rectified but tried merely to show the vital importance of this branch of learning which "concerns itself with matters which among us occupy more than nine tenths of human effort, and perhaps nine tenths of human thought." He defined economics in this wise, compressing much of his philosophy into a few sentences:

In its province are included all that relates to the wages of labor and the earnings of capital; all regulations of trade; all questions of currency and finance; all taxes and public disbursements—in short, everything that can in any way affect the amount of wealth which a community can secure, or the proportion in which that wealth will be distributed between individuals. Though not the science of government, it is essential to the science of government. . . . If you trace out the laws of production and exchange of wealth, you will see the causes of social weakness and disease in enactments which selfishness has imposed on ignorance, and in maladjustments entirely within our own control.

And you will see the remedies. Not in wild dreams of red destruction nor weak projects for putting them in leading-strings to a brainless abstraction called the state, but in simple measures sanctioned by justice. You will see in light the great remedy, in freedom the great solvent. You will see that the true law of social life is the law of love, the law of liberty, the law of each for all and all for each; that the golden rule of morals is also the golden rule of the science of wealth; that the highest expressions of religious truth include the widest generalizations of political economy.[10]

The students appeared to like the lecture. But the faculty gave it a politely chilly reception which made George suspect that he would not be invited to appear at the University of California again. And, to his deep regret, he was not invited.[11]

Perhaps this was because of the following conscious digression, in which George expounded much of his theory of education:

For the study of political economy you need no special knowledge, no extensive library, no costly laboratory. You do not even need textbooks or teachers, if you will but think for yourselves. All that you need is care in reducing complex phenomena to their elements, in distinguishing the essential from the accidental, and in applying the simple laws of human action with which you are familiar. . . . All this array of professors, all this paraphernalia of learning cannot educate a man. Here you may obtain the tools; but they will be useful only to him who can use them. A monkey with a microscope, a mule packing a library, are fit emblems of the men—and unfortunately they are plenty—who pass through the whole educational machinery and come out but learned fools, crammed with knowledge which they cannot use—all the more pitiable, all the more contemptible, all the more in the way of real progress, because they pass, with themselves and others, as educated men. . . .[12]

Whatever reason the University Board may have had for not asking George to deliver a second lecture, his friendships with President John LeConte and his brother, Professor Joseph LeConte, the physicist, Professor William Swinton (brother of John Swinton), authority in the field of belles-lettres, and others among the faculty were in no way diminished.

Of course, he did not get the appointment to the new chair of political economy.

A few months after the Berkeley lecture George was chosen by citizens of San Francisco to be the principal orator at the Fourth of July celebration held in the California Theater. The hall was crowded. He delivered a long and scholarly address which was prophetic in the sense that it antedated by many years the League of Nations and even the United Nations. At one point he asked, "Is it too soon to hope . . . that it may be the mission of this Republic to unite all the nations of English speech, whether they grow beneath the Northern Star or Southern Cross, in a league which, by insuring justice, promoting peace, and liberating commerce, will be the forerunner of a world-wide federation that will make war the possibility of a past age, and turn to works of usefulness the enormous forces now dedicated to destruction?"[13]

Ending with an apostrophe to liberty, this oration called forth wonder from his friends and commendation from most of the newspapers, although the *News Letter* stated that the "gas measurer . . . kindly spoke for several hours on the Goddess of Liberty and other school reader topics."[14]

And now the "gas measurer" declined the nomination for state senator offered by a group of workingmen who were strongly anti-Chinese. Instead, he retired from public life for a time and after the day's diminishing meter inspections were done, read history and wrote an inquiry into recurring industrial depressions. When the essay was finished he read it to his friend Dr. Taylor.

Edward Robeson Taylor, one year older than George, had served as purser on a Sacramento River steamboat, had set type, and had written for a newspaper. Later he became private secretary to Governor Haight, and was now the former Governor's law partner. (Taylor was a doctor of medicine as well as a doctor of laws. After the San Francisco earthquake of 1896 he served a term as mayor and later became dean of the University of California Law School.)

When Dr. Taylor heard this latest product of Henry George's economic thinking—this article on progress and its shadow, want —he was greatly impressed and urged the author not to give it to a magazine but to expand it into the book which another friend, James McClatchy, editor of the *Sacramento Bee*, had been urging him to write. George himself had realized, after finishing "Our Land and Land Policy" in 1871, that someday he would have to write a longer work to give the fullest expression to his views. Now, in this lull in the pressure of his personal concerns, after six years of newspaper work and study of public affairs, at last the time had come to write that book.

The entry in his diary for September 18, 1877, read: "Commenced 'Progress and Poverty.'"

CHAPTER XIII

PROGRESS AND POVERTY

IN THE WINTER of 1877-78 when Henry George began *Progress and Poverty* the whole country seemed to be passing through a period of hard times. Railroad strikes resulted in riots and the calling of troops in several of the Eastern states. In California drought had injured the crops, the output of the mines was reduced, and at this low ebb in the state's resources the Central Pacific Railroad proposed a wage cut.

Hard times did not spare the family of the inspector of gas meters, whose income had dwindled. George began lecturing to eke out a living. A group of his friends had organized what they called the Land Reform League of California, the pioneer organization devoted to the propagation of his teachings, which stemmed from a meeting at the law office of James G. Maguire on Clay Street, above Montgomery. There, in late 1877, the group began meeting to discuss "Our Land and Land Policy."

Early the following year these meetings resulted in the formal launching of the Land Reform League. One of its first projects was the sponsorship of a George lecture, "Why Work Is Scarce, Wages Low and Labor Restless." [1] The author stopped work on his book to prepare it. Speaking on the night of March 26, 1877, in Metropolitan Temple before a small audience, George prophesied, "The standard that I have tried to raise tonight may be torn by prejudice and blackened by calumny; it may now move forward, and again be forced back. But once loosed, it can never again be furled!" [2]

The small crowd disappointed him. But while his lecture reached few ears and caused little stir in San Francisco, the results were somewhat better when he repeated it in other parts of California. It was an ambitious undertaking and, as he wrote John Swinton, it was "an attempt to put into popular form a great truth which marries political economy with com-

mon sense, and which once appreciated is the key to all the
social problems of our time. . . . The seed that I have for years
been sowing is springing up on every hand. I have made to
principle, sacrifices that were very bitter, but in my own time,
I can see what at first I never expected to see, the result of my
work. Where I stood alone thousands now stand with me. The
leaven is at work. And there can be but one result. But the
struggle will be long and fierce. It is now only opening." [3]

Less than three months after the Metropolitan Temple
meeting George was asked by the Young Men's Hebrew Association to address them at their first meeting. He wrote and
delivered before this group a lecture which he called simply,
"Moses." In general, it redeveloped his economic theories.
"Moses," he said, "saw that the real cause of enslavement of
the masses of Egypt was what has everywhere produced enslavement, the possession by a class of the land upon which
and from which the whole people must live.[4] He saw that to
permit in the land the same unqualified private ownership that
by natural right attaches to things produced by labor, would
be inevitably to separate the people into the very rich and the
very poor, inevitably to enslave labor—to make the few the
masters of the many, no matter what the political forms: to
bring vice and degradation, no matter what the religion."

The audience was deeply moved. Some of George's friends
who heard the address considered it to be the finest he ever
gave. One, Dr. Taylor, was thrilled but insisted that there be
no more interruptions in the work on the book which George
had begun.

But some further interruptions were inevitable. George put
aside his pen to help organize the Free Public Library of San
Francisco which later, with its branches, was to become the
most complete library west of the Rockies.[5] He was the first
secretary of the original board of trustees and the early minutes
are in his handwriting, inscribed with the same blue ink which
he was using in the neatly written manuscript of the book.

The chief interruption came when George ran for delegate
to the convention to be held for the general amendment of the
state constitution. Knowing that if he were chosen delegate he
might succeed in having written into the laws of California his
plans for the taxation of land values, he issued an appeal "to
the voters of California," advising them that, since "justice is
the only firm foundation of the state, I shall endeavor, as I

have power, to so amend the constitution that the weight of taxation may be shifted from those who ... produce wealth to those who merely appropriate it, so that the monopoly of land and water may be destroyed ... and an end be put to the shameful state of things which compels men to beg who are willing to work." [6]

The Land Reform League worked vigorously in his behalf. The Democratic party and the new Workingmen's party both nominated him. With these groups pledged to him, election seemed assured. At the Workingmen's ratification meeting, however, he was asked to acknowledge the leadership of the political boss, Dennis Kearney, and to accept his platform. But George did not like several planks of the platform and he refused to have any man his master. His independence was stated so emphatically that the crowd began to hiss. Of course, the nomination was revoked. George was left with only Democratic support, and at the polls the Democratic ticket was beaten soundly. But he had the satisfaction of receiving more votes than any other candidate of the party.

The George family had now moved to First Street near Harrison, the exact spot where the Oakland Bridge now begins. Reduced circumstances forced them to live simply. Though there were debts and difficulties to be met and sacrifices to be made, these things did not touch the happiness which the Georges found in one another.

The author's work room, though cluttered with books and papers, was cozy and cheery.[7] Three large windows looked out on the San Francisco hills and the blue bay and on boats of all kinds and on swirling sea gulls. A large table in the center served as Henry George's writing desk. Most of his reading or planning was done as he stretched out on the lounge, although often, when he was pondering some point, he would pace the floor or else stand by a window, humming a tune and beating the rhythm on the pane with his fingers.

The eldest child, Henry Jr., having finished grammar school, became secretary to his father. Mrs. George helped by checking the "fair" with the marked copy of the manuscript. His friends were in frequent consultation and gave him their encouragement.

At last, in March, 1879, nearly eighteen months after he had begun it, the book was finished. He had thought to call it "Must

Progress Bring Poverty," or "Wealth and Want." But these
titles were cast aside in favor of the one entered in his diary.
He felt that "Progress and Poverty" "covered too wide a scope
for one volume" [8] and that the part relating to the development of civilization was but a skeleton of what he wanted to
present. "But at least an outline seemed to me essential, and I
did not know, even if I lived, if I should ever find opportunity
to write again." [9]

The work had not been easy. He had been striving for clarity
and simplicity. For, as he once said, "What makes easy reading
is hard writing." And on the night when he finished the final
chapter, as he later recalled, he "felt that the talent entrusted
to me had been accounted for—felt more fully satisfied, more
deeply grateful than if all the kingdoms of the earth had been
laid at my feet." [10]

This was no mere sentiment or a flush of satisfaction at a
job finally done. Four years later, in a letter revealed only after
his death, he wrote Father Thomas Dawson of Glencree, Ireland:

Because you are not only my friend, but a priest and a religious,
I shall say something that I don't like to speak of—that I never before have told to anyone. Once, in daylight, and in a city street,
there came to me a thought, a vision, a call—give it what name you
please. But every nerve quivered. And then and there I made a
vow. Through evil and through good, whatever I had done and whatever I have left undone, to that I have been true. It was that that
impelled me to write *Progress and Poverty* and that sustained me
when else I should have failed. And when I had finished the last
page, in the dead of night, when I was entirely alone, I flung myself
on my knees and wept like a child. The rest was in the Master's
hands. That is a feeling that has never left me; that is constantly
with me. It has made me a better and purer man. It has been to me
a religion of which I never like to speak, or make any outward mani-
festation, but yet that I try to follow....

The prodigious task of writing the book was now behind him.
Getting it published was quite another matter. He had written
his friend John Swinton, "Any man who tries to do what I
have for a good while tried to do—any man who is in advance
of his time, and who is true to his convictions, this is all he can
have—the good opinion of some few men. Wealth is not for

him, nor power—in his time, nor popular applause. I have long known that." [11]

Since D. Appleton & Co. had published the works of Herbert Spencer and "The International Scientific Series," George submitted his manuscript to this firm as his first choice.

Meanwhile, meter inspection was bringing in less and less money. Time hung heavy after the manuscript was off his desk and shipped East. This combination of circumstances led him to start *The State*,[12] a four-page "weekly journal of politics and opinion," with faithful William Hinton's plant doing the printing. Occasionally contributions were made by some of George's friends, but for the most part it was a one-man periodical.

The little paper was launched on April 6, 1879, shortly before news came from the East that Appleton had rejected his book. Other rejections followed. Then came an offer from Hinton to bring out the author's edition. Accepting his friend's generosity, George stopped *The State*, which however was paying for itself, after the eleventh issue. He needed time to revise *Progress and Poverty* and to write a new conclusion.

The manuscript had ended with the chapter "The Central Truth," in which he incorporated the apotheosis to Liberty from the Fourth of July oration which he had delivered in the California Theater. He now added one more chapter, which he called "The Problem of Individual Life."

The rejection from Appleton had brought a note: "We have read your MS. on political economy. It has the merit of being written with great clearness and force, but it is very aggressive. There is very little to encourage the publication of any such work at this time and we feel we must decline it." [13]

Hinton's offer to make the plates followed other rejections. Thomas George, the author's brother, had taken over the task of finding a publisher. Leaving his home in Philadelphia he made the rounds in New York, acting on the advice of Professor William Swinton who had moved East from California. "I have just telegraphed you that 'it seems impossible to get a publisher without plates,'" Thomas George wrote at one juncture. He had tried Harper's and also Scribner's, writing that "Harper considered it [the book] revolutionary and all that sort of thing." The publishing field seemed exhausted, for in truth no work of economics up to that time had been a profitable publisher's venture.

Making the plates involved an expenditure of one thousand

to fifteen hundred dollars. George wrote the new conclusion, then turned his own hand to setting type at Hinton's shop. The entry in his diary for May 17, 1879, reads: "Commenced to set type on book. Set first two sticks myself." [14]

Thus, standing on a board, as he always had to do to bring himself to the proper level of the case, George turned back to the trade which he had followed for years. His son, Henry, now sixteen, joined in with George's old printer friends to produce the plates. Dr. Taylor read proof and even joined those at the case who were donating their services in their spare time.

Long afterward, someone remarked, "All the bum printers in San Francisco claim the distinction of having set type on the author's edition of *Progress and Poverty!*"

"Well," replied James Barry,[15] "then I must accept the soft impeachment and be numbered among the 'bum printers,' for I am very proud of the fact that I set type on the first edition." He recounted having overheard one of the journeymen, who as it happened was not donating his services, growl when his own proof was returned peppered with corrections by George's practiced hand, "The little red-headed son of a gun! Who does he think is going to read his old book but himself, anyway?" [16]

"Little" George was now growing bald, but he retained much of his red hair and a rich, red beard. By September the "author's proof edition" of five hundred copies was struck off. One of the first finished copies went to Richard S. H. George, now eighty-one, in Philadelphia with a note from his son: "It is with a deep feeling of gratitude to Our Father in Heaven that I send you a printed copy of this book. . . . It will not be recognized at first,—maybe not for some time—but it will ultimately be considered a great book, will be published in both hemispheres, and will be translated into different languages. This I know, though neither of us may ever see it here. But the belief that there is another life for us—makes that of little moment." [17]

A MAJORITY OF ONE

THE AUTHOR'S EDITION of *Progress and Poverty* sold well enough at three dollars a copy to pay for the plates. Now that he had these, Henry George approached D. Appleton & Co. again and they agreed to bring the book out at once in a commercial edition.

It was not until the new year (1880), however, that the edition issued from the press. The sale of the book, at two dollars a copy, was slow. George wrote jocularly to a friend, "If the professed economists will only refute the truths I have tried to make clear, their acceptance will come so much the sooner." [1]

But the first disinterest and apathy of the reading public meant lean days for George. He had to give up his job as inspector of gas meters to an appointee of the recently elected Republican governor.[2] Nevertheless, his faith in his book and in himself did not falter. Later John Russell Young, who had been managing editor of the *New York Tribune* at the time of George's trip East in quest of the Associated Press franchise, wrote that "I never see *Progress and Poverty* without recalling and honoring the courage of the author. George never for a moment—even when under the grinding heel of bitter conditions—doubted the truth of his mission to mankind and its ultimate success." [3]

Copies of the author's edition had been sent to notable figures in the United States and abroad. Herbert Spencer made no acknowledgement but William E. Gladstone and the Duke of Argyll sent brief notes of thanks. Sir George Grey wrote enthusiastically from New Zealand. Joseph Chamberlain sent a gracious letter in which he said, "It appears to me a very interesting study of a most important subject." This diplomat added cautiously, "At the same time I must not be supposed to agree with all your conclusions."[4] Flattering word came from one scholar, Dr. Montague R. Leverson, an Englishman who was living in San Francisco. He was so much impressed by George's doctrines that he withdrew his own published primer of political economy, declaring that not another copy should be sold until it was rewritten.

The Appleton edition carried *Progress and Poverty* farther afield. However, the publishers had not thought it necessary to bother about foreign copyrights.* This was caused, no doubt, by the failure of their London agent to get a single British firm to handle it. "Unless the author could pay all the expenses no one would take the book," he wrote.[5] Indeed, one of the English publishers had stated that even if the plates were sent to him free of cost he would not print it. Appleton reported to George, "The only plan remaining is to send copies to our own agency, advertise them and thus introduce the book to the English people. English publishers generally would not look with much favor on your book as it overthrows old notions and views of political economy."[6]

So little faith had the American publishers that they told George they saw no advantage in putting "rights of translation reserved" in their edition. However, others placed a higher value on the work. A request soon came for the privilege of bringing it out in German. The first translation, made by C. D. F. von Gütschow of San Francisco, was followed by two others. All three were eventually circulated in Germany, where the existing land reform movement promptly assimilated George's theory.

That the author had periods of doubt about the immediate influence of *Progress and Poverty* appears in a letter to Charles Nordhoff, one of the chief editorial writers of the *New York Herald* whom he had met early in the 1870's in San Francisco:

I wanted so much to see it published [he wrote] that comparatively I do not care about its future fate. At least I do not fret and worry. My work is done; the rest is not my business. And my faith in it, or rather in the truth which I believe it embodies, is so profound that I do not think anything that could be said of it could either flatter or abash me.

* This circumstance makes it practically impossible to compute the exact circulation of the work.—Editor

I appreciate the difficulty of reaching those most deeply concerned in any social reform, and the difficulty of holding them, even when you have reached them—of preventing ideas which you got in, from taking most distorted forms. It is the general fact that those who suffer most are least able to help themselves. It is certain efforts for amelioration of the condition of the lowest class have come from above, not below. The most terrible thing about unjust social enactments is not the physical suffering they cause, but the mental and moral degradation they produce. It is this that gives the demagogue his advantage and enables tyranny to turn the rabble against their best friends.[7]

But at last important notice was beginning to be taken of the book. The first criticism to arrive from Europe was in the Parisian *Revue Scientifique* and was signed by Emile de Laveleye. "The chapter on the Decline of Civilization," wrote the Belgian economist, "is worthy of being added to De Tocqueville's immortal work."[8] A month later a review covering the larger part of a page appeared in the *New York Sun*. Other reviews appeared in important papers and magazines and there were demands for a paper-covered, cheaper edition of the book. An enthusiastic letter from a young man named A. J. Steers, in the Appleton Company, brought a grateful reply from George, in which he said, "Many a man does his work and in his life sees no result. And no matter how much of a success the book may become in my lifetime, I do not think I shall be proud of it, as men are proud of writing a successful novel or history. The feeling is one of deep gratitude that it has been permitted me to do something.... But it is not the result so much as the effort to do what we can, with which we are concerned."[9]

George was straining to pay his debt for the printing and at the same time to support his family. He wrote John Swinton that "the book has done better than in this time I would have reasonably hoped. Appletons have already published their second edition and contemplate a third, and of the obligation which I assumed in bringing it out, I have already paid all but about $120."[10]

Several articles written by George had been published in the *Popular Science Monthly* but they brought in little revenue. A contract he had hoped to make with a lecture bureau fell

through. Once again he considered going East, and he wrote
facetiously to a friend that "if they would reduce the fare a
little further—say to $10.00—I would go myself." [11] It seemed
like an answer to a prayer when John Russell Young sent word
that there was a chance for a writing position on the *New York
Herald*. Since Young had voluntarily advanced the money for
the trip, George availed himself of this opportunity and left
for the East.

"I came third class after all," he wrote Taylor, "and Young
thought there was something to be made by writing up the
emigrant trip. I am enjoying it and am full of hope. The spell
is broken and I have taken a new start." [12] When he arrived in
New York, however, he found that the position on the *Herald*
which Young and Charles Nordhoff had tried to obtain for
him was not available and that no other definite work could
be obtained.

Hoping to further the cause of free trade, he entered into
the Hancock-Garfield presidential fight. The Democratic campaign committee had sent for him and asked him to talk to
working men on the tariff question. Agreeing to this, he made
a straight free trade speech which was a success with the
audience but so distressed the "tariff reformers" controlling
party policy that they cancelled his other speaking dates.

In Brooklyn there was a group of fearless young Democrats—
Charles O'Connor Hennessy among them—who were fighting
the party machine. They invited George to speak at one of their
rallies in Jefferson Hall. There he was at liberty to make an
unqualified plea for free trade. Sure of his subject, he spoke
forcefully and powerfully. The speech made many admirers
and friends, one of them being Andrew McLean, managing
editor of the *Brooklyn Eagle*.

Pressed for money, George nevertheless determined to remain in New York in the hope that he could find work. When
a magazine article, previously accepted, was returned for
changes which the editor wanted but which made it unpub-
lishable, George wrote Taylor, "These little stumbles are only
to be expected but when a fellow carries the weight I am carrying, every little stumble hurts and it is very hard to recover
spirit and elasticity." [13]

The George family was still in San Francisco; Henry, Jr. had
a job in a printing office and Mrs. George had taken in board-

ers.* Henry wrote to Annie on their wedding anniversary, December 2, 1880:

We have been married nineteen years. Yes, more than half of your life has been that of a married woman, and I have been your husband for very near the half of mine, and that by far the most active part. And here we are with the whole continent between us, and about as poor as when we started. Well that won't be long, my darling. But this little separation amounts to nothing except to make us feel, as we may have felt before, the value of each other. I think I love you more truly and more deeply than I did when, nineteen years ago, you trusted yourself to me. I know that I have never regretted and I know that you have not. For I know I have your love and you have mine.[14]

Although the book was slowly attracting readers, the royalties were meager. Sending brave letters to his wife and wearing a brave front for the world, he showed occasional glimpses of the real state of his affairs only to Taylor during the winter of 1880-81. "I have been trying to hold on as long as I could in hopes of a chance of some kind. Don't think me a Micawber," he wrote to his friend. "I shall go to work if I have to go to the case." [15]

But at last an opening came. Abram S. Hewitt, a wealthy manufacturer and a member of Congress from New York City who had expressed an interest in *Progress and Poverty,* engaged its author to do some research on a congressional report which Hewitt had to make. George, who through stress of circumstance was now forced to break his resolution never to sell the product of his pen unsigned, wrote confidentially to Taylor:

I don't think I will get back for manifestly this is the best place for me unless I have something sure there. I say no more on the indications than in the actualities. I have taken the job from Hewitt to get up a report on labor investigation to be presented to the next Congress. He agrees to give me $50.00 a week for three hours' work a day. I have done about three weeks' work so far, and I don't know how long it will last. But there is some magazine work I have in mind and there is newspaper work to fall back on, to say nothing

* Henry George's family now consisted of his wife and four children—Henry, Jr., Richard, Jane Teresa, and the author, Anna Angela, born October 2, 1877, in San Francisco in what she said was the first brick house erected there.— Agnes de Mille

of lecturing. I have only delivered one lecture yet, receiving $50.00 for it, but will have more if I want to do it.[16]

After telling Taylor that he had received copies of part of the German translation of *Progress and Poverty*, which was to be completed and out in a few weeks' time, he chronicled some of his personal experiences:

Last night I dined with Dana of *The Sun*, the company consisting of his family, Hazeltine, the reviewer, John Swinton and myself. He lives in magnificent style. I have plenty of chance to go into company, but have hitherto kept out of it for until last week had only my old clothes, and last night felt rather out of place, when seated on the right of the hostess, yet the only man in the room in a business suit. However!

My wife thinks she can get along cheaper at boarding than keeping house, and so I have told her to sell out. . . . So life goes. My pleasant little home—that I was *so* comfortable in—is gone, and I am afloat at 42, poorer than at 21. I do not complain; but there is some bitterness in it.[17]

Early in March, 1881, he reported to Taylor that the business between him and Hewitt was terminated. He had read the matter he had prepared to Hewitt, who was exceedingly pleased with it and had given George one hundred dollars. This was far below the price they had agreed upon but George did not demur. When Hewitt indicated that he wanted some further work done on the investigation, George explained that he would have to charge another one hundred dollars. Whereupon Hewitt decided it was costing too much and he would have to stop.

George needed the money badly. But he did not confide in Hewitt. He said that he was relieved; that he knew he had been doing the work too cheaply; that he had done the job because he had undertaken to do it. There the matter ended.

The one hundred dollars, however, was a help. George was able to buy the suit of clothes he needed so badly and to send money home. But to clear up all the matters that worried him, such as a loan Taylor had made to him some time previously, he wrote his friend, "I found if I sent you $20.00 it would leave me only $5.00, and kept it to help out on this week's board. (It is in just such times as this when one is feeling for foothold

that the terrible weight of family comes in.).... There is no
one here I can talk to as I can to you, especially when I feel
blue and down. What weight I have carried no one knows. The
worst of it is the terrible mental strain, the waste of energy
and time and opportunity it involves. But it is only temporary.
If I can keep my strength. . . ." [18]

A paper edition of *Progress and Poverty* was to be printed
and a preface had to be written. He wrote and rewrote it.
Finally discarding what he had done, he ended up with a
simple summary of the book. That summary was used in this
and all subsequent editions. Worry made it difficult to think
and write, and as late as March 14, he explained to Taylor, "I
know what is wanted—rest and freedom from anxiety. But that
is what I can't get. I see a great work ahead of me—it opens
larger and larger, but sometimes I fear that I can't hold out.
God knows that I try my best." [19]

But at the end of December the sale of *Progress and Poverty*
began to pick up. Every copy of the previous editions and one
thousand of the cheap edition had gone and orders and inquiries were piling in on D. Appleton and Co. The German
notices were good. And the book was being discussed critically
at colleges in this country.

It was reported to the author that Leland Stanford had read
the book and had told James McClatchy that he had become
"a disciple of Henry George." [20] However, so far as George was
able to determine, the report was false. But Michael Davitt,
the Irish nationalist, openly pledged the Land League to push
Progress and Poverty in Great Britain. Of a sudden, its author
was attracting attention.

George received fifty dollars from *Appleton's Journal* for an
article [21] and orders for an encyclopedia article as well as one
for the *North American Review*.[22] The money pressure was
lessening a little. By May 12, he was able to pay back the twenty
dollar loan from Taylor. He wrote to his friend in San Francisco:

You do not know and I cannot readily tell you how much this
little accommodation has been to me. It is not so much the want of
money as the mental effect it produces—the morbid condition. The
man who does not understand that, does not know how it is possible for people to commit suicide. This thing has weighed on me
very much. Could I have felt free and been relieved of the terrible
anxiety, I could have, in the same time, accomplished many times as

much. But yet it has seemed as though a Providence helped me through.

When I drew on you for this $20.00 it seemed my darkest hour. I was weak and weary in mind and body.[23]

By the end of May something of the old lightness had returned. "Why do you allow the papers there to abuse me without sending me a copy?" he wrote Taylor. "To be abused and not to know of it is almost as bad as not to be abused at all." [24]

John Russell Young was the only one of George's intimate friends who never became converted to his philosophy. But a deep love linked them and they were almost daily companions during those long months of worry and struggle. Young later wrote:

It was a daring experiment—this unknown gentleman, with no aid but his own high spirit, nothing in his carpet-bag but one book of gospel, coming at 42 to make his way to the heart of mighty Babylon. The more I studied George under heavy conditions, the more I admired him. His ability and courage, his honesty, independence and intellectual power were those of a leader of men.

We took walks on the Battery, whither we went under the flush of strenuous midnight work, the great city at peace and no companions this side of the stars; strolls in the Park, in Westchester and the suburbs of Brooklyn—the brave, intrepid soul wrapped up in his book and smiling upon fate.... It was the courage which, as has been written, makes one a majority.[25]

CHAPTER XV

IRISH FREEDOM

IN 1879, the land question in Ireland was a burning issue. The Irish peasants, ground down by poverty and oppressed by their landlords, most of whom were absentee owners, were being subjected to widespread eviction. The Irish National Land League had been formed "to bring about a reduction of rack rents." During that same year Henry George had written an article on the situation in the *Sacramento Bee*. Rack rent, he explained, was "simply a rent fixed by competition at short intervals.... In our agricultural districts, land is rented from season to season to the highest bidder. This is what in Ireland is called rack rent." [1]

Charles Stewart Parnell was then president of the Irish Land League. But Michael Davitt, who was one of the honorary secretaries, seemed to be the soul of the organization. He proclaimed the principle of "the land for the people." In 1880, he was released from Portland Prison after having served seven years for his adherence to the cause of Irish independence.

Visiting New York that summer, he met Henry George and read *Progress and Poverty*. The experience led him to pledge the Land League to push the book in Great Britain.

George was deeply stirred by firsthand information on the Irish situation. He undertook to write an article on the subject for *Appleton's Journal*, but the work grew under his pen until it became a small book of seventeen chapters. He called it *The Irish Land Question: What It Involves and How Alone It Can Be Settled*.

The book argued that in order to relieve Ireland of the abomination of rack-renting and to give the Irish people the benefits of their labor, it was necessary to spare industry and thrift from taxation and to take the rental value of the land alone for the community needs. Under such a system the laborer would get what he created; no one would have an advantage as a mere landholder. Even though the landowner might be an Englishman living in England, the value of the land of Ireland would accrue to the Irish people as a whole.

D. Appleton and Co., George's publisher, brought out the little book early in March. "First edition exhausted the first day and not enough to fill orders that have already come in," George wrote Taylor. Shortly afterwards editions were published in London, Manchester and Glasgow. *The Irish Land Question* enjoyed splendid reviews. One in the *New York Times* —a column and a half of small type—began, "One rises from a reading of this weighty pamphlet with a conviction of the justice of the theory advocated and with admiration for the clearness with which it is stated by Mr. Henry George. He had the advantage of having got rid in *Progress and Poverty*—a masterly book on the reasons for the spread of pauperism in the modern social fabric—of most of the prejudices which beset writers on similar topics." [2]

In the meantime George's family had joined him in New York. They were boarding at Fort Washington, at the northern end of Manhattan Island. Living there afforded a quiet place for work and yet gave easy access to the center of the city. His financial burden was lightening; a demand had sprung up for his lectures and for magazine and encyclopedia articles. He earned $130 when he spoke in Chickering Hall at a meeting in charge of the Reverend R. Heber Newton, his classmate of the Philadelphia day school and Sunday school period who was now rector of All Souls Episcopal Church in New York. A Brooklyn lecture, arranged by Andrew McLean of the *Brooklyn Eagle,* netted $200. On this occasion the corporation lawyer, Thomas G. Shearman, friend and attorney of Henry Ward Beecher, was present. It was the beginning of a fruitful and inspirational friendship which gradually developed into Shearman's ardent promotion of George's theories.

Through the introduction of Poultney Bigelow,[3] George became a member of the New York Free Trade Club. Bigelow was a convert to *Progress and Poverty* and had translated from the French, for the American economist, excerpts from the writings of the Physiocrats. Soon after joining the club, of which Theodore Roosevelt was at that time a member, George attended one of their dinners. The experience disillusioned him; the tone of the affair was, he felt, timid and reactionary.

"As you said," he wrote to Bigelow, "only worse! worse!! worse!!! I told them four minutes of horse sense, however." [4]

In the early summer he began lecturing for the Irish Land League through New England and Canada. "Best ever have done," was the entry in his diary appraising a speech in Montreal. But the lecture tour was cut short so that he could make a business trip to California for a friend. While in San Francisco he spoke in the same Metropolitan Temple where, three years previously, when he was a "gas measurer," he had delivered an address in an all but empty hall. [5] On this occasion the auditorium was packed by an enthusiastic audience. For an hour and a half he lectured without notes on "The Next Great Struggle." From Scandinavia to Italy, he observed, Europe was in the ferment of social change. What is it? he asked, answering, "It is a quickening of the seeds cast here, a renewal of the light focussed here and of the spirit proclaimed in that Immortal Declaration of Independence that all men are created equal. . . . But Europe is striving not alone for what we have attained. It is seeking for social and not merely political reform. . . . The same feeling of unrest exists in this country. All was not accomplished when our forefathers instituted the Republic and the ballot. . . . Giant forces are arising which must make their way." [6]

The visit to his scenes of early struggle was indeed a happy one, made more so by the fact that he was able to pay off nearly all the debts he had contracted while working on his book. California had become even more receptive to his message and aware of his influence. He had learned that spring, for instance, that when the legislature named a new United States senator, two votes had been cast for him. In nominating George, Warren S. Chase of Santa Barbara and Ventura had said, "I shall name neither a lawyer nor a soldier, but a political economist who has distinguished himself and acquired a national reputation; who is throughout the world recognized as the peer of such intellects as Ricardo, John Stuart Mill and Malthus." [7]

Good news awaited him back in New York. *Truth*, a one-cent daily with a circulation of between 75,000 and 100,000, was arranging to reprint *Progress and Poverty* in installments. George received no compensation; he was grateful enough for another outlet for his message.

The editor of *Truth* was Louis Freeland Post. A printer by trade and a member of the bar, he preferred to devote his ener-

gies to the discussion of public questions. He had complained
one night of "the deadly dearth of subjects for editorial com-
ments." William McCabe, one of the printers on the paper,
asked if he had heard of *Progress and Poverty*. Post replied that
he had, but there was "nothing in it." McCabe retorted, "Maybe
so; but just the same, there are enough editorial subjects in
that book to last you a lifetime." [8]

A few days later Post found a copy of *The Irish Land Question* on his desk. He read the book and was convinced by the
author's reasoning of the evils of land monopoly. He acknowledged this in an editorial, explaining, however, what he believed
to be the fallacies of the proposed plan for abolishing the land
monopoly. After seeing his remarks in print, the "cock-sured-
ness" [9] of his rebuttal worried him; he felt compelled to send
a copy to George for criticism. George merely sent back a
copy of *Progress and Poverty* with a friendly note requesting
that Post "read the book carefully from beginning to end, for
it was 'a linked argument.'" [10]

Post read the book—in one day! He was completely convinced
that George was right. Thereupon he decided to reprint it in
Truth.

Louis F. Post was ten years younger than Henry George.
Short, stocky, with a mop of thick brown hair, his dark eyes
sparkling behind thick spectacles, he exuded strength and goodness. A man of great courage, he was extremely tolerant of men
and their ideas. He had the rare gift of trying to find the other
fellow right, not wrong; the priceless gift of making you like
yourself. His sense of humor and convincing, simple delivery
made him a delightful raconteur and speaker. He became one
of George's staunchest followers and most beloved friends.

Another friendship which started at this time was with Francis George Shaw, a man of great culture and beauty of spirit.
Shaw, a member of a wealthy Boston family, professed he had
lost hope of solving social problems until he read *Progress and
Poverty*. It so excited him that he ordered one thousand copies
to be sent to libraries throughout the United States. [11]

At the same time word came from England that Alfred Russell Wallace had also been endorsing *Progress and Poverty*,
calling it "undoubtedly the most remarkable and important
work of the century." [12] George could write happily of his recognition on two continents, "So the seed has begun to sprout."

Meanwhile in Parliament the Liberal government, headed

by Gladstone, was grappling with the chaotic conditions in Ireland. Under the direction of Westminster, Lord Cowper, the Viceroy, and William E. Forster, the Chief Secretary, were both working for justice for tenants but they were also trying to repress tenant violence against landlords who were practicing eviction. *Habeas corpus* was suspended and hundreds known or "suspected" to be connected with the tenant agitation were thrown into jail without trial. The Irish Land League had been banned; Michael Davitt had been sent back to Portland Prison and Parnell was living under threat of momentary arrest.

The Irish land question naturally had aroused intense interest and feverish partisanship in the United States. In New York, Patrick Ford, editor of *The Irish World and American Industrial Liberator*, challenged the exploitation of the Irish tenant in these strong words which had appealed to George: "The strength of the land agitation in Ireland will be in exact proportion to how much or how little it accepts of the incontrovertible truth that the land of Ireland was not made for the landlord class, or any other class, but for *all Irishmen*." [13]

Ford approached George with the proposition that he go to Ireland and England to report the political situation for *The Irish World*. It seemed an excellent chance—the one "I have long waited for," as George wrote Taylor. And so he accepted readily. He was to be paid sixty dollars a week plus transportation expenses for himself and his family.

On October 15, 1881, leaving his elder son, Henry, to work as a cub reporter on the *Brooklyn Eagle* and his son Richard to study at the Art Students' League, George and his wife, with their two little girls, set out for England on the steamship *Spain*.

CHAPTER XVI

MISSION TO IRELAND

THE GEORGES had intended to land at Liverpool. News which came to Henry George in New York two days before his departure, however, caused the family to change its plans and disembark at Queenstown.

Parnell, along with John Dillon and J. J. O'Kelly, had been sent to jail, where now some five hundred political prisoners languished under the "crimes" or "coercion" act. While George was still at sea the Irish Land League issued a "no-rent manifesto" in protest, calling upon agricultural tenants to refuse to pay rent until the Government should change its policy.

In retaliation, the Dublin authorities suppressed the Land League. Patrick Egan, the treasurer, went to Paris to protect the League's funds. The women, under Miss Anna Parnell, sister of Charles Stewart Parnell, organized the Ladies' Land League (L.L.L.) to help carry on. George decided that he should hasten to Ireland to study the situation firsthand.

On the Queenstown tender the passenger agent called the American aside and offered to change his name on his luggage and on the passenger list, else—as news of his coming had been cabled to Ireland—he would certainly be dogged by the police from the moment of landing and subjected to arrest. George refused the man's kindness. Upon arrival he met with no official hostility; on the contrary, he was given a welcome which was only short of a demonstration.

Ireland, with its population of little more than five million, was being patrolled by 15,000 military constables and forty thousand picked troops. "I got indignant as soon as I landed," George wrote, "and I have not got over it yet." [1]

He went at once to Dublin to interview Parnell, Dillon, and O'Kelly. At first he was unsuccessful:

I cooled my heels during three days outside Kilmainham Jail, in an attempt to see men who really represent four-fifths of the people of this country, and as after at length getting in, I at length got out again, there were two great Englishmen whom I wished could have been alive to visit the place—Charles Dickens and John Stuart Mill. It would require the pen that described the "circumlocution office" to fitly describe the officials at Kilmainham and the pains they seem to take to make visits to the suspects, as few and as unpleasant as possible. It would require the author of *On Liberty* to fitly warn his countrymen of what such treatment of *suspected* men really means.[2]

A fortnight later he was able to report:

I have seen the most famous and best loved men of Ireland—the men who are today the real leaders and representatives of the Irish people; but have seen them with the greatest difficulty and under conditions which in other countries surround the worst male-factors....

It was the first time I had ever met Mr. Parnell. I was most favorably impressed by him. Features and bearing and expression speak a strong, well-poised, and determined character, a man fit to be the leader of men.

Our conversation was exceedingly interesting for a conversation of its kind, but it was an exceedingly provoking kind, for the two warders strained their ears lest anything contraband should be said.... Of the things I most wanted to talk to Mr. Parnell, nothing was permitted.... No politics of any kind, of any country were to be spoken of, said the warder.... So then we spoke of Bishop Nulty, but when I attempted to allude to Bishop Nulty's views, and how he believed there can be no settlement of the Land Question until land is acknowledged as the common property of the whole people, I was peremptorily stopped. There could be no allusion to land, even with the League left out, within the sacred precincts of Kilmainham.

Baffled in these directions we talked of ancient history and of the persecution of the early Church, of the triumph of Christianity over Paganism, of the course of civilization and the effects upon European thought, of the discovery and settlement of America, of the progress of astronomical science, of the laws of human thought, etc.... Not even the gold-banded chief warder, though he looked very uneasy, could sniff "politics" in such topics as these, nor yet when I sought to obtain Mr. Parnell's views on such religious topics as the perseverence of the saints, the relation between faith and works, the final triumph of the right, the ultimate chaining of the devil, etc. And so, in a conversation that, understood literally, might have been taken for that of lunatics, I managed to get something of Mr. Parnell's views. He is more than satisfied with the spirit shown by the people, and is confident of success. . . .[3]

George had been waited upon by four committees and invited to deliver a public lecture in Dublin. Delivered some weeks after his arrival, in the historic Rotunda, the address was an immense success. The enthusiasm was so great that it was only by ordering his cab driver to whip up the horse and get him away from the crowd that George escaped having his carriage unhitched and dragged by his audience through the streets. He wrote to Taylor, "I am sorry now that I did not let them do it as it would have compelled the press agents to have taken more notice of it." [4]

Dr. Thomas Nulty, Bishop of Meath, who a few months previously had written a pastoral letter which was a scholarly summation of the land question, granted the American an interview. George wrote privately to Patrick Ford that the visit "was most delightful. . . . Here," he said, "is a Christian Bishop. He treated me with the greatest honor, and what is more with the greatest frankness and cordiality. I never met a man that seemed to me more to fill the idea of a *Rev. Father in God*. How I wish he were Pope." [5]

The Irish World's correspondent reported the publication of the Bishop's pastoral letter and quoted from Dr. Nulty: ". . . I infer that no individual, or class of individuals, can hold a right of private property in the land of the country; that the people of that country, in their public corporate capacity *are*, and always *must be*, the real owners of the land of their country— holding an indisputable title to it, in the fact that they receive it as a free gift from their Creator, and as a necessary means for preserving and enjoying the life He has bestowed upon them." [6]

George's dispatch commented:

The individual who has improved land Dr. Nulty declares entitled to the benefit of that improvement, and should be secured in its enjoyment and be entitled to receive either a selling price or rent for it, but the value of the land which arises from the growth of the community and not from what any particular individual has done (that is to say, rent in the strict use of the term) belongs to the whole community and ought to be taken in taxation for the use of the whole community.

In the fact that rent proper—or that value of land which is not due to the individual exertion of the occupier or improver—constantly increases with the growth of society, Dr. Nulty sees—as everyone must see who recognizes the true relation of this fact—a most beautiful relation of creative design.[7]

George prevailed upon the Ladies' Land League to have Bishop Nulty's article printed and sent broadcast over Ireland. The result was a widespread distribution through priests and laity alike. The Tory papers reprinted it as "an outrageous *official* declaration of communism from a Catholic bishop." [8]

The persecution in Ireland continued. The official League paper *United Ireland* was seized, but the plates of the number about to be issued were spirited to George's lodgings and hidden under his bed [9] until they could be packed into a trunk and shipped secretly to England. There the League managers wasted precious time and money, getting out one edition in London, another, an entirely different one, in Dublin,[10] and a third, from the Dublin plates, in Liverpool. George sadly was coming to realize that in the Irish movement there was a lack of management and therefore a sacrifice of opportunity and resources; that the men trying to lead were showing jealousy and incapacity. He still had faith in Parnell, although he did not consider him as strong as Davitt; but he believed Parnell's sister to be an admirable organizer and secretary, and that the women's group had been accomplishing very much under great hardships.

It was when Miss Parnell learned from an informant that the Ladies' Land League was about to be proscribed, and that one of the Dublin jails was being made ready to receive her and Nannie Lynch, her assistant, that the two women lost no time in escaping to England. As a precaution they sent the official records of their organization to Mrs. George for safekeeping. George in the meantime had gone to London. The remaining members of the L.L.L. persuaded Mrs. George to preside over their business meeting. Knowing nothing of parliamentary procedure, she had consented with reluctance. Her nervousness was hardly lessened by the presence of Government detectives, reporters and correspondents. But she carried through, and the fact that Miss Parnell was absent and that an American woman had taken the chair saved the Ladies' League from proscription.

In London, George learned from Kegan Paul of the London publishing house of Kegan Paul, Trench & Co. of the astonishing success of *Progress and Poverty*. Selling an American work on economics had seemed impossible at first and the firm had difficulty in disposing of the first twenty copies of the five hundred which D. Appleton had sent to England. Then it began to sell, and an English edition was being prepared with expectations of a quick return. George wrote to Francis G. Shaw, "I find I have made a reputation quite out of proportion to the sale of the book. This, when I can utilize it, will be our power." [11]

In January, the family was together in London where "we are staying with Miss Helen Taylor," George wrote Shaw. Miss Taylor was the stepdaughter of John Stuart Mill. She impressed George as "not a Malthusian, not a materialist, but rather a mystic." [12] After the death of her mother she had become Mill's constant companion and confidante. It was the habit of the man and the girl to take long walks—sometimes for twenty miles.

This intimate contact of the young, groping mind with the mature intellect of the great economist was an extraordinary education for the girl. When the Georges became acquainted with Helen Taylor during the Irish struggle she was outwardly a typical English woman of the Victorian era—domestic, soft-voiced, gentle in manner, and wearing, when in the house, a white lace cap on her smooth, brown hair. She had thrown herself deeply into the Irish cause. Upon reading *Progress and Poverty* she had become a fervent disciple of George, saying that John Stuart Mill, had he lived, would have embraced not only the cause of Ireland but also George's teaching. As hostess to the Georges, she was most reluctant to let them go. She was able to talk politics and economics with the eldest or to teach the youngest * to make, from the tinfoil wrappings of chocolates, tiny spoons with which to shovel sugar in the big silver bowl.

After several weeks with Helen Taylor, the Georges visited Mr. and Mrs. Henry Myers Hyndman at their home in Portland Place, London. Later they were guests of Thomas Briggs

---

* "The youngest," was, of course, the author.—Editor

and his family in Dulwich. Hyndman, a journalist, had been denied employment by the British press because of his Irish sympathies. He was such an ardent socialist that George felt it "a pity to see a man of such force following so blindly such a superficial thinker as Karl Marx." [13] Hyndman tried in vain to bring George to his viewpoint. He had hoped, as he subsequently related, "to convert him to the truth as it is in Socialist economics. It seemed to me quite incredible that a man who could go so far as he had gone would not traverse with ease the remainder of the distance, and thus obtain a sound conception of the whole subject." [14]

Hyndman had found in the British Museum a copy of the lecture delivered by Thomas Spence in 1775, proclaiming common rights in land and proposing that land values be taken for public purposes. George had never heard of Spence. But instead of being disconcerted by the discovery of a predecessor who had anticipated several of his own independently achieved positions on the land question, he reasoned that his theories would be accepted more readily if it could be proved that they were old. Therefore he persuaded Hyndman to reprint the Spence lecture, a copy of which he sent to the *Irish World* for publication.

Despite the fact that he was a Marxist, Hyndman lived in a rather formal style. The informal manners of his American guest often irritated him. He related that George's "indifference to some of our English prejudices was at times rather annoying." For instance,

On one occasion we were passing the top of Great Portland street, going home to lunch, when George espied a barrow-load of whelks being sold by a coster-monger. "I say, Hyndman," quoth George, "I like the look of those whelks." "All right," said I, "if you like them I'll have some sent in for you." "No," was the answer, "I like them here and now." Expostulation was useless. So George consumed his whelks from the barrow while I, got up in high hat and frock coat of the non-whelk-eating-at-the-corner civilization, stood by and saw him do it. [15]

Hyndman considered that while the economist was "humorous, good-natured and fond of discussion, his was not by any means a first-rate intellect." [16] George left no record of what he thought of his host. But the smallest of Hyndman's American guests developed a prejudice against him. It dated from the time he almost sent her into hysterics by pretending to bite off the toes of her doll.

The same doll, Rose, and "The Babe" or "The Child," as the George family called its youngest member, were inseparable. Once when they were staying in Dublin the Babe fell down and broke Rose's crown and even her mother's magic fingers could not heal it. Indeed, Dr. James E. Kelly, a surgeon who called so often to talk Irish and world affairs, found that in this case he could not operate successfully. And then the father, who was just starting for London, entered the consultation, suggesting that there might be someone on the other side of the Irish Channel who could operate on Rose. Gently he laid the doll on a bed of compromising documents in his bag and covered her with the rest of the precious papers. A few days later he wrote to Mrs. George from London, "I have been spending the afternoon and some cab fare in moving about with Rose. All along Regent Street they wanted ten or fourteen days to fix her, which meant sending her to Paris. I found a place over Waterloo Bridge where they will head her, paint her and put back her old wig for 6/ and have left her, to be done tomorrow afternoon." [17]

While in London the Georges were entertained frequently and met many interesting people. Henry George was usually indifferent to his appearance. Now he contrived to look well groomed in the evening clothes which a fashionable tailor had made for him before he left New York. (Perhaps because they had cost so much, he took scrupulous care of them.) Mrs. George had made for herself a handsome evening gown of garnet satin and velvet. Against its dark red her arms and neck gleamed beautifully white. For less formal affairs she favored a stiff, black silk dress, without which no lady's wardrobe, at that time, was complete.

Most of her own clothes Mrs. George made herself, and all of the clothes worn by her daughters. When she found that she was to be in London for some time, she went to the English agency of the American company, Wilcox and Gibbs, to rent a sewing machine.

"We'll let you have it for £5," said the salesman.

"That's far too much," exclaimed the American woman. "I own one at home for which I paid $85, and I can't afford to pay £5 for renting a duplicate just for a few weeks' use."

"You may *buy* it here for £5, Madam, even though it does

cost $85 in your country where it is produced. You Americans, with your protective tariff, are very kind to us!"[18]

This was a vivid lesson in the stupidity of "protection" which Mrs. George quoted many times.

George wrote to Ford that "I have succeeded in passing myself off for an Englishman, but I can't for an Irishman; my accent betrays me."[19] His wife, while abroad, almost always was taken for an Englishwoman, not only because of her poise but because she did not have the nasal, rasping quality supposed to be typical of "the American voice." Greatly to her amusement, shopkeepers often took her into their confidence: "We'll be getting a 'igher price than this, mum, in the spring, when the Hamericans 'll be coming h'over."[20]

One night Mr. and Mrs. George were dinner guests at the beautiful home of Walter Wren,[21] the celebrated Oxford coach, where they met Walter Besant, novelist and founder of the Society of Authors. On another occasion they were guests of Sir Francis Jeune (afterwards Lord Chief Justice) and Lady Jeune, at one of their "small and earlies." It was in reality a large and late, for the crowd was so great that it took half an hour to get upstairs to greet the hostess. Tennyson was there, looking like a dreamer; and Browning, described by Mrs. George as looking "like a prosperous merchant draper," was also there. George met neither of them: he was more interested, in fact, in another guest—Herbert Spencer.

Although he had once written to his wife, "Instead of trying a novel, why not read Herbert Spencer on the chrystalline system, when you want to go to sleep?"[22] he admired the English philosopher, had quoted him in *Progress and Poverty*, and had long wanted to meet him. Here at Lady Jeune's the coveted opportunity came.

The two men had hardly exchanged greetings before Spencer asked George what he thought of the situation in Ireland. The American at once condemned the action of the Government and praised the work of the Land League. He expected the Englishman who, in *Social Statics*, had condemned private property in land and had declared for what is now called land nationalization,[23] would, like himself, see the solution of the agrarian struggle in Ireland only in terms of the fundamental economic principles which they both had defined.

But Spencer, to George's surprise, condemned the imprisoned Land Leaguers. "They have only got what they deserve," he said vehemently. "They are inciting the people to refuse to pay their landlords what is rightfully theirs—rent." George was non-plussed. "It is evident we cannot agree on this matter," [24] he replied in some astonishment, and walked away, bitterly disappointed in the man whose work he had revered.

Joseph Chamberlain, according to J. L. Garvin, his biographer, had read *Progress and Poverty* and had been "electrified." [25] Indeed there was much in common between the great English liberal and Henry George. After dining with Chamberlain and John Bright, as guests of Walter Wren, George wrote of the meeting to Patrick Ford:

We started in on the Irish affairs with the soup, for Bright asked me point-blank what I thought of what I had seen in Ireland and I had to tell him, though it was not very flattering. We kept it up till half past ten, when Mr. Bright had to go down to the House . . . but Chamberlain remained until nearly twelve. Bright has got to the end of his tether, and will never get past where he is now; but Chamberlain is an extremely bright man, and his conversation, which was unreserved, was extremely interesting to me, and would make a most interesting letter if I could use it, which of course I cannot, for to print private conversation with men of his position, or even to allude to them in print, without permission, would stamp a man as not fit for decent society.

Chamberlain has evidently been reading the *Irish World* for he alluded to some things in my letters, and he told me laughingly to look out when I went back to Ireland that I did not get reasonably suspected. [26]

Though the "no-rent" movement in Ireland at this time was as strong as ever, Parnell and a few of his co-workers had grown weary of the fight. They made an agreement with the Government to "slow down" Land League agitation in return for release of the suspects and extension of the Land Act. When Parnell, O'Kelly, and Dillon were released from Kilmainham Prison on May 2, 1882, surprise and joy were general among the Irish factions. Those on the inside, however, suspected the compromise. George wrote to Ford that members of the Ladies' Land League seemed deeply depressed.

But the authorities who freed Parnell, who had been denounced for treason, were at once discredited. Viceroy Cowper and Chief Secretary Forster resigned. On the evening of Saturday, May 6, 1882, when the new Chief Secretary, Lord Frederick Cavendish, and the Under Secretary, Thomas Burke, made their official entry into Dublin, they were assassinated in Phoenix Park by a band of fanatics who called themselves the "Invincibles."

News of the deed quickly spread around the world and did much harm to the Irish cause.

Davitt, who had been jailed again after his return from the United States, had been released from Portland Prison, near London, early that day. George had been with him until late that night. Early on Sunday morning George was awakened by the arrival of a telegram from his Dublin friend, Dr. Kelly, telling of the assassinations.

There were no Sunday papers in London. George, dressing rapidly, sped from his lodgings to Westminster Palace Hotel, where Davitt was staying. "At five o'clock," Davitt relates, "Henry George entered my bedroom with an open telegram in his hand and a scared look in his kindly blue eyes. 'Get up, old man,' were his words. 'One of the worst things that has ever happened to Ireland has occurred.'" [27]

George recounts that when Davitt read the telegram he exclaimed, "My God! Have I got out of Portland for this!" The Irishman added, "For the first time in my life I despair. It seems like the curse that follows Ireland!" [28]

George took the message to Dillon and O'Kelly. Dillon went for Parnell, who joined the others at the hotel. By the afternoon nearly all the Parnellites had gathered there.

In the meantime a manifesto had been written by a few of Parnell's followers,[29] condemning the crime in the name of the Irish people and their leaders. "It was sent at once," writes Davitt, "to the press agencies in Great Britain, cabled to John Boyle O'Reilly of Boston, for the widest publication in America, and wired to Mr. Alfred Webb of Dublin, to be printed as a placard and despatched by Sunday night's last train to every city and town in Ireland, so as to be posted on the walls of the country on Monday morning." [30]

George reported to *The Irish World*: "The feeling of the Irish members was the same horror and dismay felt by Davitt and expressed in the Manifesto. They felt that a great disaster had overtaken their cause and the stigma of a great crime had been laid upon it. . . . Nothing could better have served the purpose of the worst enemies of Ireland, nothing could have given more grief and shame to her best friends than this tragedy." [31]

On that black Sunday night, the Georges were guests at a dinner given by a Member of Parliament. The guests felt there would be violent retaliation against the Irish in England, and therefore the Irish leaders should flee to France. Mrs. George, who regarded moral courage as almost the highest human attribute, argued that Davitt "should go to Ireland by the first train and be as a leader to his people in this hour of dismay." Her statement was received with amazement. "But fury and bitterness are running so high—he might be killed by a Government supporter," someone objected. "How could Michael Davitt die better than with his people," asked Mrs. George.[32]

Her husband was to remind her of these words years later.

CHAPTER XVII

INTERNATIONAL INCIDENT

SURPRISINGLY ENOUGH, the Phoenix Park murders did not provoke any public disturbances. However, the Government was compelled by public opinion to abandon its proposed lenience toward the Irish Land League. "Gladstone," wrote George five years later, "was not wise enough or strong enough to resist the frantic English demand for repressive measures." [1]

The old, dreary round of coercion was resumed. The grief and abhorrence which had swept Ireland at the violent deeds in Phoenix Park were quickly forgotten. Yet the murders caused some apparent defections in the ranks. Although Parnell, speaking in the House of Commons, openly opposed the renewed policy of oppression, in the Land League he quietly did all he could to "slow down" and kill the old movement. In a few months he had swung away from "the land for the people" to the old and rather vague program of "home rule." George believed, and wrote privately to Ford, that Parnell by his change of heart had missed the greatest opportunity any Irishman ever had.

But Davitt stuck to his guns. Seven years in prison had not broken his spirit. Unwilling to be a party to Parnell's "Kilmainham treaty," he made his position clear when he presided over a large meeting in Manchester where George had been invited to lecture. Davitt spoke so long that he left the guest of honor barely fifteen minutes. Although George hardly did himself justice, any chagrin he might have felt was overshadowed by Davitt's ringing stand against the "treaty."

Now the cry was raised that George and Ford, together with Davitt, were trying to split the ranks. George wrote to Francis G. Shaw:

The truth is that Parnell is tired, that the conservative influences in the management of the League have come out in full force, and that they want to settle the land question before it goes too far. . . . Michael Davitt is full of the idea of popularizing *Progress and Poverty*. That was the first thing he said to me. He had read it twice before, and he read it twice again while in Portland and as you may see from his speeches and letters, he believes in it entirely. He says if a copy of that book can be put in every workman's club and Land League and library in the three kingdoms the revolution will be made. His first act was to demand of Parnell and Dillon £500 to use in the English propaganda, £300 of which he wanted to put in my hands for as many copies of *Progress and Poverty* as it would bring. Parnell and Dillon at first agreed, and he went to Paris to get Egan's consent. Egan refused; but afterwards wrote that what Davitt wanted would have to be granted, and then after the Manchester speech Parnell and Dillon refused.

The fact is that the line is really drawn and the split made, but not publicly. . . . I am glad I have been here if for nothing but my influence on Davitt. But the others taunt him so much with the idea that "Henry George has captured him" that he didn't want me to go down to Galway with him. The Land League leaders—that is, the "Parliamentarians"—have fought shy of me ever since I have been here.[2]

A few days later Davitt, speaking at Liverpool, caused a sensation when he brushed aside Parnell's objections and came out for "land nationalization" in opposition to peasant proprietorship. This differed from the method that George advocated for bringing about land reform. He desired the absorption of economic rent through taxation of land values and was flatly opposed to touching the titles to land.

But Davitt's speech had the old lilt—"the land for the people." George, knowing that it was not yet time to quarrel over details, and realizing at the same time that the right principle was being promulgated, was overjoyed.

On June 10, George delivered a second Dublin lecture at the Rotunda. It was so well received that the "Kilmainham Treatyites," as the Parnell faction came to be known, began to turn their fire on him. They also brought great pressure on Davitt, who had gone to the United States to try to raise money for propaganda.

Despite this opposition from Irish leaders, the American won the friendship of George O. Trevelyan, the new Chief Secretary for Ireland, and the enthusiastic support of the Reverend Harold Rylett of Belfast, of Father Thomas Dawson, O.M.I., of Glencree, and of Dr. James E. Kelly of Dublin. Other lesser figures in Ireland rallied to his cause.

In England and Scotland he found enthusiasm for his ideas among men like Joseph Cowen, proprietor of *The Newcastle Chronicle;* Thomas F. Walker, a manufacturer in Birmingham; and William Saunders, president of the Central News Agency in London. He was invited to speak in Glasgow at two large meetings which kindled great enthusiasm and which are considered by many to mark the beginning of the radical land movement in Scotland.

George had written to Shaw, "*Progress and Poverty* is slowly and steadily making its way—eating in as I am inclined to think no book of this kind ever did before, and the little *Irish Land Question* has certainly produced a considerable effect. And soon now, I think the big discussion is to open and the oxygen blast will be turned on the smouldering fire." [3]

Crossing this letter was one from Shaw which enclosed a draft for $500. In thanking him, George wrote that the money "seems to me like the fulcrum for a lever that will help move the world." [4]

Nine days later Shaw wrote again to say that $3,000 had been pledged for the circulation of *Progress and Poverty* by someone who wished to remain anonymous. [5] With part of this money Shaw had ordered Appleton to send one thousand copies of *The Irish Land Question* and to follow them with an equal number of the larger book, specially bound, to members of the Society for Political Education in the United States.

"The great movement we have so often talked about is coming," George wrote to Dr. Taylor. [6] For now, thanks to the Shaw money and the cooperation of Dr. James C. Durant, who had a printing office in London, a six-penny edition of 12,000 copies of *Progress and Poverty* was issued and circulated throughout the United Kingdom. A three-penny edition of 5,000 copies of *The Irish Land Question* followed.

An amusing incident occurred during the preparation of this English paper-bound edition of George's master work.

One day a stranger sauntered into the composing room of the Durant plant. Explaining that he had been a printer, he said he would like to try his hand at the case. Permission was granted

and the stranger began chatting with another compositor named
Boyle as the two set type. At last Boyle broke in, "You are an
American and a compositor, and from what you've been telling
me you've been a sailor and a miner. The man who wrote this
book we're working on, was all those things. Can it be that you
—are—?"

"Yes," admitted Henry George, "I am!" [7]

In August, 1882, the American set off on a jaunting-car trip
to western Ireland to study and write of conditions there. With
him went an Englishman, James Leigh Joynes, a master of Eton,
who had been engaged to write articles for *The Times* of
London.

They arrived at the small town of Loughree, which swarmed
with soldiers and constabulary. As the correspondents drove
down the street to the only hotel, the police seemed to leap
from the houses on each side and follow them.

A month earlier George had written from London to America, "It has been very hard work ever since I have been here.
Every word I write or telegraph has been watched on the other
side (Ireland) and I have been in a much more difficult place
than a mere newspaper correspondent." [8] Indeed, now in
Loughree his position became acute. Later he wrote of it to
his wife: "A lot of police were waiting for us and arrested us
(under the Crimes Act) the moment the horse stopped in front
of the hotel. Police jumped up (on the jaunting-car) and drove
us to the barracks where, in a barred room, each valise was
searched, each paper read. It was very funny to see them going
through everything like a parcel of monkeys." [9]

George was particularly amused by a constable who, with
intense interest, studied a manuscript which he held upside
down. Indeed, the whole episode struck him as highly farcical.
Joynes was not amused. His companion, wrote George, was
"indecently disconcerted and frightened." [10] He went on in
this vein:

The Eton men are brave. Whatever else he may get at the old
school, a boy gets the lesson that he must not flinch drilled into
him with his Greek and Latin. But this notion of being arrested
and being paraded through the streets as a would-be assassin of
landlords, was evidently more horrible at first blush to my friend
than being fired at from behind a stone wall—the danger that his
friends had warned him he was risking.[11]

An Englishman who comes to Ireland in the right way gets some
new notions. I have no prejudices against publishers, but I would
like to have had Kegan Paul on one side of the car and W. H. Appleton on the other.

The whole thing struck me as infinitely ridiculous. There was
after all, a good deal of human nature in Artemus Ward's declaration that he was willing to sacrifice all his wife's relatives to save
the Union. And in my satisfaction at seeing an Eton master lugged
through the town as too suspicious a stranger to be left at large,
I lost all sense of annoyance at my own arrest.

The Magistrate who examined them concluded there had
been some mistake. After three hours the correspondents were
released. They spent the night in the local hotel, paid a visit to
the prior of the Carmelite Order and to the shops of several
"suspects," and drove off to the nearby town of Athenry. In
this hamlet, which was too small to support a doctor and which
boasted only one pump for the entire town, twenty-six constables and fifty-six soldiers were quartered. The correspondents
visited Father McPhilpin, did some sight-seeing, and made for
the railroad station. The police, who had been loitering about,
arrested George again but permitted Joynes to go free. The
American related:

The charge against me was being a stranger and a dangerous
character who had conspired with certain other persons to prevent
the payment of rent. The police surrounded me and forced me into
what in some parts of this country would be called the hoodlum
wagon. I was carried to the police station under a formidable guard,
and after being cross-examined was locked up. . . . I was taken to
the mansion of the squire for examination. I shall never forget the
contrast it presented with the misery of the village. Well-dressed
people were playing lawn tennis on its beautiful grounds. It had
stately trees around it and an air of the utmost respectability and
comfort. The squire sent me back to the subordinate magistrate
and I was recommitted to the lock-up.[12]

Several hours of detention followed, with a long examination
of papers and endlessly stupid testimony regarding the prisoner's movements. George, as he wrote later, "was very hungry,
for all I had to eat since morning was a bit of bread and cheese.
. . . It was near midnight and I was very tired, and if I had to
sleep in Galway Jail, as I expected, there was a long ride yet

before me, so I said nothing about the effort of kissing a 'swear book,' nor further bothered the inspector." [13]

The magistrate, who, oddly enough, was the same one who had examined him at Loughree, summed up with a justification of the police for having arrested the American. Then he proceeded to discharge him. Whether the decision was due to the telegram which Mr. Trevelyan, the Chief Secretary for Ireland, stated in the House of Commons that he had sent to Ireland, or whether it was due to the magistrate's native wisdom, George could not determine. "My papers," he continues in the account of the incident, "were restored to me, and as the magistrate expressed a desire to read the whole of *The Irish Land Question,* I asked him to accept a copy, and gave one each to the Sub-Inspector and the constable who had personally been very polite to me.[14]

Next morning the two correspondents wasted no time climbing into the jaunting car behind their Irish driver and the fleet little mare. As to further adventure, George only indicates: "... how the police followed us into the wilds of Connemara, and how we lost them by the aid of a horse that could understand Irish, if she could not speak it." [15]

Irish friends who learned of the American's predicament hurried to his wife to apologize and commiserate with her, and were quite amazed to find her unworried. Her sense of humor reassured her—and besides she had received a note from her husband saying, "Am enjoying the trip and seeing a lot." [16]

Yet George knew that such treatment as he had experienced could on occasion prove most annoying. When he reached Dublin he sent a letter to President Arthur protesting against "wanton annoyances, unreasonable inquisitions and imprisonment upon frivolous pretexts" suffered by American citizens abroad without adequate intervention by American diplomats. In reality, the letter was aimed at James Russell Lowell, the American Minister to the Court of St. James's. This assignment, as George afterward wrote in a critical yet humorous vein, was "a place for the spoiling of good poets."

After he returned to the United States, Henry George received a letter from Secretary of State Frelinghuysen who passed on to him "the regret of Her Majesty's Government that this incident should have occurred," [17] and invited him to enter a claim for damages. George declined to do this.

The publicity given the arrests in Ireland, the reference to it in the House of Commons, the spread of the cheap editions of his books, and the laudatory criticism in the *Times* of London brought George and his theories to the forefront of popular discussion. When the *Times'* review of *Progress and Poverty* appeared, George's English publisher sold out every copy of the book on hand.

Back in London, he made his first address in Memorial Hall with Alfred Russell Wallace in the chair.[18] It was a chance hearing of the American at this meeting that changed the life of a young Irishman, George Bernard Shaw, and (according to Archibald Henderson) "fired him to enlist, in Heine's phrase, 'as a soldier in the Liberative War of Humanity.'"[19] Following "the clarion call" of the author of *Progress and Poverty*, Shaw said subsequently in a message to America, "my ambition is to repay my debt to Henry George by coming over some day and trying to do for your young men what Henry George did nearly a quarter of a century ago, for me."[20]

A few days later George spoke to another gathering, one that gave him inspiration and satisfaction—three hours of serious discussion with Church of England clergymen.

That same evening he was guest of honor at a two-shilling workingmen's banquet. Then he said farewell to England—but not for the last time. His admirers were eager for him to stay but he told them that the movement was strong enough to go on without him; that perhaps he could be of help but no one man was necessary to the movement now. And with the glad tidings that another edition of 20,000 copies of *Progress and Poverty* was to be printed in a few days, he left for Ireland.

In Dublin a farewell dinner was given him. On October 4, 1882, he sailed with his family for New York.

CHAPTER XVIII

RETURN TO AMERICA

WHEN Henry George returned to the United States in the autumn of 1882 after a year's absence he found himself "pretty near famous." Newspapers heralded his arrival and he was given a formal welcome by labor union members at Cooper Union and a ten-dollar-a-plate dinner at Delmonico's by leaders in science, letters, politics, and law.[1]

The toastmaster at the banquet was Algernon Sidney Sullivan, and the speakers included Justice William H. Arnoux, Justice Van Brunt of the New York Supreme Court, the Reverend Henry Ward Beecher, Thomas G. Shearman, Andrew McLean, Francis B. Thurber, Thomas Kinsella, and Representative Perry Belmont of New York. Henry George, mistaking the hour, arrived at the dinner late, and although he was carefully dressed in his smartly cut evening clothes, characteristically he had forgotten to have his shoes polished.

The *New York Times* reported on the following morning (October 22, 1882):

In introducing Mr. George, Mr. Sullivan . . . said he had "been to a great many dinners in that room. . . . Never before in all New York had representative men from all the classes of Society been assembled for the single purpose of making an acknowledgement to one whose sole claim to fame was that he was a philosopher and author". . . . When Mr. George arose he was greeted with three cheers, the whole company rising to deliver them. He began by saying he could hardly express how much he appreciated the compliment tendered him: "You honor me for my ability and personal worth—so your invitation runs. I have read in the newspapers that I am a communist, a disturber of social order, a dangerous man, and a promoter of all sorts of destructive theories." *

---

* In *The Philosopher of San Francisco* Louis F. Post contributes an interesting sidelight on the honor tendered George by these leaders of New York business, political and social life. He writes:

Let the *Herald* take it up from here:

What is the terrible thing I want to do? I want in the first place to remove all restrictions upon production of wealth and in doing this I want to secure that fair distribution of wealth which will give every man that which he has fairly earned. What I contend for is that the man who produces, or accumulates, or economizes; the man who plants a tree, or drains a marsh, or grows a crop, or erects a building, or establishes a business, should not be fined for so doing; that it is to the interest of all that he should receive the full benefit of his labor, his foresight, his energy or his talents. In other words, I propose to abolish all taxation which falls upon the exertion of labor or the use of capital or the accumulation of wealth, and to meet all public expenses out of that fund which arises, not from the exertion of any individual, but from the growth of the whole community. . . .

Consider, Gentlemen, how this city would grow, how enormously wealth would increase, if all taxes were abolished which now bear on the production and accumulation and exchange of wealth. Consider how quickly the vacant spaces on the island would fill up could land not improved be had by him who wanted to improve it, without the payment of prices now demanded.

Before George's return from Europe, Michael Davitt had come to the United States in search of aid for the Irish cause.

The eulogies pronounced at that dinner, both from the guest table and the floor, with reference to this American with whose teachings none of the speakers but Mr. Kinsella, Mr. Shearman, and Mr. Saunders had any acquaintance, would have puzzled me beyond hope of solution if I had not stumbled upon the probable explanation of that large attendance of distinguished New Yorkers. Having occasion at the banquet lull between eating and oratory to carry a message to the guest of honor from my place in the rear of the room to his at the front, I was caught by the arm by Recorder Smythe as I returned.

"What part of Ireland does this man George come from?" the Recorder asked me.

"He isn't an Irishman," I explained; "he was born in Philadelphia, and his father before him."

The Recorder looked puzzled, as he murmured half to me and half to himself: "No-o-o; that can hardly be; I was told that he was born in Ireland."

After further and positive assertions to the contrary, I left Recorder Smythe in a reflective mood which seemed to have seized him. One seized me, too. As I came out of it I brought with me the astonishing success of that Delmonico banquet to Henry George. Our guests having doubtless heard of him as a British prisoner in Ireland, had probably leaped to the conclusion that he was an Irish patriot—a kind of patriot hardly less popular with New York politicians in those days than American patriots of the 100-per cent variety became some years later.—Editor

In the opening speech of his campaign which he delivered at the New York Academy of Music on June 26, the Irish leader went out of his way (evidently under pressure from the Parnellites) to protest that he had not "fallen into Mr. George's hands." [2]

On this occasion the Reverend Dr. Edward McGlynn, rector of one of the largest Roman Catholic churches in the city, St. Stephen's on East 29th Street, came out openly for George's solution to questions of economic injustice—much to the delight of George when he heard of the incident.

Father McGlynn was a native of New York and of Irish parentage. Two years George's senior, he had enjoyed a brilliant career in the priesthood, studying at the College of Propaganda in Rome and becoming, after his ordination at the age of twenty-two, assistant to the Reverend Dr. Cummings at St. Stephen's. Dr. Cummings, a man of somewhat liberal views, had considerable influence in the community. When McGlynn succeeded him at the age of thirty, the younger man continued to serve St. Stephen's in this tradition.

Father McGlynn appeared with Davitt on three other occasions. In the second speech he rebuked the Irishman, "Michael Davitt is only a pilot engine that goes before the head of the train. Let him not apologize for the truth that is in him." He added, "I am entirely of the opinion of Henry George as a matter of political economy . . . and therefore [think] that the plan of Henry George and Michael Davitt is the true one." [3]

Again, at the huge meeting held in Union Square on July 5, McGlynn exhorted Davitt:

Explain away not one tittle of it, but preach the gospel in its purity! It is a good gospel, not only for Ireland, but for England, for Scotland and for America, too. And if in this country we do not yet feel quite so much the terrible pressure of numbers upon the land, the same terrible struggle between progress and poverty, as is felt in other lands, no thanks are due our political system, but thanks only to the bounties of nature, and to the millions of acres of virgin lands with which God has blessed us. But when these virgin lands have been occupied; when the population shall have increased here as it has elsewhere in proportion to our extent of territory, we shall have precisely the same problem to solve, and the sooner we solve it the better. [4]

The priest's acceptance of his teachings meant very much to George, who had written from Ireland, "Sure as we live the world is moving. A Power infinitely superior to ours is forcing it on!" [5]

Father McGlynn's outspoken support of George could scarcely go unnoticed by the enemies of the Irish cause. Soon word came from Cardinal Simeoni, Prefect of Propaganda in Rome, ordering the American priest's suspension unless Cardinal McCloskey of New York should rule otherwise. An interview followed with the Cardinal and Father McGlynn sought to clear up his superior's misunderstanding of the doctrine which he had been advocating. The upshot of the interview was that the priest promised not to make any more speeches for the Land League, "not because I acknowledged the right of any one to forbid me, but because I knew too well the power of my ecclesiastical superiors to impair and almost destroy my usefulness in the ministry of Christ's Church to which I had consecrated my life."

Shortly after George returned to New York he called upon his new advocate. He found in the tall, handsome, dark-haired man with the resonant voice and gracious manner, the strength that endeared him to his huge congregation. The meeting convinced McGlynn, as he said later, that "Mr. George's genius and intellectual gifts do not exceed his gifts and graces of heart and character and his profoundly reverent and religious spirit." [6]

It was only a few weeks after this meeting that George's beloved friend, Francis George Shaw, died after a short illness. [7] The loss of this wise and learned man, who had been a bulwark in time of need, hurt him deeply. As a last reminder of the faith and generosity of Shaw came a gift of $1,000 in his will to the younger man—his "proxy."

"What a curious life mine is," George told a friend, "literally from hand to mouth; yet always a way seems to open." [8]

The Shaw bequest, he believed, was intended to relieve him from the strain of hack writing. Turning down Charles Nordhoff's appeal that he run for Congress, early in the new year, George started work on a book dealing with the tariff question. He found time, however, for other writing. In March of 1883, the *North American Review* [9] published an article "Money in Elections" in which George advocated the Australian ballot, even as he had advocated that reform in his "Bribery in Elections" published in *The Overland* of December, 1871.

In the meantime the cheap English edition of *Progress and Poverty* was meeting with so much success that the author was able to negotiate an American twenty-cent paper-covered edition through the publishing house of John W. Lovell. *The Irish Land Question,* paper-covered and selling for ten cents, followed this venture. (Since it did not deal exclusively with Ireland it was retitled *The Land Question*).

Both books did well. Although George received 10 per cent—the same royalty which Appleton had paid for the finer edition—he gave away so many copies of *Progress and Poverty* and made such large discounts and concessions to those who bought in quantities for educational purposes that his own earnings were small.

On both sides of the Atlantic appreciation of George's work was growing swiftly. He wrote to Taylor, "In England our ideas are spreading with extreme rapidity. A Birmingham gentleman, Thomas F. Walker, states that he himself has bought and distributed to the active men of the Liberal party two thousand three hundred copies of *Progress and Poverty*." [10]

In the United States, George found another advocate in T. V. Powderly, Grand Master of the Order of Knights of Labor. The organization had started among the garment workers of Philadelphia fourteen years earlier. By 1883, it had spread all over the country. Speaking in New York the previous December, Powderly had said:

In my opinion the main, all absorbing question of the hour is the land question. . . . The eight-hour law, the prohibition of child labor and the currency question are all of weighty moment to the toiler. But high above them all stands the land question. . . . You may make the laws and own the currency but give me the land and I will absorb your wealth and render your legislation null and void. . . . Give heed to the land question. . . . It were better to be called a communist than to be a party to the plundering of a people of the inheritance ordained for them by God. [11]

Powderly was instrumental in placing copies of *Progress and Poverty* and *The Land Question* in local assemblies of the Knights of Labor. In this way the American laboring man became acquainted with "Georgism."

About this time Allen Thorndike Rice of the *North American Review* proposed that George edit an economic weekly.[12] After considering this flattering offer, George decided instead to contract with *Frank Leslie's Illustrated Newspaper* for a series of thirteen articles at one hundred dollars each.

The articles, called "Problems of the Time" and starting with the April 11 issue, dealt with different aspects of economic questions. The fifth one, discussing "The March of Concentration,"[13] showed that there was an increase in the size of land holdings in the United States and that the Census reports for 1870 and 1880 contradicted the figures which were given to prove that the average size of farms was decreasing. Therefore, he said, the reports were unreliable and without any worth.

Both censuses had been supervised by Professor Francis A. Walker, the Yale political economist who had been president of the Massachusetts Institute of Technology. Walker was the author of books on money, history, economics, and statistics. Angered because of the criticism of his work, he wrote to *Frank Leslie's* offering to send George "a more elementary study," illustrated with diagrams, to prove that the average size of farms was decreasing."[14] In the same periodical George replied, Walker rejoined, and a lively little debate developed.

The *New York Sun* found the controversy amusing because, while the paper considered George suave and dignified, "his opponent squirms and sputters as one flagrant blunder after another is brought forward and the spike of logic is driven home through his egregious fallacies."[15] Later the Census Bureau admitted that the 1870 tables had been based on improved area while those of 1880 were based on total area—which made Walker's comparison of the two impossible and proved George's charge of carelessness.

After these thirteen articles were finished, George arranged them as chapters, added eight more chapters, and a conclusion, and brought them out as a book entitled *Social Problems*. He dedicated the volume to the memory of Francis G. Shaw. Selling the English copyright for £400 cash, he wrote to Taylor, "This makes nearly $3,600 I have had out of the book before the first copy is issued, which is a considerable difference from *Progress and Poverty*."[16] Some weeks later he added, "I did let *Social Problems* go too low; but I wanted the money badly and snapped at the first good offer. But I rely on the United States to give me more." [17]

Easy to read, this book was the one the author himself used to recommend to beginners in political economy before they tackled *Progress and Poverty*.

It was before he published *Social Problems,* however, that George had told Taylor, "I have met with a misfortune. You know I put considerable work this spring on a free-trade book. I have lost the manuscript. . . . It cannot be found anywhere and has evidently gone into the ash barrel." [18]

The Georges had been boarding at the time on Fourteenth Street, near Seventh Avenue. His precious manuscript, which would have made about one hundred printed pages, evidently was carried off and destroyed by a servant who had been given an accumulation of waste papers to dispose of when George's study was cleaned.* He wrote again to Taylor, "Writing well on exact subjects is of all work the hardest. Yet I should be delighted if I could see my way clear to keeping at it. How blessed are they for whom the pot boils of itself! I have now just $25 in the world, about half a week's living with economy; no, not that. However, this is no new experience for me. That MS. is a very serious loss even in the financial aspect." [19]

For all of this, George spent no time bemoaning his misfortune but set himself to reading thoroughly Adam Smith's *Wealth of Nations* with the idea of abridging and annotating it. He started the work but was never able to finish the annotation.

His own works had begun to command widespread attention. But Henry George never allowed fame to distract him from the tender things which he held most dear. During their separations there was a steady stream of letters—almost daily—

* The loss has an interesting though tenuous link to what is perhaps the most famous parallel of this kind in literary history. Forty-five years before, Thomas Carlyle had lost the manuscript of the first volume of the *French Revolution* in much the same manner. He had given it to his friend John Stuart Mill for reading and annotation. Mill lent the material to his friend, Mrs. Taylor (Harriet Hardy), and while it was in her care a serving maid carelessly committed it to the flames so that nearly all of it was lost. Mill later married Mrs. Taylor, and it was her daughter, Helen, who had entertained the Georges in England.

Mill induced Carlyle to accept £100 in compensation for the loss of the first volume of the *French Revolution* but Henry George had no one to recompense him for the loss of what was to become *Protection or Free Trade.*—Editor between Henry and Annie George. After they had been married for twenty-three years he could write his wife:

You used sometimes to say that you liked to feel necessary to me. You don't know how thoroughly that wish is gratified. I know it even when I am with you; but feel it more when I am away. I often think how more and more you have grown into my life, so that in everything that draws a man there is only one woman in the world for me. I not only love you with all the fervor I did when I first clasped you to my heart; but with a deeper love. I have learned to respect your judgment and value your advice: your caresses, if they cannot seem more sweet, seem more needed, and even when you assume the imperious tone and art of the mistress there is a charm I would not feel from anyone else. I think the people who grow tired of each other are never truly married. There is in the perfect confidence—the absolute oneness of the truly married—something which far surpasses any fresh charm.[20]

Throughout the years he had kept in close touch with his family in Philadelphia. He sent financial help as often as he could. The bond between him and his father had not weakened with time and Richard Samuel Henry George's interest in his career had been an inspiration despite the fact that the older man, who was nearly eighty when *Progress and Poverty* was published, never fully understood the book or recognized its significance. This lack of intellectual kinship was shared by George's mother, though she, like her husband, gloried in the acclaim which her son had received.

Henry George's sister Kate and her husband Jerry Chapman were the members of his generation who more nearly comprehended both his proposed fiscal reform and his economic philosophy—and enthusiastically championed both. If George had any mental or spiritual loneliness within the family circle it was far outweighed by the devotion which deepened with the years.

To his father, who wrote thanking him for a present received on Mr. George's eighty-fifth birthday, it seemed "only yesterday when you came to me saying that you would go to California and that you would try your fortune there. I did not object; and now the result has been all I could have wished." [21]

This was the last letter he wrote to his son; a few days later he was stricken with pneumonia. All his children gathered around the bedside of the patriarch in time to receive his blessing before he died. One week later, his wife, made ill by grief, followed him. And Richard Samuel Henry George and Catherine Vallance George, who had been such loving partners through their long life together, were buried in the same grave in Mt. Moriah cemetery.

CHAPTER XIX

GREAT BRITAIN IN '84

HENRY GEORGE met the death of his parents with a serenity which expressed his faith in a life hereafter and in whatever might be in store for him. One day, while walking on Broadway with his son Richard, he stopped suddenly, threw back his head, and, gazing upward, exclaimed, "Yes, I could die now!"

"Why do you say that?" the boy asked in some surprise.

The father, who had been musing aloud, was jerked back to reality. "I was thinking," he explained, "that I could die now and the work would go on. It no longer depends upon one man. It is no longer a 'Henry George movement'—a one-man movement. It is the work of many men in many lands. I can help it while I live; but my death could not stop it." [1]

However, his followers did not share this opinion. Those in England who were members of the Land Reform Union importuned him to return for a speaking campaign and guaranteed his expenses.

Taking his elder son, Henry, as secretary, he left in December, 1883, just before Christmas.

The two Americans were met at Liverpool by Michael Davitt and Richard McGhee, M.P. George found that discussion of his "theory" was widespread. The sale of the Kegan Paul, Trench and Company editions of *Progress and Poverty*, together with 40,000 copies of the sixpenny editions, had taken the book into all quarters. It had been discussed and "answered" by a number of English economists, including the Right Honorable Henry Fawcett, Postmaster General and professor of political economy at Cambridge, and the brilliant young Oxford lecturer on economic history, Arnold Toynbee, who had died only a few months before at the age of thirty-one.

Arriving in London on January 6, 1884, George was greeted

by a large delegation from labor organizations. He delivered
an address from the roof of a "four-wheeler," thanking them
for their welcome and explaining his purpose in coming to
England.

Although the campaign was being financed by members of
the Land Reform Union, including Helen Taylor, William
Saunders, Richard McGhee, J. L. Joyce, H. H. Champion, and
R. P. B. Frost, the last two mentioned, the one treasurer and
the other secretary of the Union, strangely enough leaned toward the doctrines of Karl Marx.[2] George promptly had to
make clear to these and a few other Socialists, who threatened
to obstruct his campaign if he did not adopt their program,
that he not only opposed the nationalization of capital, including machinery, but that he stood firmly for the principles enun-
ciated in his own books.[3]

Let us make these principles clear.

George's philosophy was one of freedom as against regimen-
tation; individual liberty as against collectivist restriction. He
believed with Jefferson that the best governed people were
those the least bound by governmental restrictions. When the
state stepped in to regulate capital or labor, it thereby interfered with the rights of the individual. Instead of regulation
of wages, George wanted the release of natural opportunity
("land") which determines wages. For since all wealth, and
therefore all capital, comes from the application of labor to
land, he argued that land would afford for labor a just return
if freed from private speculation and monopoly.

Finally, Henry George put it in these words: "An equitable
principle already exists in natural laws, which if left unob-
structed, will, with a certainty that no human adjustment could
rival, give to each who takes part in the work of production
that which is justly his due."

The Marxists Champion and Frost, realizing that their American guest could not be swayed, quietly acquiesced in his plans
for the speaking campaign.

Karl Marx himself conceded that George was a "writer of
talent" but believed him to have "however the repugnant arro-
gance and presumption which inevitably mark all such panacea
breeds." According to Henry M. Hyndman, who was an un-
shakable Marxist, Marx looked through *Progress and Poverty*
and "spoke of it with a sort of friendly contempt; 'the capitalist's
last ditch' he said." The contempt was evidently reciprocated,

for George wrote Hyndman that he considered Marx unscientific and "a most superficial thinker, entangled in an inexact and vicious terminology." Years later he summed up his feelings in a letter to Thomas F. Walker, "As for Karl Marx, he is the prince of muddleheads."

George had to clarify his principles for another group besides the Socialists.[4] He had to reaffirm that he did not believe in compensating landlords in the application of the taxation of land values. If the land belonged "in usufruct" to the people, there was no justice in making the people buy back what was by right their own. "Because I was robbed yesterday and the day before, and the day before that, is it any reason that I should suffer myself to be robbed today and tomorrow, any reason that I should conclude that the robber has acquired a vested right to rob me?"[5] he had asked in *Progress and Poverty*. He did not believe in buying out the land profiteer, but rather in taxing him out.

These things settled, Henry George's second English tour began. He spoke first at a meeting in St. James's Hall, London.[6]

Ordinarily he did not prepare for a speech except to meditate on its subject beforehand in his favorite posture—stretched out on a sofa and smoking. But this event was of such overriding importance that he spent most of two days and two nights dictating to his son and another stenographer alternately, continuing until time to dress and hasten to the lecture hall.

Even though the London correspondent of the *New York Tribune* reported that "people of the better sort find a difficulty in taking Mr. George seriously,"[7] every one of the four thousand seats in the great hall was occupied and scores of his listeners stood in the back aisles and along the walls. John Ruskin was to have presided, but he was detained by ill health and his place was taken by Henry Labouchere, M.P., editor of *Truth* (London). To quote briefly from the long account of January 10, 1884, in the *London Daily News*:

The Chairman, in introducing the lecturer, said that like Byron, Mr. George had written a book, and had awaked to find himself famous. In all parts of Great Britain Mr. George's name was a household word.... In *Progress and Poverty* Mr. George did two things, he pointed out lucidly and eloquently the evils of our system of land tenure and he suggested a remedy for them. With the denunciations of the present system he thought they must all agree.

It was a matter of wonder that a nation pretending to some degree of intelligence should have assented so long to allow the landlords of this country to legislate in their own exclusive interests.

Only the synopsis of the written speech was delivered, for George had put aside the manuscript which had been prepared so laboriously. Despite his fears that he would talk too long, the talk—and it *was* long—seemed a magnificent success. The *Daily News* reported that he closed with the question, "How could they defend the right of a few in England to own the land on which they all must live?" And he exhorted his audience, "Let English people make England truly the free home of free men—men equal in their rights, men who knew their duties and would perform them; and in doing what they could for that end they would be doing it, not for their country alone, but for the whole civilized world."

An ovation followed. It produced such an effect that all the English, Scottish, and Irish papers commented upon it. Some of the Tory papers, however, took offense at the part of the speech where George said that if the unearned increment were collected for public needs, among those benefited would be orphans and also there would be enough to "give every widow, from the lady who sat upon the throne to the poorest laborer's widow, a pension." Long afterward George explained, "At my remark 'that every widow from the Queen down ought to have a pension, not as a matter of charity, but as a matter of justice' I meant no disrespect to Her Majesty, but it was misinterpreted by part of the audience." [8]

After this great meeting in London, addresses followed in many towns of the United Kingdom, north as far as Wick and Keiss and in the west. George wrote to Taylor that "I have been riding all day and far into the night over hills of Skye and speaking on hillsides to gathered crofters. . . . I have been working hard this trip, speaking every night but have stood it well though I am very tired. I have been sowing good seed and it would not be long in germinating." [9]

He spoke twice in Glasgow, both times in the City Hall. On the first occasion he made his "Scotland and Scotsman" speech which became famous. [10] In it he pictured the hideous poverty of the crofters and the colliers as well as the laboring class in the cities. He did not mince words:

OVER-PRESSURE.

He. "DID YOU GO TO HEAR MR. GEORGE'S LECTURE?"
She. "NO. WHO'S MR. GEORGE?"   (*Pause.*)
He. "DID YOU GO TO HEAR JOACHIM?"
She. "NO. WHO'S JOACHIM?"   (*Pause.*)
He. "HAVE YOU HEARD ST. PAUL AT THE ALBERT HALL?"
She. "NO. WHO'S ST. PAUL?"   [*Gives it up.*

A Du Maurier cartoon appearing in *Punch*, August 1, 1885.

You people in Glasgow not merely erect church after church, you have the cheek to subscribe money to send missionaries to the heathen. I wish the heathen were a little richer, that they might subscribe money and send missionaries to such so-called Christian communities as this—to point to the luxury, the very ostentation of wealth, on the one hand, and to the barefooted, ill-clad women on the other; to your men and women with bodies stunted and minds distorted; to your little children growing up in such conditions that only a miracle can keep them pure! ... In this great, rich city of yours there are today numbers of men who cannot get employment. Such a state of things is but typical of that which exists everywhere throughout the world. There is just the same state of things in America. It is due merely to the selfishness and ignorance of men. And when you come to ask the reason of this state of things, if you seek it out, you will come at last, I believe, to the great fact, that the land on which and from which it was ordained that all mankind must live has been made the private property of a few of their number. This is the only adequate explanation. Man is a land animal. All his substance must be drawn from the land. ... And as land is absolutely necessary to the life of man, the man who commands the land on which and from which other men live, commands those men. ... Proclaim the grand truth that every human being born in Scotland has an inalienable and equal right to the soil of Scotland. ... It is not necessary to divide the land. You can easily take the revenue that comes from the land for public purposes. There is nothing very radical in this; it is a highly conservative proposition.[11]

When George had finished speaking some five hundred persons remained to organize what Richard McGhee [12] named the "Scottish Land Restoration League." At a second and over-flow meeting held a week later in City Hall nearly two thousand names were enrolled. Similar societies sprang up in Dundee, Aberdeen, Inverness, Edinburgh, Greenock, and other communities. Still, there were those who thought George a crank. Frederic Harrison, the Positivist, delivered lectures against him in Edinburgh and New Castle. And John Bright, in Birmingham, inveighed against the "wildest" reform "imported lately by an American inventor." [13]

George had set out on his speaking tour braced for opposition from special privilege, vested interests and from intrenched intolerance, but the most difficult experience he had to face came when he spoke at the University of Oxford. True, he did not share Michael Davitt's experience of being locked in a hotel room by students so that he could not get out to speak; but nevertheless the American's experience was an unhappy one. And all this despite the fact that, during his two days' stay at the ancient center of learning, he was the guest of that rare gentleman and distinguished Oriental scholar, F. Max Müller.

From 7 Norham Gardens, George wrote to his wife, "Here we are at Max Müller's: a beautiful place, splendid man, nice family, everything charming only I am suffering from my old enemy, sleeplessness. I hardly got any sleep last night; have been like a drowned rat all today and now tonight it is as bad as ever until in desperation I have got up and started to write. ... I am to lecture before a magnificent audience of University people tomorrow night. The only thing I fear is my condition." [14]

Thus he may have been ill-prepared for what happened.

The lecture, delivered in Clarendon assembly room, was attended by men and women prominent in the University. But in the audience, which consisted chiefly of undergraduates, sat a group of ill-mannered young Conservatives who kept up a disturbance throughout the proceedings. While George was always prepared for heckling, this activity made a smooth discourse almost impossible. So he cut short his address and invited questions.

Instead of questions, he got harangues, statements of private, biased opinions, and a chain of argument which lacked even the dignity of debate.

Alfred Marshall, lecturer on political economy at Balliol, announced that he had "read Mr. George's book from one end to the other; there was nothing in it both new and true; what is true is not new, and what is new is not true." To which the American replied quietly, "I accept your statement. It is a correct criticism; social truth never is, never can be new; and the truth for which we stand is an old truth; a truth seen by men everywhere, recognized by the first perception of all men; only overclouded, only obscured in our modern times by force and fraud." [15]

The speaker won over a large part of the audience but disorder flared up again when one of the prime disturbers denounced Henry George's proposal as a "nostrum" that was "scandalously immoral," and delivered his condemnation in a tone that, although it produced cries of disapproval as well as those of assent, cut George to the quick. He retorted that he would have to withdraw the compliment he had paid the University earlier in the evening when he spoke of its learning and good manners. The uproar was only stilled when the chief attacker arose and said that he had meant only to criticize Mr. George's ideas, not his character.

It was not until the disagreeable performance was over that the American realized that his tormentor was the son-in-law of Max Müller. George apologized to his host for having permitted the young man to arouse him. Müller was much moved and apologized to his guest for having been subjected to a public insult by a member of his family. For it also developed that the young man had not even read *Progress and Poverty* and therefore did not know what he was talking about.

The incident, ugly as it was (George later told his wife that it reminded him of the hoodlums of San Francisco), resulted, however, in tightening the bonds of friendship between the Oxford professor and the American economist.

The lecture which George delivered later to a large audience at Cambridge went off with dignity and order. A sidelight on this experience comes from the diaries of Mary Gladstone, daughter of the then Prime Minister. She had read *Progress and Poverty*, "supposed to be the most upsetting and revolutionary book of the age." [16] She had "finished *Progress and Poverty* with feelings of deep admiration—felt desperately impressed, and he is a Christian." [17] At the time of the Cambridge lecture she met George at the home of Professor James Stuart and wrote of his "earnestness, conviction and singleness and height of aim." [18] Her diary criticism of his lecture says, "Certainly he had a good deal of the genius of oratory about him, and sometimes the divine spark—he is also the man possessed, and he often carried one away. Questions were asked him of all kinds at the end. He did not flinch, and had a wonderful way of leaping to his feet and answering with great spirit and manliness." [19]

After the Cambridge lecture she wrote to her cousin Lavina, wife of Bishop Talbot, "Alfred Lyttleton and Prof. Stuart went with me. They both were struck. We mean to tackle him [George] once more." [20]

And "tackle" him they did, some days later, in London, at the home of Lady Stepney. "There," continues Miss Gladstone, "we had over tea and muffins a conference with Mr. George—Herbert [Herbert Gladstone, M.P., later created Viscount on being appointed governor-general of the Union of South Africa] and Prof. Stuart chief questioners and examiners, Alfred Lyttleton listening and putting in much sympathizing with Mr. George. A great success, for they liked and softened toward the good little man, and as for Maggie [Lady Stepney] she was converted." [21]

The good little man realized that he had made a good little impression for he wrote to his wife, "They are at least three quarters with me." [22]

George made four more speeches in London, and then his three and a half months' of continuous lecturing in Great Britain was brought to a close at a farewell banquet given by the Land Restoration League. Crossing over to Ireland, he spoke to a large audience in Dublin before he sailed, on April 13, for New York.

The visit had been strenuous but George drew from it so much encouragement and inspiration that he counted the work light. During his journeyings there had been the usual lapses into absent-mindedness and the frequent forgetfulness about his belongings. On one railroad train he mixed his luggage with that of another passenger and found to his dismay, and too late, that he was carrying a bag which resembled his own but which contained a much worn pair of woman's shoes instead of his precious manuscripts. Wiring back along the line for information, he received a complaint against the man who had "stolen a valuable pair of lady's shoes and stuffed in their place a bunch of waste paper!" [23]

Always and everywhere he asked questions. Frequently they seemed to the questioner to be abrupt, but that was because he made straight for the point without wasting time on preliminaries. Not a diplomat in the narrow sense of the word, he could win through the wall of reserve to a man's heart by his understanding and sympathy. He often joked with a serious face, only the corners of his eyes laughing. He rarely indulged his power for sarcasm. His manner was genial; he was kindly, especially to the little people, the lowly, the defenseless. Certainly he measured up to Robert E. Lee's definition of a gentleman as "one who never willingly reminds another of inferiority." A great respecter of persons, he had no feeling for caste or worldly position. ("Don't you ever let me hear you use the expression 'our class' again," he said years later to his youngest child. "There are no 'classes.'") It was typical of him, also, that to try to get the other man's point of view he would eliminate himself in conversation.

He delighted, while in England, in hearing unbiased criticisms of Henry George when sometimes talk with strangers would turn upon the "American inventor." Often their reactions were amusing, for occasionally he found himself described as "a Yankee with a Yankee's money-making scheme," a "pestilential agitator," or such.[24] By keeping his identity unknown he was sometimes able to argue so skillfully against his own ideas, using the *reductio ad absurdum,* that he had the erstwhile antagonists finally defending the stand they had at first condemned. He was attacked constantly by the unsympathetic press and sometimes by anonymous letter. "An Indignant Briton" asked angrily why he "did not before coming over here, endeavor to convert his own nation to his most immoral and dishonest doctrines?"[25]

During his second English trip, old friendships were cemented and new ones formed. Wilfred Maynell, editor of a Catholic paper, *The Weekly Register,* tells the story:

It was my great privilege to introduce Henry George to Cardinal Manning. I have a vision of the two profiles facing each other in the dim light of the growing dusk, and I recall the emotion of tone in which each man made frankly to the other a sort of profession of faith. They had travelled to the same goal from opposite directions. "I loved the people," said Henry George, "and that love brought me to Christ as their best friend and teacher." "And I," said the Cardinal, "loved Christ, and so learned to love the people for whom he died."[26]

CHAPTER XX

PROPHET OF SAN FRANCISCO

O N HIS return to New York in April, 1884, Henry George was given an official welcome a second time at Cooper Union by working men of the city.

Many Americans who had heard his speeches before he started on either of his European tours might have agreed with William Saunders, M.P.,[1] who had asked after hearing George in New York, "Why does this man, who writes so well, try to do what he cannot do at all, and what he probably never will do well—speak in public?"[2]

Louis F. Post had long felt "there was nothing attractive about his speeches but the message they bear."[3] He now felt confirmed in his belief that the reports which had been coming from England of the eloquence of his friend were exaggerated since "there was nothing at all moving in his response to the welcome at Cooper Union." At the end of this address Post left the hall for a smoke. When he returned he discovered that George was speaking again—and with a thrilling eloquence. "It was not many minutes," says Post, "before I knew why the British press had exalted this man as 'as great an orator as Cobden or Bright.' "[4]

A few days after the Cooper Union meeting George was given a complimentary dinner at the Cosmopolitan Theater.[5] But this banquet lacked the brilliance of the one held two years before at Delmonico's. Few men of any great prominence were present. His real adherents were being sifted out of the mass of those who had flocked to him, not because they understood his message, but merely because he was in vogue. No longer a dramatic novelty, he was disclosed as a menace to vested rights and special privilege. Those content with or fearful of altering the *status quo* were shying away from this man who seemed bent upon making a fundamental change in the economic order.

A paid lecture at the Academy of Music proved such a financial failure that, with characteristic generosity, George offered to release the managers who had contracted with him for a tour of the United States and Canada.

The lecture tour cancelled, he set himself to writing an answer to an attack made upon him by the Duke of Argyll in the April, 1884, issue of *The Nineteenth Century*. The article written by the nobleman and scathingly called "The Prophet of San Francisco" was to become a title which Henry George wore with the greatest pride.

The Duke, who was titular chief of the great Campbell clan and whose son had married Princess Louise, fourth daughter of Queen Victoria, had served in the cabinets of Aberdeen and Palmerston and had lately resigned as Lord Privy Seal under Gladstone when he differed with the Prime Minister on the Irish land question. But what was more important, he was a man of letters and a philosopher. As author of *The Reign of Law* (1866) he had been much admired by the American whom he now attacked.

The Duke did not disapprove so much of George's theories as he disapproved of what was his own grotesque misinterpretation of those theories—he erected a scarecrow and then knocked it down. Proving his ignorance, he wrote, "In the first place, is it not a little remarkable to find one of the most extreme doctrines of communism advocated by a man who is a citizen of the United States."

Having labeled George to his satisfaction, he continued, "But like all Communists, Mr. George hates the very name of Malthus."

Although far from being a Communist, certainly George did hate the theory of Malthus: that population would overtake subsistence—a theory which the Duke evidently accepted.

Moreover, the Duke of Argyll disregarded the difference between the meanings of "ownership" and "possession." He disregarded the fact that George, who believed that land belongs in usufruct to the living, claimed that under the system of taxation he advocated, the *title* of the individual's holdings would be as inviolate as it is today. Evidently he overlooked the passage in *Progress and Poverty* which reads: "The value of land expresses in exact and tangible form the right of the community in land held by an individual; and rent expresses the exact amount which the individual should pay to the community to satisfy the equal rights of all other members of the community. Thus, if we concede to priority of possession the undisturbed use of land, confiscating rent for the benefit of the community, we reconcile the fixity of tenure which is necessary for improvement with a full and complete recognition of the equal rights of all to the use of land."

The Duke had also overlooked a passage in *Progress and Poverty* which George had taken the trouble to underline: "Let the individuals who now hold it still retain, if they want to, possession of what they call *their* land. Let them buy and sell, and bequeath and devise it. *It is not necessary to confiscate land; it is only necessary to confiscate rent.*"

The Duke asserted that George "is not content with urging that no more bits of unoccupied land should ever be sold, but he insists upon it that the ownership of every bit already sold shall be resumed without compensation to the settler who has bought it, who has spent upon it years of labor, and who from first to last has relied on the security of the State and the honor of the Government. There is no mere practice of corruption which has ever been alleged against the worst administrative body in any country that can be compared in corruption with the desolating dishonor of this teaching."

Page after page (there were thirty-nine) the Scotsman dedicated to his attack, really epitomizing his opinion of the "villainy advocated" by the American in his cry: "The world has never seen such a Preacher of Unrighteousness as Mr. Henry George."

George lashed back. "The Duke declares it has not been his aim to argue," he wrote. "I wish it had not been his aim to misrepresent." He restated his economic plan, and since he had travelled through much of Scotland where he had seen the crime of landed privilege and its consequent poverty, he was able to meet the Duke of Argyll on his own ground by giving proofs and citations which were irrefutable, fighting always for the rights of "the men who all life long must spend life's energies in the effort to maintain life!"

The *Nineteenth Century, Fortnightly,* and the *Pall-Mall Gazette* all offered their columns for George's reply. He chose the first, since it was the one that had printed the attack. His answer was called "Reduction to Iniquity." It appeared in the July issue of the magazine.

The Scottish Land Restoration League published the two articles under the name of "The Peer and the Prophet" and spread the pamphlet throughout Great Britain. It appeared in the United States under the title of "Property in Land." [6]

After this controversy, George turned again to his book on the tariff. Installing himself with his family on the Long Island farm belonging to young Walter Cranford, son of John P. Cranford, a devoted adherent, he focused his attention to the rewriting of *Protection or Free Trade,* the first manuscript of which had been lost. "I find it will be just as hard to do as though I had never attempted it," he wrote to Thomas F. Walker.[7] From his study window he used to watch the stupid bull who periodically got himself tangled in the tether rope—which is described in the opening paragraphs of the book.

This work demanded great concentration. But there were periods of relaxation, as for instance when the Thomas Georges came to visit.

Henry loved to tease his beautiful, black-eyed sister-in-law, Susan. The two shared a fondness for ice cream. And while agreed that Philadelphia ice cream was the best in the world, they indulged in a running argument as to where one could buy the biggest portion for ten cents—in Philadelphia or New York. George argued for New York. She insisted that the helpings were larger in Philadelphia. One afternoon they drove to Jamaica in the Cranford surrey, and after Henry had left his sister-in-law at a store where she wished to shop, he drove to the confectioner's where they had planned to meet. He ordered three portions of ice cream—two on one plate which he left for Susan. He began eating the single portion, and when she came in her brother-in-law explained that he had started on his ice cream because the weather was hot and the stuff was melting. Her gaze fell on the huge mound of ice cream at her place. She flashed her radiant smile, and then her face clouded. "Oh, Henry!" she exclaimed. "I guess you win after all. You do get bigger portions over here than we do in Philadelphia!" She had forgotten to look for the little telltale crinkles in the corners of his eyes.

Work on the tariff book was interrupted, first by a speaking invitation from the Ninth Congress of the Episcopal Church, which met in Detroit. George attended and spoke on the subject, "Is Our Civilization Just to the Working Man?" Soon after that came another call to Great Britain from the Scottish Land Restoration League.

Henry George made his third trip abroad in the autumn of 1884, this time traveling alone. His first speaking engagement was in familiar St. James's Hall in London. The speech drew a tremendous crowd. Helen Taylor, Michael Davitt, and William Forsythe, president of the Scottish League, appeared with him and made brief addresses. The meeting caused so much comment in the press that wherever George spoke on his two-month tour meeting halls were crowded. His Glasgow address, a pay affair, drew such an audience that many persons had to be turned away.[8]

His brief tour, with speeches in rapid succession, ended as it had begun—in London. Denied the use of the Guildhall by the Lord Mayor, the English League conducted the meeting outdoors.[9] Some seven thousand persons, mostly unemployed, attended. Two extra meetings—one in Liverpool and the other in Belfast and both enthusiastic—were rung in before George sailed for home.

This third visit to Great Britain was as stimulating as the two earlier ones. The crowds were large and the press was most attentive. Men in high places were taking his ideas much more seriously. "A book has happened," wrote James L. Garvin, "Henry George appeared and like a few since Thomas Paine he awakened new imaginings and aspirations amongst Radical working men; they thought they saw a great light. Amongst them that passionate and ingenuous work *Progress and Poverty* went like wildfire. Chamberlain read it, electrified: the effect on Morley was the same." [10]

The most encouraging sign of all, however, was a report made by the Royal Commission on the Housing of the Working Classes,[11] whose members included the Prince of Wales, Cardinal Manning, and Lord Salisbury. The Commission recommended that a tax of 4 per cent of the selling price be placed upon vacant or inadequately used land. This would discourage the existing speculation in land holdings and encourage the freeing of building sites. Unfortunately, however, the attempt of the Royal Commission to discourage speculation in land was quashed by its Tory members.

On this trip, too, George made the acquaintance of James

Bryce, historian and author of *The American Commonwealth*. The two men had a long talk. George came away much impressed.

He had planned, on his return to the United States,[12] to resume lecturing. But the times seemed unfavorable. So George kept the pot boiling by writing articles for the *North American Review*, the while concentrating on his manuscript of *Protection or Free Trade*. Work on this powerful appeal for freedom in production as well as for freedom in exchange had been interrupted several times, notably when he had lost more than a hundred pages of the first draft. George worked diligently. In the fall and winter of 1885 some of the chapters appeared serially in seven newspapers.[13] The $3,000 received for this more than paid for publication of the book.

This was done by the author himself under the firm name of Henry George & Co., which became the sole American publishers of the cloth editions of the George books.[14] His son Richard was associated with him in this enterprise and was jokingly known by friends as "Co."

One day late in 1885, while George was busy with the publication of *Protection or Free Trade*, a stranger—a Kentuckian—called upon him. He was Tom Lofton Johnson. Thirty-one years old, of average height but so heavy as to be termed "fat," his face was so beautiful and his smile so beguiling that it charmed even his enemies. He looked like an adult cherub.

At the age of fifteen Tom Johnson had started to retrieve his family fortune, which had been lost in the Civil War, by selling newspapers. Later he became a street car conductor, made some small but lucrative inventions, and gradually achieved wealth through more inventions, the acquisition of street railway franchises, and the manufacture of steel rails.

Once, when Johnson was traveling between Indianapolis and Cleveland, his home town, a train "butcher" recommended that he read *Social Problems*. The youthful industrialist turned it down with the remark that he was "fed up on sex stuff." The conductor overheard the conversation and urged him to buy, explaining that it wasn't "sex stuff" and offering to refund the half dollar if the book proved uninteresting. So Johnson read. And soon after he was reading *Progress and Poverty*. Its arguments converted him, though it seemed against his interest to be converted. He took the book to his lawyer, L. A. Russell.

"I want you to read it," he said, "and point out its errors to me and save me from becoming an advocate of the system of taxation it describes."

Although the lawyer was paid to criticize the book, he failed to convince his client of its fallacies. Whereupon Johnson gave a copy to his partner, Arthur J. Moxham, president of the Johnson Steel Manufacturing Company of Johnstown, Pa., who read it, "carefully marking all the places where, in his opinion, the author had departed from logic and indulged in sophistry."

Moxham read it a second time and erased some of the marks. He went through it again, and then reported, "Tom, I've read that book for the third time and I've rubbed out every damn mark."

The two partners then went to work on Russell. Whether they converted him to the philosophy of Henry George matters less than the fact that their discussion clarified and strengthened their own understanding of *Progress and Poverty*. Johnson's opinion thus reinforced, he mustered courage to call on the author. George at once put him at his ease, placing him in a comfortable chair, while he himself stretched out on his lounge close by and smoked.

Johnson relates:

I was much affected by that visit. I had come to a realizing sense of the greatness of the truth that he [George] was promulgating by the strenuous, intellectual processes which have been described, but the greatness of the man was something I felt when I came into his presence. Before I was really aware of it I had told him the story of my life, and I wound up by saying:

"I can't write and I can't speak, but I can make money. Can a man help who can just make money?"

He assured me that money could be used in many helpful ways to promote the cause, but he said I couldn't tell whether I could speak or write until I had tried; that it was quite probable that the same qualities which had made me successful in business would make me successful in a broader field. He evidently preferred to talk about these possibilities to dwelling on my talent for money-making.

Johnson became so interested in the new book *Protection or Free Trade* that he ordered two hundred copies to be sent to lawyers and ministers in Cleveland.

His publishing venture well launched, George worked on the

Henry George and his daughter, Anna Angela, in a jaunting car.
Queenstown, Ireland, 1889.

Henry George,
Henry George, Jr.,
and Anna Angela George, 1896.

Mrs. George in 1897.

preparation of a series of articles on "Labor in Pennsylvania" for the *North American Review*.[15] He wrote to Taylor, "The Primer is something I have intended to write for a long time— ever since I wrote *Progress and Poverty*, but have not done so for want of time. I had intended to write it this summer but it is very doubtful whether I will be able to do so." [16]

Instead, he made plans to start a weekly paper. But an interruption came which caused a complete change in his plans— indeed, in his life.

CHAPTER XXI

THE FIRST MAYORALTY CAMPAIGN

IN THE summer of 1886, Henry George was waited upon by a committee representing 165 labor organizations who asked him to be their candidate for mayor of New York.[1]

Busy with his writing, he explained that he could not accept the nomination without interrupting the work he had planned. But in a few days the committee returned and made an even more insistent appeal. George was in sympathy with the platform of the Labor party, but he questioned the group's ability to break the iron grip of Tammany Hall—especially since the trade union movement had made a poor showing at the polls the year before. He did not wish to expose his cause to ridicule through political failure. Again he declined the nomination.

The request was then made a third time. The committee assured George that labor had closed its ranks, that the organizations which embraced some 50,000 members were in solid agreement, and that this was a firm offer of support. These guarantees were not to be brushed aside. George felt compelled to make a formal reply, and so he wrote:

My personal inclinations are to say "No." I have no wish to hold office and my hopes of usefulness have run in another line. But there are considerations which under certain conditions, would compel me to say "Yes.".... In this great city, the metropolis of the Western Hemisphere, municipal government has reached a pitch of corruption that, the world over, throws a slur and a doubt upon free institutions. Politics has become a trade and the management a business. The organizations that call themselves political parties are little better than joint stock companies for assessing candidates and dividing public plunder.... It is time for a body of citizens of New York to take some step to show that they have a deeper interest in the government of this great city than whether this or that set of politicians shall divide the spoils, and to demonstrate their power in a way to make their influence felt in every branch of administration.[2]

George had solicited some of his friends for advice. Father McGlynn thought he should run. Louis F. Post was at first dubious. But George went on to say that although failure would harm the cause which "earnest men" wished to help, he would accept the nomination if 30,000 citizens should express a desire over their own signatures that he be their candidate.

He expected that this letter, which he wrote to James P. Archibald, secretary of the Trade and Labor Conference, would end all discussion of the mayoralty. Instead, it was greeted with enthusiasm by the labor groups which had importuned him three times to run. They set about collecting signatures to the petition and invited him to review the annual Labor Day parade with Mayor William R. Grace from the stand in Union Square.[3]

Tammany was to be his unyielding foe as George's candidacy under the Labor banner took spirit and substance. The famous "Hall," once an idealistic force with the inspiration of Jeffersonian democracy, had degenerated into a group of professional politicians bent upon power and graft. In the 1870's the scandals of the notorious "Boss" Tweed ring gave rise to a faction called the County Democracy. But this group, too, became corrupt. On the eve of the 1886 election New York City was a byword for crooked politics.

Both Tammany and County Democracy saw in George a potential menace to their almost undisputed dominance. Together, they chose William M. Ivans, Chamberlain of the City of New York, to talk to George and dissuade him from running.

George and Ivans met in a private room in Seighortner's restaurant on Lafayette Place. The economist was informed that he could not possibly be elected Mayor of New York, no matter how many men might vote for him. Ivans had a proposition. If George would refuse the nomination, the two Democratic groups would run him for Congress in a city district where nomination to Congress was tantamount to election. Ivans explained that George could then go to Europe—or anywhere he desired—and on his return would receive a certificate of election to the House of Representatives.

"You tell me," said Henry George, "that I cannot possibly be elected Mayor of New York. Why, if I cannot possibly get the office, do you want me to withdraw?"

Ivans replied, "You cannot be elected, but your running will raise hell!"

George quickly responded, "You have relieved me of embarrassment. I do not want the responsibility and the work of the office of the Mayor of New York, but I do want to 'raise hell!' I am decided and will run." [4]

George wrote privately to Taylor that the campaign would achieve more in bringing the land question into practical politics than all the writing he could do. "This," he said, "is the only temptation to me." [5]

The formal nomination took place at Clarendon Hall [6] on September 23. George was chosen candidate by the Trade and Labor Conference on the first ballot, with only a scattering of votes for other candidates. The convention accepted the platform which he wrote and in which he asked for taxation of land values, abolition of other taxes, municipal ownership of railroads and telegraph, and a reformed ballot system.

But the interest in his nomination was not confined to labor unions. During the Tweed days a group of Democrats calling themselves "Irving Hall" had seceded from Tammany. Now they came out for George against the other Democratic candidate and formally endorsed him at an acceptance meeting in Irving Hall. On this occasion George said, "The Tammany faction and the County Democracy faction have seen fit to join hands in an effort to put down a movement of the men who always have been the strength of the Democratic party.... Again, the true democracy, the party of Thomas Jefferson and Andrew Jackson, is coming to the front. This is no petty contest for the mayoralty of a city, for the administration of a great municipality, it is the new birth of a great party that is destined to go on conquering."

Intense enthusiasm for George had also been voiced in a crowded meeting held in Chickering Hall, at which the Reverend Dr. John W. Kramer, an Episcopal clergyman, presided and at which the Reverend R. Heber Newton, a boyhood friend, Professor Thomas Davidson, Dr. Daniel De Leon, Charles F. Wingate, Professor David B. Scott, and Father McGlynn all spoke. [7] Resolutions endorsing the Labor party nomination were passed with acclaim. [8]

A few days before this meeting Father McGlynn had received word from Archbishop Corrigan virtually ordering him not to associate with George's meetings or to "coincide with socialism." [9] At the priest's suggestion, the economist called on Archbishop Corrigan and tried in vain to explain his doctrines. The church dignitary was courteous but he pointed out that Father McGlynn had violated an understanding of four years before according to which he was to make no more political speeches. The Archbishop then informed George that he had called his council to meet at noon to consider the McGlynn case.

The priest looked at it a different way. He understood the agreement of 1882 as a promise not to speak further on the Irish land question. As for domestic politics, he had spoken in the meantime in behalf of Grover Cleveland—and without any censure. He felt that even should he be forbidden to speak at the Chickering Hall meeting, "he could not, now that he had been announced to speak, refrain from doing so consistent with his own self-respect and without publicly renouncing the rights of an American citizen."

The upshot of his defiance was suspension for two weeks. George did not learn of the Archbishop's action until later. When he took Father McGlynn to task for failing to mention his punishment, the priest replied:

"Why man, telling you would only have worried you. Why should I add to your worries?" [10]

On October 5, George delivered his formal speech of acceptance at a meeting in Cooper Institute Union. [11] This famous hall had been dedicated by Peter Cooper to free speech. It was there that Abraham Lincoln made his first address before an Eastern audience. The immense auditorium was so crowded that George himself had difficulty in entering. (An immense overflow meeting was held outside, where from trucks stationed in different spots the candidate later made short speeches.) The Reverend Dr. Kramer again presided and John McMackin, chairman of the executive committee of the Labor party, tendered the nomination. Large bundles containing the signatures of some 35,000 voters who had pledged their support to George were placed on the edge of the platform.

The nominee began his speech of acceptance by saying that he did not take the nomination lightly; that at first he could not consider it. "I did not desire to be Mayor of New York. I have had in my time political ambition, but years ago I gave it up.... Another career opened to me ... that of the men who go in advance of politics, the men who break the road that after they have gone will be trod by millions. It seemed to me that there lay my duty and there lay my career." [12]

If elected, he went on, he would attempt to root up political corruption. "Without fear and without favor" he would "try to do my duty. I will listen as readily to the complaint of the richest man in the city as I will to the poorest." [13] He made it crystal clear that his object was reform; that he believed in the equal rights of *all* men; that he was opposed to privilege of whatever kind.

The packed hall listened intently as he continued:

Look over our vast city, and what do we see? On one side a very few men richer by far than it is good for men to be, and on the other side a great mass of men and women struggling to get a most pitiful living. . . . What do we propose to do about it? We propose, in the first place as our platform indicates, to make buildings cheaper by taking the tax off buildings. We propose to put that tax on land exclusive of improvements, so that a man who is holding land vacant will have to pay as much for it as if he was using it, just on the same principle that a man who should go to a hotel and hire a room and take the key and go away would have to pay as much for it as if he had occupied the room and slept in it. In that way we propose to drive out the dog in the manger who is holding from you what he will not use himself. . . . The value of the land of this city, by reason of the presence of the great population, belongs to us to apply to the welfare of the people. . . .

I am your candidate for Mayor of New York. It is something that a little while ago I never dreamed of. Years ago I came to this city from the West, unknown, knowing nobody, and I saw and recognized for the first time the shocking contrast between monstrous wealth and debasing want. And here I made a vow, from which I have never faltered, to seek out and remedy, if I could, the cause that condemned little children to lead such lives as you know them to lead in the squalid districts. It is because of that that I stand before you tonight, presenting myself for the chief office of your city—espousing the cause, not only of your rights, but of those who are weaker than you. [14]

Henry George set up campaign headquarters in the Colonnade Hotel on Lafayette Street near Astor Place. Most of the campaign funds were collected at meetings and solicited by volunteers. But there was little to fight the combined strength of Tammany and the County Democracy, which together under the banner of the Democratic party chose Abram S. Hewitt for their candidate.

Hewitt has appeared in this story before. It was he, who, in 1880, had engaged George to do some private research on a Congressional report. He now took upon himself the role of saving society from "the ideas of anarchists, nihilists, communists, socialists and mere theorists." [15] He exhorted his fellow citizens to "distrust the men who make it their business to prate of the rights of men. It is a very convenient stepping-stone for such people to the property of other men. It pays to be a demagogue." [16]

Hewitt and his supporters hoped that the Republicans would rally behind this "candidate of law, order and progress" and scourge the wild agitator from out of the West. But the Republicans nominated their own candidate—a young man of ability and private means, Theodore Roosevelt.

Roosevelt's campaign, conducted mostly in the strongholds of his own party, was feeble. Hewitt and George exchanged open letters in the newspapers but did not meet on the platform. Hewitt seemed obsessed with the Roosevelt candidacy and warned the third candidate's followers, "If by the action of the Republican Party Henry George should be elected Mayor of this city, or even come very close to it, the men engineering this Republican movement had better go out onto Henry George's unoccupied lands and hang themselves."

This tangential attack sorely tried the patience of the Republican *New York Tribune*. It cried out:

Mr. Hewitt and Mr. George have each assailed with great vigor the weak points of the other. Neither succeeds in defending himself against the attacks made because both are in positions absolutely indefensible. Mr. Hewitt ought to be beaten because he is the candidate and *(will he, nill he)* the instrument of the Democratic ring. Mr. George ought to be beaten because he is the candidate and instrument of men who are hostile alike to true freedom of labor and to the right of labor to its savings. Both are laboring for Mr. Roosevelt by demolishing each other.

To say nothing of this opposition to Hewitt as well as George, the press of New York was arrayed almost solidly against the Labor candidate. The only exceptions were the *Irish World* and the German *Volkszeitung*. Louis F. Post wrote the editorials for the latter.

Some of the campaign reporting was highly distorted and unfair. But George was hardened to such tactics. Three years before he had written Josephine Shaw Lowell, who had been worrying about twisted statements attributed to him, "I expect to be misrepresented and misunderstood by very many and care nothing for it except in the case of those I esteem. It is useless to try to get correction. I can only trust that there are some people who know I am neither a crank nor an idiot." [17]

Apparently many editors who had been misrepresenting him quite agreed with James Gordon Bennett, who wrote in a letter to Poultney Bigelow, "In my humble opinion Henry George is a 'humbug' and a 'busybody'. . . . If the *Herald* does anything it will be either to ignore Mr. George and all his nonsense, or if he should happen by chance to become dangerous, pitch into him roundly." [18]

During the mayoralty campaign George apparently was considered "dangerous," for "pitch into him" the New York papers did. In a note to Mrs. Lowell, George said, "I think of you every night as I read the lies of the *Evening Post* and have been wondering how much you believed. The best reports will probably be in *The Leader,* the newspaper started today." [19]

This little daily was a singular venture in journalism. Edited by Post, it was launched in an attempt to give the George cause honest reporting. The editorial and reportorial work was contributed without pay by many of the copy editors and reporters on the larger dailies who would repair to *The Leader's* office after their regular stints and work long hours in George's behalf. The paper was self-supporting and jumped quickly to a circulation of thirty-five thousand.

Since George could not draw Hewitt to the platform for joint debate he had to be content with dozens of speeches, in personal appeals to voters of all degrees. He spoke from trucks on docks, in factory yards, and at street corners in a "tail-board campaign." It was one of the fiercest mayoralty contests in New York's history. George was called not only "demagogue" and "revolutionist" and an "enemy of civilization and the social order" [20] but also was accused of attacking the sacred rights of property and of preaching anarchy and destruction.

He took all of this in stride, and a year later he could write: "Falsehood and abuse are ever the weapons employed against truth, and the man who attempts to do battle against a great social injustice must expect them, and will, if he be wise, learn to be careless of them, content with knowing that—

> '... never yet
> Share of truth was vainly set
> In the world's wide fallow.' " [21]

But commendation and praise came amidst the calumny and slander. George drew support from men representing many different factions: T. V. Powderly of the Knights of Labor; Samuel Gompers, president of the newly organized American Federation of Labor; Father J.O.S. Huntington, the "Protestant Monk"; George Inness, the painter; and Colonel Robert G. Ingersoll, "the great agnostic." One of the largest contributions made to the campaign fund was a check for one hundred dollars from a manufacturer, August Lewis, until then unknown to Henry George.

Lewis was a man of great charm, conservative manners and quiet dignity. Patron of the arts and friend of writers, musicians, and painters, he was one of the founders of the New York Oratorio Society and of the Philharmonic Orchestra and had given money to help build Carnegie Hall. As a member of the Society for Political Education he had received in 1882 a copy of *Progress and Poverty* through a gift of Francis G. Shaw. He had not read George's work until the mayoralty campaign, and at once he became a convert. A long and devoted friendship followed, and toward its end George was able to epitomize Lewis's outstanding characteristic in one sentence, "Your delicate kindness is as obvious in what you don't say as in what you do." [22]

As election day approached the rumor spread that Father McGlynn had deserted George. At the risk of another reprimand from his ecclesiastical superiors, the priest stated to the press: "Each day, more and more earnestly, I desire to see his [George's] triumphant election. I know of no man I admire and love so much. I believe that he is one of the greatest geniuses that the world has ever seen and that the greatness of his heart fully equals the magnificent gifts of his intellect." [23]

To his superiors, Father McGlynn's crime evidently was not in taking part in politics but in supporting George, since the Right Reverend Monsignor Preston, Vicar General of the Archdiocese, did not find it incompatible with his own priestly

duties to step into the campaign. While not openly champion-
ing Hewitt, he wrote a formal letter condemning the candidacy
of George, declaring his principles "unsound, unsafe and contrary to the teachings of the Church." He added, rather naively,
"And although we never interfere in elections, we should not
wish now to be misunderstood at a time when the best interests
of society may be in danger." [24]

Meanwhile, the two other candidates were leaving no stones
unturned. In his final speech on October 30, Hewitt said:

> I am a candidate for Mayor only for one purpose. I regard the
> election of Henry George as Mayor of New York as the greatest
> possible calamity that could menace its prosperity and future hopes.
> But I have no fear that he will be elected, or if he is elected, I have
> no fear that the doctrine of confiscation which he preaches will ever
> be put in practice in this city. . . . What I do fear is lest by the divi-
> sion which exists among those who have no faith in the doctrines
> which Henry George has been disseminating in this city, and in
> consequence of this division he may receive a larger vote than he
> would fairly be entitled to, the man who will be elected may not
> receive so great a majority as to give a final and fatal blow to these
> doctrines of anarchy and destruction which this new apostle is
> preaching to the working people.

Hewitt again appealed for the Roosevelt vote, arguing that
"the only success that can attend" Roosevelt's efforts "would
be the election of Henry George," in which case "Mr. Roosevelt himself would lament in sack-cloth and ashes and ask
forgiveness of his fellow-citizens for the calamity he had helped
to bring about."

But young Theodore Roosevelt, then twenty-eight, had no
intention of throwing his vote to Tammany. He said:

> There are curious circumstances in this election. The George
> vote from the Democratic party is so large and from the Republi-
> can so small that we have a right to regard his candidacy as simply
> a split from the Democratic party. To stop the growth of the split
> the Democrats have tried to force the fight for the mayoralty on
> false issues. They try to make it appear that it is a contest between
> anarchy and order. Mr. Hewitt, they say, represents order, while
> Mr. George represents anarchy. This I say is false. I oppose Mr.
> Hewitt not because he is not a good man, but because he is simply
> a new figurehead of the same party that has misgoverned this city

for the last quarter of a century. I believe that there should be a change in the government and it is on that issue that I am making the fight.

On the Saturday night before election George's rank-and-file supporters engaged in a giant demonstration which must have given his opponents even further pause. A crowd of working-men variously estimated at from twenty thousand to sixty thousand strong paraded through Union Square past the small wooden reviewing stand where George greeted them. The parade was without uniforms, without bands, without any of the usual political trappings. Carrying torches, trade union banners and signs, the marchers clumped rhythmically through the cold rain chanting "George! George! Hen-ry George!" or "Hi! Ho! the leeches-must-go!" or yet "George! George! Vote for George!" [25] The parade took two hours to pass.

In the meantime Monsignor Preston's letter inferentially condemning George had been given to the newspapers. On the morning following the parade, the Sunday before the election,[26] it was distributed at church doors and made the subject of sermons. Thundered from Catholic pulpits, the denunciation of Henry George doubtless had great weight in the election.

The candidate himself had made few attacks on his rivals. He had merely stressed his conviction that "a civilization cannot stand that is not based on justice." He made his last address at Cooper Union on election eve.

The only thing I regret in this campaign [he said] is that my opponent [Hewitt] saw fit to refuse my challenge to debate face to face before our fellow citizens the principles that he says are living issues in this campaign.

The campaign is over. I have done my part. Now it remains for you to do yours.... I ask no man to vote for the candidate, but to vote for the principle....

But elected or not elected we have won a victory. Elected or not elected, I thank God from the bottom of my heart that it has rested upon me to begin what I believe will prove the grandest work ever begun in America.... And I am glad that in this city of New York, where years ago, unknown I took into my heart of hearts the cross of a crusade that I have never faltered from, that it has devolved upon me to lead in this first movement....

Closing with an eloquent appeal, he called upon his followers to "do your duty tomorrow and tomorrow night we may begin a cheer that will echo through this land and around the world."

But merely to vote was not enough. New York had no Australian secret ballot. Under the election laws each party had to print its own ballots, distribute them, and provide its own voting booths. The new party was under a cruel disadvantage. The counting of ballots was a careless, slip-shod procedure easily open to mishandling and fraud.

The George men were desperate over their own inadequacy. In some voting places there were no George ballots. Some places had no Labor party watchers, though every effort had been made to man each district.

Early on election night a Puerto Rican named Antonio Molina, who was one of the staunchest and most loyal of Georgists, called on Mrs. George. He was in a frenzied state. Tears of anger streamed from his dark, blazing eyes as he told how, at one of the polling places where he had been a watcher, he had seen twenty ballots "for the Prophet" counted for Hewitt.

This was not an isolated case. Gustavus Myers testified that "the vote of the labor forces was so overwhelming that even piles of fraudulent votes could not suffice to overcome it. One final result was left. This was to count out Henry George. And that is precisely what was done, if the testimony of numerous eye-witnesses is to be believed. The Labor Party, it is quite clear, was deliberately cheated out of an election won in the teeth of the severest and most corrupt opposition." [27]

Charles Edward Russell, the author, recalls: "When the last vote had been deposited that day, Henry George was elected Mayor of New York. In the next three hours he was deprived of his victory by the simple process of manipulating the returns. Twelve years later Richard Croker, speaking to an intimate friend, admitted the manipulation. His version of it was simple but sufficient. 'Of course,' he said, 'they could not allow a man like Henry George to be Mayor of New York. It would upset all their arrangements.'" [28]

The "official" vote was:

Abram S. Hewitt 90,552
Henry George 68,140
Theodore Roosevelt 60,435

The next morning the defeated candidate was back in the office of the Henry George Publishing Company. "I shall buy a bottle of ink and some pens and again go to writing," he announced cheerily to a *New York Sun* reporter. [29]

Letters of congratulation on the size of his vote poured in from all over the world. A crowded meeting was held in celebration at Cooper Union.[30] In his speech before this gathering George demanded the Australian ballot system for the United States in line with articles urging its adoption which he had begun writing as far back as 1871.

The newspaper comment was, for the most part, surprisingly sympathetic:

The *New York Times:* "[The George vote] surprised even those who did not make the common mistake of declaring his following to be made up of cranks and Anarchists."[31]

The *Baltimore Sun:* "When we remember that he was not well known in the politics of the city, having been principally before the public as a writer upon economic subjects as related to the labor element, and that the machinery of both the old parties was against him, to say nothing of Wall Street and property interests generally, it is remarkable that he should

A SURPRISING RESULT.

A cartoon on the 1886 mayoralty campaign, from a
New York newspaper.

have succeeded in bringing to the polls nearly 68,000 supporters." [32]

The *New York World:* "It is an extraordinary thing for a man without political backing, without a machine, without money or newspaper support, and without any logical, fixed, practical principles to have polled 67,000 votes * for Mayor of this city. It was something that no man has ever done before, and the achievement carries with it a great compliment to the integrity of Mr. George's character and to the aim of his life. Mr. George's energy in the canvass has been almost phenomenal, and his capacity for leadership must henceforth be admitted to be equal to his ability in purely intellectual work." [33]

The *Pall Mall Budget:* "[Henry George] stood as the incarnation of a demand that the world should be made a better place to live in than it is today; and his candidature was a groan of discontent with the actual, and therefore of aspiration after the ideal."

Henry George set his own seal on the "defeat." Knowing, late on election night, that he had lost, he addressed his tired and disheartened followers at headquarters:

I congratulate you tonight upon the victory we have won.... I did not accept your candidacy for the office nor did you nominate me for the office. What we sought was to bring principle into American politics. The future is ours. This is the Bunker Hill. We have been driven back as the Continental troops were driven back. If they won no technical victory, they did win a victory that echoes around the world and still rings. We have begun a movement that, defeated, and defeated, and defeated, must still go on. All the great currents of our time, all the aspirations of the heart of men, all the new forces of our civilization are with us and for us. They never fail who die in a good cause.[34]

* The discrepancy of more than 1,000 votes is not explained.—Editor

CHAPTER XXII

FATHER McGLYNN

"EVER SINCE reading your books I have ardently wished that you could see your way to some measures for more extensively circulating your views on political and social reform; and I cannot refrain from expressing my great gratification at seeing in the *Pall Mall* a notice that you are starting a paper for this purpose. I wish you God speed, and though my peculiar position forbids my public advocacy of your views I shall not fail in private circles to recommend your paper wherever I can.

"I believe you have found the true solution of our greatest social difficulties, so far as any temporal solution can avail; and although the task before you might well appall and discourage a Gabriel I believe if you are true to the interests of righteousness in the conduct of your paper, God will gird you for the battle and let you live to see (at least) the beginning of victory." [1]

This was one of many letters of encouragement which were received by Henry George when, in fulfillment of a lifelong ambition, he launched his own weekly newspaper. It was *The Standard*. And the letter came from Mrs. William Booth, of Salvation Army fame, in London.

Money for the new enterprise came from subscriptions paid in advance and from a $500 loan by Thomas Briggs of London. With George as editor, William T. Croasdale as managing editor, and Louis F. Post as editorial writer—a staff in all of eleven men, besides the compositors—*The Standard* first appeared on January 8, 1887. In his salutation George wrote, "I shall endeavor to be fair to opponents and true to friends. I do not propose to make everything that shall appear here square to my own theories, but will be willing to give place to views which

155

may differ from my own when they are so stated as to be worthy of consideration." [2]

The outstanding feature of the first issue was his own eight and one-half column article on "The McGlynn Case." It proved to be a sensation.

The Roman Catholic church had not allowed its criticism of George to end with Monsignor Preston's statement [3] before the election that the economist's teachings were "unsound and unsafe." [4] Archbishop Corrigan attacked him in a pastoral letter a few weeks after the election.[5] Believing it his duty "to be quick in discerning dangerous movements and prompt in sounding timely alarms," [6] he commended Catholics to be "on guard against certain unsound principles and theories which assail the rights of property." [7]

The attack did not name George but it was pointed squarely at him. Father McGlynn, who had been staying clear of politics, felt compelled to respond. In an interview in the *New York Tribune* [8] he defended the principles which the Archbishop had condemned, saying they were not contrary to the teachings of the church.

The Archbishop promptly struck back. He suspended McGlynn for the remainder of the year and wrote to Rome.[9] Father McGlynn was ordered to come to the Vatican.

The priest replied that several grave reasons, among them heart trouble (which, with other complications, ultimately was the cause of his death), prevented him from complying. Anyway, his doctrines about land had been made "clear in speeches, in reported interviews and in published articles." [10]

The Archbishop then extended McGlynn's suspension until either Cardinal Simeoni, Prefect of the Propaganda, or the Pope himself should act. George had written an open letter in answer to the Archbishop's attack.[11] Now he made a long and full statement of the case in *The Standard,* where he said in part:

Let it be observed that there can be no pretense that Dr. McGlynn in taking part in politics has done anything inconsistent with his duty as a Catholic priest. . . . The Catholic Church does not deny the propriety of the priest exercising all the functions of the citizen. To say nothing of the past when bishops and cardinals held the highest political offices, in Germany and France and Italy, the Catholic clergy have been in recent times energetic politicians and sometimes held elective office. . . .

Henry George at the time of the second mayoralty campaign,
September, 1897.

The author, Anna Angela George, in 1897.

In the last Presidential election Dr. McGlynn made some vigorous speeches in behalf of the Democratic candidate without a word or thought of remonstrance.[12]

While George refrained from attacking the church, he condemned what he called the "Bourbons" in its fold, asking in reference to the call to Rome, "What chance would a simple priest —a suspended priest at that—with his own Archbishop against him, have before a tribunal where united Ireland could barely get consideration?"[13]

The article appeared in the first number of *The Standard*. It attracted so much attention that two extra editions of the paper had to be printed. Seventy-five thousand copies were sold. Few other New York papers backed Father McGlynn; practically all of them sided with the Archbishop.

George fought on. "Is it not time," he asked, "that we should demand that American priests should be released from the abuse of ecclesiastical authority which makes them political slaves?"[14] He asked the further question, "Is an American citizen, because he is also a Catholic priest, to be held to answer before a foreign tribunal, because of his actions in American politics?" This was answered, it would seem, by Father Sylvester Malone, who said, "Archbishop Corrigan has no right whatever to interfere with Dr. McGlynn in the exercise of his political opinions, freedom to express which his American citizenship entitled him...."[15] He is not accountable to Rome for his opinions on political economy."

On January 14, Father McGlynn was removed from St. Stephen's. Father Arthur Donnally (brother-in-law of a former treasurer of Tammany Hall) was appointed to succeed him. The new priest took possession without any notice, even attempting against the resistance of two maids to install himself in the private room which McGlynn had used for twenty years and giving the banished rector no time to remove his books, papers, and personal effects.

Not only that, but Father Donnally proceeded to remove Father McGlynn's name from his confessional and, attended by a police captain, ordered two of the eight assistant priests who had been hearing confession, and those parishioners who had come for devotion, out of the place.

Feeling ran high in the parish of St. Stephen's, where Father McGlynn was immensely popular. "Archbishop Corrigan has done his worst and has done his worst in the worst possible way," wrote George. "Dr. McGlynn has been removed from the church he has helped to build up, and from the people to whom he was the very ideal of all that a pastor ought to be: and the removal has been accomplished by circumstances calculated to scandalize the church, outrage the priest, irritate the congregation and disgust the public." [16]

Mass on the first Sunday [17] of Father Donnally's pastorate was held under difficulties. The church was bitterly cold, for the engineers had refused to make the fires. The choir and the altar boys also had gone on strike.

The anger of thousands of Catholics boiled up at a meeting in Madison Square Garden which was called to honor Michael Davitt but which was turned into a protest on behalf of McGlynn.[18] Through most of this excitement the suspended priest maintained a dignified silence. But on March 29, he held a meeting at the Academy of Music and delivered a fiery address on "The Cross of the New Crusade" to a large audience composed chiefly of his old parishioners.

Following this meeting a group formed to educate the public on the land question and to promote social justice. It had its inception in the mind of Thomas L. McCready of *The Standard* staff. Its name was the Anti-Poverty Society. As George explained:

The purpose of the Anti-Poverty Society is not that of forming a new church. It will welcome to its ranks those of all creeds who desire to join it. It is not a political society, for though its aims may be practically realized through politics its purpose is that to which political action is secondary—to arouse conscience and excite thought. It is not a class society. Its object is to secure justice to all— to the capitalist as to the workman, to the employer as well as to the employed, to the rich as well as to the poor. It is not a charitable society. It does not propose to give alms or to attempt to alleviate poverty by half-way measures. It declares war against the cause of poverty itself. . . . On this broad platform men of all classes and all creeds may stand.[19]

Father Edward McGlynn was chosen president and Henry George was named vice president. The first public meeting was held at Chickering Hall on the night of May 1, 1887. Thousands unable to enter were turned away. McGlynn made the chief address. George wrote of it in *The Standard*:

The significance of the great meeting of the Anti-Poverty Society at Chickering Hall is the marriage again of what too long have been severed—the union of a religious sentiment with the aspiration for social reform: of the hope of heaven with the hope of banishing want and suffering from the earth. . . .

The simple words, "Thy kingdom come, Thy will be done, *on earth* as it is in heaven," as they fell from the lips of a Christian priest who proclaims the common Fatherhood of God and the common brotherhood of man; who points to the widespread poverty and suffering, not as in accordance with God's will but in defiance of God's order, and who appeals to the love of God and the hope of heaven, not to make men submissive of social injustice which brings want and misery, but to urge them to the duty of sweeping away the injustice—have in them the power with which Christianity conquers the world.[20]

On the following Sunday the Anti-Poverty Society met in the Academy of Music with Henry George as the chief speaker. The attendance was heavy, with many enrolling as members. Denunciation and ridicule meted out by the press only served to advertise the weekly gatherings (for the Society now met every week) and to stimulate the growth of the audience.

Early in May, Archbishop Corrigan informed Father McGlynn that he had been summoned to Rome and that he had forty days to comply or be excommunicated. McGlynn stoutly refused, citing his former reasons. A giant parade (estimated at upward of 75,000) composed mostly of Catholic workingmen was held in protest at the order.[21]

Forty days later, on July 3, the church he had served for twenty-five years excommunicated Father Edward McGlynn. Nor was this all. Other priests who had sympathized publicly with him were shifted to other parishes or demoted. Archbishop Corrigan went so far as to deny burial in Catholic cemeteries to two persons who had attended the Anti-Poverty Society meetings.

In the meantime Henry George maintained his active interest in politics. On August 17, a New York state convention of the United Labor party, organized in the winter of 1886-87, was held in Syracuse. The Socialists, who had supported George and his platform the year before, now tried to swing the party in their direction. Just as in England George had refused to accept the socialistic dictum of state regulation, so now in America he must reject it. The majority of the United Labor party sided with him in refusing to advocate the nationalization of capital or the abolition of all private property in the "instruments of production." After a bitter session, which Louis F. Post had opened as temporary chairman, the Socialists withdrew from the convention.

George was urged to accept the nomination for secretary of state, the chief state office in New York below the governorship. After some misgivings he agreed—perhaps because of implied criticism that he feared another defeat at the polls. Accepting the nomination,[22] he said, "For my own part it concerns me little what the result shall be. All that concerns me is that I shall do my best. For no matter what the setbacks, no matter what the temporary defeat, in the long run the good will triumph." [23]

He waged an active campaign all through the state, accompanied by several reporters who, early in the trip, complained to Mrs. George that since the candidate spoke extemporaneously and never repeated a speech, they had to keep on the alert and could get no rest.

This campaign brought to the forefront the scholarly publicist, William Lloyd Garrison, son of the great abolitionist. He had been won to George's doctrines through reading *The Peer and the Prophet,* and now was spreading it from the lecture platform.

Father McGlynn, Louis Post, the Reverend Hugh O. Pentecost, minister of a large Congregational church in Newark, New Jersey, Judge James G. Maguire of San Francisco, one of the first of George's converts, and others traveled over the state, campaigning for what was then beginning to be known as the "Single Tax" movement.

This term was first used as the title of an address delivered before the Constitution Club of New York [24] by Thomas G. Shearman, who took it from Book VIII, Chapter 4, of *Progress and Poverty.* It was there that the author suggested "substituting for the manifold taxes now imposed a single tax on the value of land." The label came into wide use although Henry George and many of his followers knew it did not describe their philosophy of freedom but only indicated the fiscal means for applying that philosophy.

Money for the campaign was scarce. However, enough was collected at meetings, from small outside donations, and from a huge Labor Fair held for three weeks at Madison Square Garden, under the auspices of the Anti-Poverty Society, to pay for the distribution of nearly a million tracts and to carry on widespread and effective propaganda.

But all of this was to no avail. George drew only 72,281 votes as against a total of nearly one million for his Republican and Democratic opponents. One of the disappointments of the campaign was the defection of Patrick Ford, who in three successive articles in the *Irish World* took the part of church authorities against George, making no distinction between priests as men with political preferences and as spiritual teachers.

Ford seemed to have forgotten that five years before it was he who had invited Father McGlynn into the Land League fight at the time when Michael Davitt had come over from Ireland and when the priest had made speeches that brought upon him his first ecclesiastical censure.

As usual, George had attracted few "respectable" personages. Chauncey M. Depew sneered at "the strange and extraordinary theories of Henry George" [25] and Theodore Roosevelt delivered a speech against the "utterly cheap reformer" [26] in which he said "it is only a step from land confiscation to anarchy." [27] (Roosevelt was just then getting in stride.) Henry George never advocated confiscation of land and, at that time, to link him with "anarchy" implied contempt.

CHAPTER XXIII

PUBLIC AFFAIRS AND THE STANDARD

LOUIS F. POST had been candidate for district attorney on the local ticket of the Labor party. He, too, was defeated. Carrying the sad tidings from the *Herald* bulletin board to campaign headquarters, the two men rode uptown on the front platform of the streetcar.

Knowing his friend's deep faith in Divine Providence, Post suddenly asked George, "Do you see the hand of the Lord in this?" And George, looking at him "with an expression of simple confidence," instantly replied, "No, I don't see it, but I know it's there." [1]

The two men arrived at the United Labor party headquarters to find their co-workers crushed by the political defeat. But George at once sprang to the little platform to encourage his despondent followers, who afterward clustered around him— first weeping, then cheering—to grasp his hand.

"Through strife, through defeat, through treachery, through opposition," he said a few nights later at a meeting of the Anti-Poverty Society, "the great cause will go on. There is something behind it more powerful than we; there is something behind it that will urge it on, no matter what we may do or what we may not do. . . . When a truth like this comes into the world, when it gets as far as this has done, then the future is secure." [2]

George's showing in the New York State election, where he admitted the hand of Providence, was owed to factors besides his Republican and Democratic opposition.

The year before, on May 4, 1886, an event in the neighborhood of the Haymarket, in Chicago, had shaken the country. A mass meeting called by a group of avowedly violent-action Anarchists, who however had devoted their gathering to advocacy of the eight-hour day with ten-hour pay, ended in a bloody riot. While the speakers were descending from the truck they had used as a platform, a bomb hurtled into the ranks of a body of policemen who had suddenly appeared and ordered the crowd to disperse. One officer was killed. Many others were wounded. Swift retaliation followed, with the death of one civilian and injury to dozens. This tragedy, with its resulting toll of eight dead and at least eighty-two wounded,[3] threw the whole country into a ferment which continued during the long criminal trial of eight Anarchists before a jury chosen from 981 talesmen.

Henry George had expected to draw much of his voting strength from among the groups today vaguely defined as "leftists." The stand he took as a consequence of the Haymarket trials certainly prejudiced his chances of election with support from this quarter. Some of the circumstances of the case, therefore, need to be recalled here.

Defense attorneys for the eight Anarchists did not deny that the accused men had for years advocated the use of force. They did not deny that the accused had, on that very May 4, printed and distributed exhortations "To arms!" and "Revenge!" and "Workmen arm yourselves and appear in full force!" [4] The Chicago area in that year was a center of much industrial unrest and some considerable unemployment. Clashes between laboring men and Pinkerton detectives hired by employers were not infrequent. At the trial the defense could not even deny that one of the accused had been making bombs, similar in workmanship to the one that was hurled into the policemen's ranks.

But the defense did deny there was *proof* that any one of the eight defendants had thrown this particular bomb.[5] On the other hand, the prosecution contended that although there might be no proof that one of these men had thrown the bomb, all eight were responsible for its having been thrown.

The eight were found guilty on October 9, 1886, and were condemned to die. The case was then carried to the Supreme Court of Illinois, where on March 13, 1887, the judgment of the lower court was affirmed.

In October, 1887,[6] in Union Hill, New Jersey, a public meeting was held to express sympathy with the men who now faced the gallows. Police broke up the meeting. Outraged at this invasion of free assembly and free speech, George wrote a protest in *The Standard* and also urged, publicly and privately, to the Governor of Illinois, that the death sentences be commuted to life imprisonment. He had believed the Anarchists were unjustly accused of the crime until he read the "summary of evidence which is embraced in the decision of the Supreme Court of Illinois." [7] One of the eight men originally accused had committed suicide. George's mind was changed. He wrote in *The Standard:*

It was not indeed proved that any of the seven men threw the bomb, nor even was it proved who did throw the bomb, but it was proved beyond any reasonable doubt that the men were engaged in a conspiracy, as a result of which the bomb was thrown and were therefore as guilty as though they themselves had done the act. . . .

In this country where a freedom of speech which extends almost to license is seldom interfered with, and where all political power rests upon the will of the people, those who counsel to force or to the use of force in the name of political or social reform are enemies of society, and especially are they enemies of the working class. What in this country holds the masses down and permits the social injustice of which they are so bitterly conscious, is not any superimposed tyranny, but their own ignorance. The workingmen of the United States have in their own hands the power to remedy political abuses and to change social conditions by rewriting the laws as they will. For the intelligent use of this power they must be aroused and reason invoked. But the effect of force, on the contrary, is always to awaken prejudice and to kindle passion.[8]

Not satisfied with his own opinion, George sought the legal advice of Judge James G. Maguire, who also studied the summary and was convinced that the Anarchists were guilty. This confirmed George in his decision. "Our bench is not immaculate," he wrote, "but I could not believe that every one of the seven (judges) men, with the responsibility of life and death hanging over them, could unjustly condemn these men." [9]

A final appeal was made to the United States Supreme Court, where, after a six-hour hearing, the Federal judges denied a writ of error. The Governor of Illinois refused to pardon the condemned men, and on November 11, four of them were hanged. George felt more sorrow over the tragedy and understood the deep cause of it more profoundly than those who were accusing him of heartlessness. "With the mass of the so-called Anarchists," he wrote in *The Standard* on November 19, "anarchy is not a theory but a feeling that workingmen are oppressed by an intolerable class despotism, and that the breaking down of governmental power by acts of violence is the only sure and speedy way of release. Anarchy is the child of despair. It is the impulse of men who, bitterly conscious of injustice, see no way out."

George thought that anarchy was a foreign importation, born of repression and class governments abroad, and that the new-comer would soon lose his anarchism "if he found here that political liberty brought social justice." But this was not always the case. "What great bodies of the foreigners who come here actually do find," he wrote, is that our political equality is little better than a delusion and a mockery, and that there exists here the same bitter social injustice which presses down the masses of Europe. . . ."

Who was to blame for the attitudes of violence? *The Standard* article went on:

And if it is true that there are among working men many who are disposed to condone acts of violence when committed by those who assume to be the champions of oppressed labor, is it not true that there is the same blind class feeling among the well-to-do? When Pinkerton detectives shoot down strikers; when superservice-able policemen club Socialists, is there any outcry from those who deem themselves conservative?

The Anarchists are not our most dangerous class. Back of the men who died on Friday in Chicago with a fortitude worthy of a higher cause; back of the men who sympathize with them in their deed, is a deep and wide sense of injustice. Those who are most responsible for the existence of this are those who, having time and opportunity and power to enlighten the public mind, shut their eyes to injustice and use their talents to prevent the arousing of thought and conscience and to deny any peaceful remedy that may be proposed.[10]

Several of George's friends, including Post, later declared that if he could have had access to the full testimony in the case and not merely the summary, he would have had greater belief in the probable innocence of the Haymarket rioters. *The Standard* articles which condemned both extremes doubtless lost him votes even though he was accused by other radicals of "simply trading his earlier sympathy with the condemned men for votes."[11] But he was philosophical about it all, writing von Gütschow that "the man who acts solely by conscience must often be misunderstood and seem to others as if he were acting from low motives, when in reality he is acting from the highest." [12]

The campaign of 1887 behind him, George turned to national affairs. President Cleveland, in his message to Congress, had advised a reduction of the tariff. It was a plea for tariff reform, not a demand for free trade, but George liked its courage. Since the Tilden campaign in 1876 he had fought to abolish the tariff. He had written a 356-page book discussing protection and free trade and now he felt he could serve his cause much better by supporting Cleveland for re-election than by supporting a candidate nominated by the United Labor party who could not possibly win. In *The Standard* he wrote:

I regard the general discussion of the tariff question as involving greater possibilities of popular economic education than anything else. And as I have often said when myself standing as candidate, what I care for is not how men vote but how they think. . . . . I will support Mr. Cleveland, not as the best thing I would like to do but as the best thing I can do. When the wind is ahead the sailor does not insist on keeping his ship to the course he would like to go. That would be to drift astern. Nor yet for the sake of having a fair wind does he keep his yards square and sail anywhere the wind may carry him. He sails "full and by," lying as near the course he would like, as with the existing wind, he can. He cannot make the wind, but he can use it.[13]

Most of George's supporters in the New York State campaign agreed with him, but some of them preferred to stick with the Labor party. One of these was Father McGlynn. Although an ardent free trader and on friendly personal terms with Cleveland, the priest did not want to ally himself with the Democratic party since it was represented in New York by Tammany Hall, which had played an influential part with Archbishop Corrigan in attempting to crush the Single Tax movement and those who espoused it. George, in refusing to try to make a national party out of the United Labor party, believed however that "parties are not to be manufactured; they grow out of existing parties by the springing forward of issues upon which men will divide." By supporting Cleveland he thought he could "bring the whole subject of taxation, and through it the social question, into the fullest discussion." [14]

The split over Cleveland also split the Anti-Poverty Society. For the sake of harmony, George and his followers withdrew. He wrote in confidence to von Gütschow: "You of course only know what had appeared in the papers, and I, as far as possible, have refrained from 'washing dirty linen in public.' ... The truth is our little [United Labor] Party early developed a little 'party machine' using to the full measure his [Dr. McGlynn's] influence. ... I would not assent to this, and finally the Dr. and the machine which was really using him, read me and my friends out of the Party and the Anti-Poverty Society. I would not contest this, but with my friends, left the whole thing to them." [15]

Despite the "pain" of separation from McGlynn, George felt that his movement was "rid of the floatwood and the people who aim to use a movement as soon as it begins to show influence." Besides, he had plunged whole-heartedly into the Cleveland campaign, speaking many times in New York and in other cities for his own absolute doctrine of free trade. Some of Cleveland's supporters, however, were fully as protectionist as the Republicans. The Single Taxers for their part argued so strongly that the tariff reform men felt constrained to temper this preachment by chanting, as they marched in Democratic party parades

> Don't, don't, don't be afraid—
> Tariff reform is not free trade!

When Cleveland and Thurman lost to Harrison and Morton, George believed this was due to the lack of radical, aggressive tactics on the part of the Democrats.

Despite his seeming preoccupation with politics, George was quite as occupied as ever with his editorial duties. Louise Crane, who as a young girl had been William T. Croasdale's secretary in *The Standard* office, speaks of the editor:

I never heard from anyone in or around that office any word about Mr. George that was not a tribute to some of his many noble qualities, save from the compositors who used to swear, not at him but at his manuscript. It used to be common talk that Mr. George never sent back a proof without margins filled with his closely written script. One day they threatened to cut the margins off, top, bottom and sides, but an inconsiderate foreman interfered. They might swear but they loved him, as we all did.[16]

Mrs. Crane tells a story which illustrates the patience of Louis Post, and not incidentally the kindliness of Henry George:

He [Post] had written an article for *The Standard* and had sent it to the office by a messenger, who had lost it en route. Croasdale was furious. The door opened and a mite of a boy, with tear-stained face, appeared. There followed a terrible ten seconds for the poor child before the door opened once more, this time to admit the dignified figure of Henry George, champion of the weak. Putting a hand on the boy's shoulder he offered him a coin, and, pushing the sobbing wretch out of the room, he looked over at Mr. Post who had seated himself at the desk. Croasdale's eyes followed his, and approvingly he said: "That's right, Post—writing a complaint. Have the miserable whelp—"

"Complaint?" asked the imperturbable Post, with a chuckle. "I'm re-writing the article." [17]

After the McGlynn sensation the circulation of *The Standard* had leveled off at approximately 25,000 copies. Because of high costs and its inability to attract advertising, the paper brought the owner little money. Election defeats not only cost circulation but also "took the spirit out of many of our most earnest friends through the country," George wrote his friend von Gütschow in San Francisco. "I would have been unable to continue, but for the generous assistance of some friends—particularly of Tom L. Johnson of Cleveland." [18] Indeed, George had contemplated giving up the venture a few months after starting publication. He feared that he was not doing his best work and thought "the strain of the last two years has been very great and has made me much older." But things brightened after the presidential election, *The Standard* began to gain back some circulation, and now "hopefulness and consciousness of doing something" was "succeeding the first dispirited feeling." [19]

This was in late 1888. Soon afterward, William Saunders, now a Member of Parliament, came to the United States on business and took George back to England with him for a short holiday.

He had last visited England in 1885, and he found that in the interim much progress had been made in the advancement of his ideas. The visit lasted only two weeks but it was scarcely a holiday. He spoke before gatherings of clergymen of various denominations, before the Knights of Labour at a meeting near Birmingham, before the Council of the Financial Reform Association, and before several other meetings of mixed groups.

The effect of this brief tour, George's fourth in Great Britain, was so important that friends extracted from him a promise to return soon and make an extended speaking campaign, with expenses guaranteed. After a few weeks in the United States devoted to lecturing and to attending a tariff reform conference as a delegate from the New York Free Trade League, he departed for England in March, 1889, with his wife, his two daughters, and a young friend, Mary Cranford.

Beginning with a joyous greeting at Southampton from a large group who came out on the tender to meet them, the Americans had an unforgettable experience. They were entertained graciously and traveled about England and Scotland. George spoke often. Perhaps his outstanding address was one entitled "Thy Kingdom Come," delivered in Glasgow City Hall [20] under the auspices of the Henry George Institute. It was more of a sermon than a speech:

Early Christianity did not mean [said George] in its prayer for the coming of Christ's Kingdom in heaven but a kingdom on earth. If Christ had simply preached of the other world, the high priests and the Pharisees would not have persecuted Him, the Roman soldiery would not have nailed His hands to the cross. Why was Christianity persecuted! Why were its first professors thrown to wild beasts, burned to light a tyrant's gardens, hounded, tortured, put to death by all the cruel devices that a devilish ingenuity could suggest? . . .

What was persecuted was a great movement for social reform—the Gospel of Justice—heard by common fishermen with gladness, carried by laborers and slaves into the Imperial City. The Christian revelation was the doctrine of human equality, of the fatherhood of God, of the brotherhood of man. It struck at the very base of that monstrous tyranny that then oppressed the civilized world; it struck at the fetters of the captives, at the bonds of the slave, at the monstrous injustice which allowed a class to revel on the proceeds of labor, while those who did the labor fared scantily. That is the reason why early Christianity was persecuted. And when they would no longer hold it down, then the privileged classes adopted and perverted the new faith and it became, in its very triumph, not the pure Christianity of the early days, but a Christianity that, to a very great extent, was the servitor of the privileged classes. . . . There has been no failure of Christianity. The failure has been in the sort of Christianity that has been preached.

This tour through England and Scotland was trying, for all of his lectures save only the "Moses" which he had delivered first in San Francisco years before were extemporaneous.

Sidney Webb wrote to him on March 8, 1889: "I want to implore your forbearance. When you are denounced as a traitor and what not, by Socialist newspapers, and 'heckled' by Socialist questioners or abused by Socialist orators, it will be difficult not to denounce socialism in return. But do not do so. They will only be the noisy fringe of the Socialist Party who will do this and it will be better for the cause which we both have at heart, if you will avoid accenting your difference with the Socialists." [21]

George did not accentuate the differences between the Single Tax and socialism at the debate which he and H. M. Hyndman held at St. James's Hall in London.[22] Rather, he spent most of the time allotted to him in explaining his own philosophy and school of economics. He followed much the same strategy at the National Liberty Club in a debate which he held with Samuel Smith, M.P., who defended established interests and attacked the Georgist program as immoral.

Soon after, the George family and a group of English, Scottish, Irish, and American friends went to Paris to attend a land reform conference called by Michael Flürscheim, an ironmaster of Baden-Baden whose great works turned out everything from inkwells to cannon. He had written George, "You have done more for humanity in these ten years than all the benevolent societies of the whole world." [23] George delivered the opening speech at this, the International Conference for Land and Social Reform. Translated from French to German and then into English, it read in part:

The land question, with which we are concerned, is the bottom question. It is the starting point for all reforms. It is an error to believe that the land question relates only to agriculture. It concerns directly or indirectly all who have to pay rent, all who produce and exchange goods. It concerns the townsman as well as the countryman, industry and trade as much as agriculture.

Everything that man produces comes from the land. It is the site of all production, of all living, of all labor. Without the earth man can do nothing.

Land monopoly is the primary cause of poverty. On the other

hand, land monopoly is the source of the accumulation of capital in the hands of the few. Through rents, royalties, tolls and tributes of all kinds which he takes under many different names, through the increase in value and the improvements of which alone he gets the advantage, whether they are the result of the labor of others or the natural effect of increase of population, the landowner acquires capital. This he then invests in the bank or in trade and industry, either in the form of loans, mortgages, stocks and shares, or in government and municipal bonds. In the course of time he builds up a tremendous financial concentration which presses heavily on the world of labor. It is from landed privilege that the great fortunes have sprung, which have become the means of oppression and exploitation. *The concentration of capital is the child of land monopoly.*[24]

This was in the summer of 1889. Paris was thronged with tourists drawn by the Exposition and by the new Eiffel Tower. But hardly had the Georges arrived when Jennie became dangerously ill with a combination of diphtheria and scarlet fever. At the first words of the doctor's pronouncement, every other family in the crowded pension moved out, bag and baggage, leaving the entire rent for Henry George to meet. When Mrs. George had nursed Jennie back to health with the assistance of a gentle little Sister of the Sacred Heart, George left the womenfolk to occupy the large apartment house and went to Holland for a brief and very successful trip.

The anxiety over Jennie's health was followed by another worry—news of dissension in *The Standard* office. Henry George, Jr., had been acting as managing editor for more than a year. But now, while the real chief was away, two of the dominant personalities on the staff had begun to show disloyalty. T. L. McCready and J. W. Sullivan had published an attack on *The Standard's* policy in a new weekly, *Twentieth Century*, founded by the Reverend Hugh O. Pentecost, who had been a follower of Henry George. At the time Sullivan was not only a member of *The Standard's* staff but, with his wife, was living in the Georges' home during their absence abroad. McCready left *The Standard* office before George returned to the United States. Sullivan remained until he was personally dismissed. A few months later he circulated an attack in the Pentecost paper entitled "A Collapse of Henry George's Pretensions." It began with abuse and ended with the statement that *Progress and Poverty* was founded upon

Patrick Edward Dove's *The Theory of Human Progression.*[25]
This charge of plagiarism was so widely noticed that George felt
compelled to answer it.

In *The Standard* he reprinted the Sullivan attack, ignored the
abuse, and contended in a twelve-column article that if similar-
ity of thought and precedence in stating it proved that he had
plagiarized from Dove, so Dove must have plagiarized from
Herbert Spencer, and Spencer from Thomas Spence, as far back
as 1775. George ended his article—and the controversy—with
the statement:

What we are struggling for is no new and before undreamed-of
thing. It is the hope of the ages. . . . To free men, what we have to
do is not to make new inventions, but simply to destroy the arti-
ficial restrictions that have been imposed, and to come back to the
natural order.

When I first came to see what is the root of our social difficulties
and how this fundamental wrong might be cured in the easiest way
by concentrating taxes on land values, I had worked out the whole
thing myself without conscious aid that I can remember, unless it
might have been the light I got from Bissett's *Strength of Nations*
as to the economic character of the feudal system. When I published
Our Land and Land Policy I had not even heard of the Physiocrats
and the *impot unique.* But I know if it was really a star I had seen,
others must have seen it too. . . . And as I have heard of such men,
one after the other, I have felt that they gave but additional evidence that we were indeed on the true track, and still more clearly
showed that though against us were ignorance and power, yet behind us were hope and faith and the wisdom of the ages—the deepest
and clearest perceptions of man.[26]

AUSTRALIA

HENRY GEORGE remained in New York only a few months after his return from Europe. On January 22, 1890, he set sail for Australia in response to invitations from the Sydney Single Tax Association, urging him to make a lecture tour similar to the ones which he had made in Great Britain.

Mrs. George accompanied him on what he called their "belated honeymoon." She had little chance to prepare for the journey around the world, for George rushed in from *The Standard* office only an hour before train time and hurled his books and papers together. He packed not one article of wearing apparel, and this task had fallen in haste to Mrs. George.

When they were ready to leave, the husband had collected so many books and papers that there was not room for all of them in his valise. So, one by one he commandeered every piece of unused hand baggage in the house. A four-wheeler had been engaged and the two daughters were to have the thrill of driving in a carriage with their parents to the station. But alas, the thrill was never experienced. Tearful farewells had to be said on the sidewalk, for after Mr. and Mrs. George and their luggage were packed into the carriage, there was no room for children and barely room for a typewriter, which had to be pushed through the cab window into the owner's lap.

Bound for the West Coast to board their ship for Australia, the travelers stopped in St. Louis for a few hours' visit with Sister Teresa Fox, Mrs. George's sister, at the convent of St. Vincent de Paul, and to attend a large dinner given in their honor. They also stopped for meetings in Kansas City, Denver, and Los Angeles.[1]

George often said that when he took his wife on trips she paid her traveling expenses in the clothes or tickets she saved him from losing. He rarely returned from a lecture tour, for instance,

with the handkerchiefs, collars, or cuffs he had started with and
frequently he had lost or exchanged umbrellas, shoes, hats,
shirts, or even overcoats. Once he wrote her, "I have done pretty
well in some respects on this trip. I wore the swallow-tail always
except in Kansas City, where I had to go straight from the train.
And I flattered myself I had lost nothing until tonight, when I
found I have left my nice new dress boots somewhere. . . . I find
it very convenient to have plenty of clothes." [2]

In spite of his wife's watchful eye, there were lapses on this
trip West. She wrote from St. Louis to her sons that "your father,
this far on the journey, has exchanged his own for other people's
hats only five times!" [3]

The return of the Georges to California was a triumph. They
were met by Dr. Taylor and a party of old San Francisco
friends [4] who boarded the train at Martinez, overflowing their
car, and escorted them into the city they loved so well. The *San
Francisco Examiner* observed on their arrival: "A gentleman
fifty years of age and no taller than the first Napoleon, looked
out of the window of the west-bound Pullman. . . . It was Henry
George, California's political economist, who had caught the
world's ear and interested its intellect. . . . He has always been
fearless and in becoming an agitator has never ceased to be a
gentleman. San Francisco recognizes and appreciates that
merit."

On February 4, from the same stage in Metropolitan Hall
where twelve years before the "gas measurer" had made his first
plea to an almost empty house, George now faced a capacity
audience which had paid to hear him. He was now a world citizen. "Ye gods, what a transformation!" exclaimed Mrs. George's
cousin, William Cleveland McCloskey, in a letter written some
years later:

From the merest tyro at public speaking to a finished, polished
orator! That night was a memorable one in Henry George's career.
The hall was packed to the dome and there was an overflow meeting
outside. There were over 100 prominent citizens on the stage, and
as he advanced to the center after being introduced, I shall never
forget the demonstration. For some minutes it was pandemonium
and he was visibly affected. He was home again among his friends.

For two hours he held his audience spell-bound, and at the conclusion the people swarmed upon the stage and showered him with
praise and congratulations. There was a marked change in the man.

He was absolutely master of himself. Without notes and with the air and assurance of a finished orator, his voice full, round and resonant, he might well have compared with the greatest orators of the day.[5]

George accounted for his years since leaving San Francisco in these tones of dedication and humility:

When after growing up here, I went across the continent, before the railway was completed, and in the streets of New York for the first time realized the contrasts of wealth and want that are to be found in a great city; saw those sights that, to the man who comes from the West, affright and appall, the problem grew upon me. I said to myself there must be some reason for this and I will not rest until I have found the one and discovered the other. At last it came clear as the stars of a bright midnight. I saw what was the cause; I saw what was the cure. I saw nothing that was new. Truth is never new. . . . I have done no more to any man than point out God's stars; every man will see them who will look.[6]

So many were unable to attend this meeting that a second one, a free one for working men, was held in the same hall a few nights later. George also spoke in Oakland and in San Francisco before a group of clergymen at the Y.M.C.A. Old friends gave a banquet for him and professed to find him unspoiled by his worldwide reputation—still "light hearted," still "little Harry George."

Before sailing he wrote August Lewis, in New York, that "I have hardly averaged three hours' sleep since reaching here, and even then have not been able to see but a small number of the old friends that have come to greet us." [7]

Bidding farewell to the crowds who went to the wharf to see them off, the Georges embarked for Sydney on the steamship *Mariposa*. During their twenty-four-hour stop at Honolulu they were given a dinner by some officers of United States warships stationed there. Most of these men were avowed believers in the Georgist philosophy. Indeed, the books of Henry George were rather popular in the Navy, where there was time, even in those days, for serious reading. One officer, William Sims, afterward an admiral and commander of American naval operations in European waters during the First World War, had been a guest in the George home on East 19th Street in New York. He had written his father that "*Progress and Poverty* [is] a truly won-

derful book" which "points to a future that surpasses all imagination.... I don't think any unprejudiced man can read it
carefully without being convinced of its truth." [8]

The *Mariposa* landed the Georges at Auckland, New Zealand,
where early on the morning of March 1, 1890, they were met by
a group of Single Taxers. The group drove first to the residence
of the venerable Sir George Grey, who had once played the role
of dictator and had four times been governor of important British colonies. Sir George, who had advocated a land tax upon
assuming the premiership of New Zealand (then a colony) in
1877, had been one of the first to read and acclaim *Progress and
Poverty*. George wrote glowingly to *The Standard* of this visit
and concluded, "I hope to return to New Zealand if only for the
purpose of seeing him again." [9]

During the few hours' stay in Auckland members of the New
Zealand Anti-Poverty Society, meeting in one of the hotels, presented George with a beautiful illuminated address. And Sir
George Grey, who incidentally was himself a large landowner,
made a speech in which he again proclaimed his faith in *Progress and Poverty*. The two men, who struck up an immediate
and fast friendship (though they were never to meet again face
to face), continued their conversation so long at the wharf,
where they had walked together, that the captain of the *Mariposa* considerately delayed the ship's sailing.

The Georges' arrival in Australia had a deep significance for
both of them. For Mrs. George it was the first visit to her native
land since she had left it at the age of five years. For George it
was a visit to the land of enlightenment. This great Pacific sub-
continent had fascinated him ever since, as a lad of fifteen, he
had sailed to Melbourne. In the later years of his social and economic awakening he had come to look with hope upon this
country where the secret ballot had originated, where railroads
and telegraph systems were publicly owned, and where savings
banks and parcel post were part of the postal service.

Their reception in Sydney was enthusiastic. George was compelled to make a brief speech from his carriage to a huge crowd
in front of the Town Hall, and then another and longer one inside, where he was officially welcomed by Mayor Sydney Burde-
kin and by city and colonial dignitaries (Australia, too, had not
yet attained dominion status). He told how he had fought to
have the Australian system of voting introduced into the United
States, and reported that ten states had adopted the method and

that others were sure to follow. "He delivered such an address," wrote John Farrell, an Australian single taxer, "as had never before been heard in Sydney and received such a hearing as had seldom been accorded to a public speaker." [10]

A bewildering succession of meetings, receptions, luncheons, dinners, and interviews followed the Georges' Town Hall appearance and continued until the day of their departure from Australia three and a half months later. "Taken altogether," reported Farrell, "we expected nothing like the success which has attended his presence here, and we did not expect to find Mr. George such a powerful and moving speaker. He has the rugged earnestness and plain honesty that most impress an audience, together with a splendid voice which he knows how to use." [11]

The Sydney newspapers devoted much space to the visitor. The *Herald* reporter noted that although the very words of Henry George could be found in the newspapers, these words "do not tell what the lecturer said. You must add the magnetic quality of personality." For George had "held his audience of various political shades spellbound, and he spoke without manuscript, notes, or other accessory" and achieved "an intellectual feat." [12]

The Australia Star, a protectionist paper, took a somewhat different view: "Let a man have an attractive literary style, or a magnetic tongue, and he can convince multitudes that any absurdity he chooses to teach represents an absolute truth. But as a rule the deluded creatures find out in a short time that they have made a mistake. Most of Henry George's American disciples have forsaken him." [13]

Generally speaking, however, the press was pleased with Henry George, whose immense reputation had preceded him but whose simplicity and geniality seemed to belie the usual conception of a world celebrity. One reporter wrote that "out of thirteen different orations, in no case was there any repetition of words or phrases, although in each case the central truth was portrayed with the utmost clearness." [14]

The campaign was repeated in the smaller towns of New South Wales before the Georges visited the other colonies. Everywhere there were receptions by mayors and other high officials, brass bands, torchlight processions, beautifully illuminated addresses. And for Annie George there were lovely bouquets, tied with ribbons lettered "Welcome Australia's Daughter." And for the couple there were such exotic and typical gifts as an emu skin, made into a rug; an emu egg exquisitely mounted in silver and onyx; and two stuffed specimens of the rare and almost extinct platypus.

Typically, too, George made friends all over Australia. He thought his audiences both intelligent and enthusiastic. But he regretted, and sought to avoid, the fuss which was usually made over him. Sometimes the train on which he and Mrs. George were traveling would stop, at a place and time not scheduled, in order that the dignitaries of a small town might come aboard to deliver a eulogy to the American. Sometimes he could not escape them. But if he got wind of an impending "reception" he would try to escape from the back of the railway carriage when his train entered the depot, leaving the acceptance of these honors to his embarrassed wife. However, he usually got caught—sometimes in the station itself in the act of sneaking away to his hotel—and was always led by enthusiastic admirers to brave the official welcome.

When George went to Victoria his admirers feared that he would have a poor welcome there because the colony was a stronghold of protectionism. Some of them were so alarmed that they urged Mrs. George to persuade her husband against talking on the tariff question. This, of course, was futile. Not long after her marriage Annie George had written her husband, "I would not give your independent spirit for all the money in California." [15] Nor would she give it now for all the warnings—friendly, of course—in Australia.

Henry George's first lecture in Melbourne was delivered in the town hall and was chiefly an exposition of the Single Tax. But he did not avoid the controversial tariff question. "I am a free trader—a free trader absolutely," he proclaimed. "I should abolish all revenue tariffs. I should make trade absolutely free between Victoria and all other countries." [16]

The audience was far from hostile. Indeed, it gave him the traditional three cheers of approval, and hundreds remained afterward to enroll in a Free Trade League. Struck by George's courage, the *Melbourne Evening Standard* remarked: "No one will question the manliness of Mr. Henry George in boldly facing a Melbourne audience and attacking their favorite doctrine of protection not only with the arms of logic, but of withering scorn; and the fact that he not only carried with him the forebearance, but continuous and enthusiastic applause of an immense audience, is more than anything a testimony to the public admiration of genuine pluck." [17]

Two meetings followed in the same hall, with audiences steadily increasing in size. His third appearance was at Exhibition Hall before an audience of three thousand, where George debated "Free Trade versus Protection" with Mr. W. Trenwith, M.P. "The debate really cannot be considered seriously," remarked *The Melbourne Telegraph.* "Trenwith never rose to George's height. In plain English the local man was utterly lost." [18] The consensus seemed to be that George's visit to Australia was "an event of more than ordinary significance." [19]

The Australian campaign closed formally in Sydney on May 31. At a huge meeting in Protestant Hall, where George spoke on "The Fallacy of Protection," the chairman, G. H. Reid, M.P., who was president of the Free Trade League, said, "You need not be told that the man whose rare eloquence and deep sympathy will soon entrance your attention has a perfect horror of flattery. Still, I don't think we should allow him to make his farewell address without the assurance that his name, famous in so many lands, has now become in Australia a household word. . . . He has thrice earned it. He has earned it as a thinker, he has earned it as a writer, and he has earned it as an orator." [20]

On the last day a reception was held in Temperance Hall. A huge, handsomely bound album containing photographs of Australian friends was presented to Mrs. George. The spokesmen for the presentation committee addressed their speeches directly to her. Always shy, she looked to her husband for help. But his face was wrinkled with merriment at her consternation. He winked at her, dropped his handkerchief on the floor, and, as he stooped to pick it up, managed to say, *sotto voce,* "How do *you* like it?" [21]

George had received cabled and written invitations from Sir George Grey to revisit New Zealand, and from the Premier and the Attorney General of Tasmania to go there. However, after three and a half months of hard traveling across the great distances of Australia, and daily lecturing (frequently he spoke twice a day), he felt too tired to prolong his tour.

More lectures were delivered in Melbourne and in Adelaide, South Australia. And then, saying a reluctant good-by to the country that had given them such precious friendships and such inspiration, the Georges left for home on June 10, 1890.

Aboard the S.S. *Valetta* they crossed the Indian Ocean, the

Red Sea and the Mediterranean to Brindisi, where they disembarked. Their tour through Italy was hurried and it was made at the worst time of the year—in the hot summer—but they were thrilled by the beauty and the historical interest of the country. From Italy they went through Switzerland and France to Great Britain, where they remained for only a few days.

George made one speech in Glasgow and another in London. Together with the Reverend J.O.S. Huntington of New York, who had supported him in the New York mayoralty campaign, he called upon General and Mrs. William Booth of the Salvation Army. Catherine Booth had written him three years before, "I believe you have found the true solution of our social difficulties so far as any temporal solution can avail." Now, to his great satisfaction, he learned that Mrs. Booth was planning to introduce economic reform propaganda into the program of the Salvation Army. Before her plans were completed, however, she became ill and died. George sensed—quite accurately—that her death ended any concrete plan for propagation of the Single Tax within the organization where she had wielded so much influence.

The sixth visit to England, short though it was, encouraged George even though men in high places seemed to be misrepresenting him. *The London Democrat* asked, "What on earth could Mr. Gladstone have meant by his reference to Mr. George in his speech at Lowestoft? Speaking of the agricultural laborers, he confessed that 'there is much to be done for them, not according to the ideas of visionary politicians, who seem, some of them, to think that under the guidance of Mr. George or somebody else, the land of the country can be taken and redistributed, and be divided among the population. These, Gentlemen, are not real and important political discussions. . . ." [22]

Mary Gladstone evidently was not at Lowestoft to instruct her famous father. "It is a thousand pities," *The Democrat* concluded, "that someone does not persuade Mr. Gladstone to read *Progress and Poverty*." [23]

FRIENDS AT HOME

THE TRAVELLERS reached home September 1, 1890. On the day they landed, Henry George plunged into the work and excitement of the first national Single Tax Conference. Delegates came from all over the United States for the sessions which were held in Cooper Union. During the two days of meetings, George wrote the platform, made speeches, and subjected himself to the constant strain of public and private interviews.

A lecture trip to New England followed the conference; then another, longer trip through the Southwest as far as Texas. Always the speeches were different, new, extemporaneous—save for the ever-popular written lecture, "Moses." At the same time George wrote editorials for *The Standard* and concerned himself with its financial condition. He worked early and late—under what pressure can only be imagined.

Finally, one day early in December, the break came which his friends had feared.

"It hurts here," said Henry George, putting his hand to his head.

"You must have a headache," said Mrs. George.

"So this is what you've meant all these years, when you talked of having a headache!" he exclaimed. It was actually his first experience of that kind.

But it was serious. Shortly afterwards he was stricken with aphasia. Dr. James E. Kelly, who was sailing for Europe, gave the case to Dr. Frederick Peterson, a brain specialist. He in turn consulted Dr. Allen Starr and Dr. Walter Mendelson.[1] The three physicians examined the patient and expressed astonishment at his physical condition. "His body is as remarkable as his mind," they concluded.

The trouble now was overwork. Nerve strain had resulted in

a slight hemorrhage in the part of the brain in which the center
of speech is located. His mind was clear, yet sometimes in
speaking he would use the wrong word or interject an alien
word. The aphasia lasted only three days but it was impossible
to keep the patient in bed for any length of time and most difficult to keep him from his desk. He even slipped out of the
house one sunny morning and walked up and down the sidewalk
when Mrs. George, his nurse, was off guard.

For Henry George simply did not know how to be ill. His
mind was busy but he was denied the opportunity to supply it
with daily papers or books. He needed the release which fiction
brings but it rarely held his interest. On several occasions he let
his youngest daughter read him stories he had given Henry
George, Jr., when he was a small lad and which he himself had,
at that time, "like a goose, spent the night re-reading." [2] These
were *The Arabian Nights*. He frequently said that memories of
the old days before the mast came back to him—of the Orient as
he had seen it in his youth.

> Adown the Tigris I was borne
> By Baghdad's shrines of fretted gold,
> High-walled gardens green and old [3]

he would quote. But it was to the Bible and to Shakespeare that
he most frequently turned.

His friends were more devoted than ever. John Russell Young
was among those who called every day. August Lewis and Tom
L. Johnson were constant in their attentions. It was Lewis and
Johnson who joined in a plan financing the Georges for a trip
to Bermuda, where they went as soon as the convalescent was
strong enough for the trip. Mr. and Mrs. Simon Mendelson
(parents-in-law of Lewis) accompanied them.

It was difficult to make the sick man relax but Mendelson
succeeded when he read Shakespeare aloud. One day Mrs.
George was able to write home happily, "We went yesterday to
St. George, starting at 9 in the morning and not returning till
nearly 7. Your father drove us all the way and wound up last
night playing euchre with us!"

But keeping him from work became increasingly difficult—
until the unexpected arrival of a young admirer, W. E. Hicks.

In a rash moment, some time before, George had consented
half-seriously to let Hicks teach him to ride a bicycle, provided
that they could find time for the lessons. There had never been

time in New York. But now Hicks appeared in Bermuda, trundling a bicycle down the gangplank of the boat from New York.

Henry George kept his rash promise. Along the white shell roads of the island he wabbled, strings binding his trousers tight to his ankles, his hat squashed down on his head, his face rosy with exertion, his blue eyes flashing—and Hicks running and panting beside him, steadying the machine.

By the time he returned to New York, George had become a confirmed cyclist. He talked it to everybody. He made his whole family learn to ride. (Mrs. George, however, gave up after a bad fall—caused, she said, by a lamp post's running into her. But her husband kept at the sport.) George and some or all four of his children—the girls dressed in the smart bloomer bicycle suits of the period—would start from their home on 19th Street and frequently ride to Grant's Tomb, collecting bicycling friends en route.

George passed on the bicycle fever to August Lewis, Louis F. Post, and others. One day Tom Johnson, who was now a member of Congress, came to call on George just as the economist was leaving to see Post through his last lesson and go with him for his first out-of-door venture. Johnson went along to the bicycle school,[4] where he watched Post circle the big room repeatedly and go through all the exercises of mounting, dismounting, and reversing.

"Let me see if I can't do that," said the portly congressman. The attendants could not find a teaching belt big enough to fit him, but finally they buckled two together, strapped them around Johnson, and hoisted him to the saddle. The strongest teacher was delegated to the job of running beside the heavy pupil and holding him on the machine. The man ran part way around the room, and then said suddenly, "Hey, you, go 'long! You know how to ride!" Johnson did, instinctively. It enchanted him so much that he decided to skip his business appointments. Accordingly, when George and Post bicycled to Central Park, Johnson followed in the coupe in which he always traveled about New York. Coming to a sequestered place, he poked his head out of the window and begged to be allowed to ride. George obligingly lent his wheel to the neophyte and Messrs. Johnson and Post followed each other around the circle in neat order. That grew tame and Johnson suggested that they reverse. Somehow there was a miscalculation and suddenly a collision. There was nothing left to do but to perch the wrecked machines on the roof, pack themselves in the coupe that was none too roomy even for Tom Johnson, and ride off hilariously to the repair shop.

It was not long after this that Henry George, Jr., writing to his father from Washington, sandwiched in between a detailed account of his impression of Herbert Spencer's *Social Statics* and word of doings in the Senate, the report that "Johnson makes the pedal mount from both sides now!" [5]

As this recreation continued it was the task of the youngest child * to keep her father's bicycle clean. One afternoon he wandered into the basement to find her at her labor. "What's happening?" he inquired in dismay at the sight of his dismembered machine.

"Oh, I took the hind wheel off and found a lot of filthy, greasy little shot," she answered. Not knowing that a bicycle was a "ballbarian," as the family afterward jokingly called it, she continued blithely, "I've lost quite a few of them but the others I've cleaned and put back."

Here if ever, was a temptation to the father to show deep annoyance. Instead, he set about recovering as many as he could of the lost "shot." But the bicycle had to go to the repair shop again.

Admirers often showered gifts on George. One morning two young girls appeared at his home with a beautiful down pillow. One side was pale pink and the other was baby blue satin, on which had been embroidered by skillful Chinese fingers a stately white stork with red legs. It was a work of art, certainly, but it was out of place on the brown rep couch in the book-strewn, paper-cluttered study.

Several years before, George had been given a boat by a friend who knew that he never really relaxed save when on the water. The tiny craft was kept at a small dock on the East River close to the George home, which was then on Pleasant Avenue (another name for Avenue A) near Nineteenth Street. The boat could be used for sailing or rowing, and if the breeze and river traffic were favorable, the economist (who sometimes still used his diary as a sea log with such notations as "East wind and Smooth sea") would hoist the white canvas and take the helm. [6] Usually one or more of his sons went with him, and often his

---

* The author usually referred to herself as "The Child," and this was her name in the household.—Editor

daughters. They would weave up the river through the big and little craft, on gala occasions going as far as High Bridge. If they were becalmed, "Captain" George, seated at the stern and quietly puffing on his cigar, would use a trick he learned as a youngster, taking one oar and propelling and steering the boat by sculling. Although he loved these hours on the water, he took time to relax in this manner far too infrequently. The boat was given up.

One day he came home with a gift brought to him from Paraguay,[7] a small covered basket, from which there came weird noises. After the assembled family had guessed the contents correctly, George opened the basket and a beautiful little Capuchin monkey jumped to his shoulder. The monkey was a lady and her name was Cleopatra, and they should not have referred to her as "him"—only they always did. Cleopatra loved his master even as that other little monkey, back in the days before the mast, had loved him. The animal had, among other accomplishments, an uncanny way of sensing when the master was arriving home, either from *The Standard* office or from a lecture tour. Long minutes before the key was heard in the latch, Cleo was waiting in the front hall. Leaping to his master's shoulder, one paw grasping the tawny beard and the other holding an ear lobe, the monkey would ride about chattering all the "gossip" of the household.

The Georges were "at home" informally on Sunday evenings. A dozen or twenty friends usually were expected, but sometimes as many as forty guests arrived. And then the celebrated George chocolate would emerge for distribution distinctly pale in color, the whipped cream as sparse as soapsuds on a small boy's washrag. The most intimate of the guests were secretly requested to show a dislike for macaroons, which usually were in short supply.

On one of these very crowded occasions, Mrs. George asked one of Jennie's beaux to find Cleo and put him to bed—Mrs. George remembering that in a moment of misplaced enthusiasm the monkey had bitten a chunk out of a perfectly good little niece, Alice George. To humor the animal, who objected raucously at being penned up by a stranger, the young guest parted with his best lead pencil. After that all was peace and quiet in the George basement for the remainder of the night. But next morning, in the crate bed, splinters of wood were all that could be found of what had once been a lead pencil, while a very sick little monkey lay snuggled on a cushion near the sitting-room fire. The household was plunged in sorrow two days later when Cleo died. "We'll never have another pet," the master decided. "It hurts too much when they go." And they did not, for a few months—that is, if one did not count the cats.

Another gift was a bequest of approximately $10,000 which was left to George for the dissemination of his books by a man of whom he had never heard before—George Hutchins, a farmer of Ancora, New Jersey. Gratefully accepting the money, the author was preparing to use it for the purpose intended when he learned that Hutchins' widow had not been properly provided for. This was in 1886. George thereupon endeavored to return the money legally to the woman, but the collateral heirs stepped in, contesting on the ground that George's philosophy was "confiscation," and tried to break the will in order to get two-thirds of the estate for themselves. He was compelled to fight the action, which he eventually won, but the legal controversy was long, drawn-out, and yielded no one anything. The widow in fact was reduced to public charity.

Later, learning from a newspaper that "the woman whose husband had left $30,000 to Henry George was in an alms-house," [8] he sent to Mrs. Hutchins money out of his own pocket from time to time. When she died in 1892, it was he who paid for the funeral.

The author of *Progress and Poverty* had visitors from all over the world. Some of them had amusing, even eccentric, ways. One was an erudite Englishwoman who wore long black trousers under her decorous skirts and bundled herself in an astounding number of coats, shawls, scarves, and furs. One correspondent sent him postcards on which he wrote in miniature script enough to cover, with normal handwriting, several sheets of notepaper. Most of those who sought him because of his writings and lectures were interested in economics. But there were others, usually artists, who might not be expected to have much interest in the "dismal science." Such a one was George Inness, the painter. Dr. Taylor wrote George, "George Inness is here on a visit and I have had some talk with him about you. He says you are the clearest thinker of the age on politico-economic subjects, and that you are logical while all the rest are illogical and muddled." [9]

Of course there was his old friend, Mark Twain, and the artist, Daniel Carter Beard, subsequently of Boy Scout fame, who drew the brilliant illustrations for *A Connecticut Yankee in King Arthur's Court*. Beard wrote in his autobiography: "I knew Henry George intimately. We would discuss things, principles and people as friends may, but all the time I was talking or listening to him I felt that I should be standing hat in hand, because I realized that back of the little man was an invisible something, big and great—bigger and greater than the generation in which he lived understood, or even George himself realized. It was the soul of the man himself." [10]

In the old days of the San Francisco Bohemian Club, Harry Edwards, the actor, had been a dear friend. And now in the East there was James A. Herne, who had become so enthusiastic an advocate of *Progress and Poverty* that he used to collect his company, when on tour, and read aloud to them passages from the book. He was a finished actor and a brilliant playwright. Henry George, who went rarely to the theater—save to see Shakespeare or to Tony Pastor's Variety Show to which Tom Johnson sometimes enticed him for relaxation—used to go delightedly to see Herne's plays. Occasionally he sat in the wings through a whole act of *Shore Acres*. After first seeing this play he wrote the author, "You have done what you ought to do—made a play pure and noble that people will come to hear. You have taken the strength of realism and added to it the strength that comes from the wider truth that realism fails to see; and in the simple portrayal of homely life, touched a universal chord. . . . In the solemnity of the wonderfully suggestive close, the veil that separates us from heaven seems to grow thin, and things not seen to be felt. . . . I did not feel like talking when I left the theater; but I wanted to grasp your hand." [11]

Franklin Garland, for years a member of Herne's company, used to go often to the house on East 19th Street. His brother Hamlin Garland, also friend and follower of George, frequently contributed poems, articles and short stories to *The Standard*, and went about to Single Tax groups in various cities where he read aloud his story, "Under the Lion's Paw." [12]

Henry C. de Mille, who had made an enviable place for himself in the front rank of American playwrights, was also numbered among George's friends.* Although their meetings had been brief and infrequent, through letters a deep spiritual

* His elder son, William Churchill de Mille, married the author, Anna Angela George. Both his sons William and Cecil were her playmates.—Editor.

understanding had grown up between them. De Mille had written:

It seems to me that, as Paul says, "in these latter times also God has spoken to us."

I was struck by the title of the Duke of Argyll's essay—"The Prophet of San Francisco." How unconsciously one's enemies speak the truth sometimes. . . .

I believe that a prophet has spoken; that a man inspired with the truth of God's Kingdom wrote the words of *Progress and Poverty*. I tell you because I know the value of a word of cheer to the toilers in the cause of light, that another has started to raise his feeble torch to illumine the way. . . . If I can make the dramatic sermon approach near the dignity, clearness and grandeur of the text book, I shall feel that I have truly done God's work.[13]

To which Henry George replied:

I speak what I know, and what many others will testify to, when I say that you will never regret having thrown yourself into the good cause. It will make life higher and happier and the thought of death easier. And now the time has come when every effort shows its result. You have power to reach those whom I cannot, and may pass the torch to those who will carry it further than you can reach. I am glad of your coming. We have needed you, for the field is ripe, and from the bottom of my heart I wish you, God speed!

De Mille had intended to impart his friend's philosophy to the theater in a play. But a few months later that rare and gifted gentleman, who was not yet forty, died. And the dreamed-of play was never written.

Among the women friends were Helen Taylor, constant as ever; Frances M. Milne, the California poet; Mrs. Francis George Shaw and her brilliant daughter, Josephine Shaw Lowell; Catherine Helen Spence, "the grand old woman of South Australia" and champion of the cause of proportional representation; Elizabeth Cady Stanton, the suffrage pioneer with whom George used to exchange funny stories; and his own sister-in-law, Sister Teresa Fox, whose deep spirituality and understanding of world movements made her a never-ending inspiration.

But closest of all was Annie George, whom he consulted in all his affairs. He trusted her instinct above his own judgment and counted her his wisest critic. Always after a speech, no matter what the adulation of the crowd, he would ask when they were alone, "Well, Annie, how did it go tonight?" And she would give him her frank opinion, telling him if he had failed to make a point clear, recommending always that he make his talks too short rather than too long.

Dr. Taylor wrote of them, "Surely, never were man and woman closer to each other in affection and sympathy than were Mr. and Mrs. George—companions ever until death stepped in between them—companions, too, of the noble sort that breasted together not only their sufferings, but the sufferings of the world around them.[14]

CHAPTER XXVI

ON EAST NINETEENTH STREET

THE GEORGE HOME revolved around the master of the house, or rather, around the work of the master of the house. Since he never exacted silence or any special concession, Henry George did not make his family conscious of his world-wide reputation. One of the remarkable things about this father was that all four of his children became, without any coaching, his staunch adherents. As the children grew up, each one of them took a turn at secretarial work for their father. But they were never sacrificed to this pleasant duty.

Mrs. George was ever anxious to help her husband in any possible way. Yet she did not neglect her own roles as mother and housekeeper. Her tact and managerial genius helped to make up for the shortcomings of their relatively small family income.

In the shabby, cozy sitting-room, the main feature was the center table, with its large lamp, around which the members of the household gathered for study, reading, games, and fancy needlework and mending. It seemed the symbol of family unity.

When *The Standard* office moved uptown to Union Square, the George family had moved downtown to 357 East 19th Street. The editor, accompanied by his brother, Val, and by his two sons, Henry and Richard, used to walk home for the midday meal. Frequently he brought guests with him—unexpectedly, as a rule, since there was no telephone. He had no inkling of the trouble this entailed, since Mrs. George never let him know what it meant to have to produce a meal suddenly. But usually, with the help of two kitchen maids, some kind of repast—however meager—could be provided even on short notice.

One noon when the father came home he spied his youngest daughter reading a book he had recommended out of his own youth. She was dissolved in tears.

"What is the matter?" he asked, kissing her.

"Masterman Ready [1] has just died," she sobbed.

"Oh, then I know how you feel," said he, sympathetically. "Don't bother to come to lunch yet awhile. I'll arrange with your mother."

Later when the red-eyed youngster crept into the dining-room, the meal was almost finished. Apparently nobody noticed her, though her food had been kept hot.

George was usually impatient for his meals; it was his after-dinner cigar that he wanted. During these years he smoked one that had been named for him. He considered it the best to be had for five cents, which indeed was the most he could afford. It became a popular brand and was widely advertised. Many supposed he received a royalty, but this is not true. The firm producing the cigar did make him a present of his first box of "Henry George Cigars"—and that was all.

He cared little for food; although he had favorite dishes, usually he did not know what he ate. One night, when guest of honor at a formal dinner and quite absorbed in the conversation, he absent-mindedly emptied the large dish of olives placed near him. His wife's agonized signal reached him from the other end of the table only as the last olive disappeared into his mouth. He rarely ate candy, but on occasion when it was offered him he would exclaim (with eyes twinkling), "My, I must save you from this terrible unhealthy stuff!" And, helping himself to a handful, he would go back to work, munching.

"Time and again," according to Carney, their little Irish maid, "he'd come home bringin' ice cream from the store at any hour durin' day or night. Glory be, but they were strong fur ice cream—the whole of them! And he was turrible fond of cold-boiled potatoes! Now where do you s'pose he got that trick? And maybe he didn't love stewed tomatoes! Once, after he'd come to the lunch table first, 'Carney!' he sez, 'an' have yer got any stewed tomatoes?' An' him, only just havin' et the dishful I'd put there, meant fur the whole family! Thinkin' about them books he wrote, I guess he wuz. Sure he wuz a lovely man! Sometimes he used to be that quiet! One time when he was travelin' to the country, sudden-like, out of a great silence he sez to me 'Carney, there's me favorite flower,' he sez, pointin' to a line of sun-flowers. 'Oh, Mr. George,' I sez, 'them yeller things growin' against a pigsty and an outhouse?' 'Shure,' sez he, 'an' bein' that brave and gay whilst they be doin' it!' But yer had ter like him all the same if he was a bit queer. I mind how after bein' free from talk he'd suddenly jump up from the lunch table and go look outer the back window at the New York tree (ailanthus) an' catchin' sight of a bit of cloud, 'Annie,' he'd call, "'tis a great white ship ter be seen. Come!' An' nothin' would do but Herself must leave her lunch and join him gazin' at the little splinter o' back yard sky—his arm around her, the whilst the omelette was fallin' flat. Wasn't he the happy man!"

Although Henry George lectured for pay, his income was always small as he so frequently reduced his honorarium. He had written to his wife from Chicago, in 1884, "I spoke at Battle Creek last night to another small audience. It was an association of Knights of Columbus and I threw off $40 of my hundred, which let them out square."

In 1887, he wrote her from Kansas City, "I was on the whole better pleased with the audience and the speech than I have been, but there was not enough in it to make the $300 I was to get for coming here, and I reduced the price to $200. I cannot go around assessing these people and if I did not feel the want of money so much I would not take that much. . . . It is hard doing anything constructive on these trips—so many people to talk to. I stayed up till 3 o'clock this morning trying to lick into something like shape the most abominable report of my speech that ever pretended to be verbatim." [2]

In order to spread his doctrines he sacrificed his copyrights and royalties or gave away his books with no thought of the financial loss to himself. In a letter to Richard McGhee of Ireland, sent three years previously, he had said, "Owing to the fact that I have just now more credit than cash I can make a larger contribution in books than I could in money, and as you say that will do as well, I have ordered sent to you for Mr. McHugh's use 1,000 copies of *Progress and Poverty* and 500 copies of *Social Problems*. When you use these I will supply more." [3]

For some reason the belief persisted that he enjoyed ample means. To Gütschow he had written:

That you should share in the notion that I have made so much money somewhat surprises me and not a little amuses. I allow all such newspaper statements to go un-contradicted and do not publish my real condition to the world; but the truth is, I have made very little out of my books—a few hundred dollars a year, that is all.

With the exception of $2,000 I got for the English edition of *Social Problems* I have had nothing from abroad. . . . The work that I have done does *not* pay. In lecturing, for instance, I have never made anything. The times that I have lectured for nothing and given up my fee have eaten all I got in at other times. I merely mention that that you may know the real truth.[4]

He might have added that he gave more money away than he could well afford. He rarely denied an appeal for help. The memories of his own dire poverty remained vivid, and he preferred to be an "easy mark" for the many than to fail the needy one. Once a friend chided him for giving money to beggars, saying that they were too lazy to work. "How can I tell about that?" George responded. "Let the responsibility for their actions rest on them." [5]

Time after time a little drama was enacted at his home. A stranger would be announced. Disliking to refuse himself to anyone who took the trouble to call, George would interrupt his work and go to the visitor. After the caller had left, Mrs. George, who had an uncanny way of sensing her husband's moods, could tell by looking at him if it had been another "hard luck story." She would ask, trying to mask a forgiving smile:

"Well, Harry, how much did you 'lend' this time?"

"Oh, only about—only five dollars," he would murmur, trying to be nonchalant. "He'll pay back—you'll see!" But although "he" rarely "paid back," somehow a "loan" was made to the next needy one who asked. Mrs. George's extraordinary ability in making the small income go far did not prevent him from deploring his own seeming inability to make or keep money, and he tried to train his children to be practical.

Once when Tom Johnson called at the house he took the youngest member of the family in his coupe to the St. James Hotel, where he made his New York home, to visit his own children. She told her parents afterwards, "On the way we stopped at Park and Tilford's, and do you know Mr. Johnson paid as much for one box of cigars as my whole month's salary!"

She * referred to the allowance her father gave her so that she might learn the use of money. It began when she was seven, at two dollars and fifty cents a month, and each year was raised fifty cents a month. It was not "pin money" to be spent on candy

* This, again, is the author, Mrs. de Mille.—Editor

and trifles but had to pay for her wardrobe. It meant tight economy although nearly all her dresses were made from her mother's or sister's, "cut down" and embellished with bits of trimming taken from a treasure chest known as the "sewing trunk."

Mrs. George taught her daughters to make their own clothes, as soon as they were old enough. But they never acquired her skill in making patterns, managing scant material, or in the use of the needle.* Often they would sing as they sewed (indeed, someone always seemed to be singing somewhere in that house) —the mother with her sweet, full voice taking the alto part in snatches from Gilbert and Sullivan, from grand operas, or from ballads. Some of these ballads Mrs. George remembered from the "tripenny song book" a seaman had given her on the sailing vessel from Australia, when she was five years old, and from which book, on that long voyage, she had taught herself to read.

Henry George did not share her love for symphonic or "highbrow" music. It was the words which caught him more than the tune. He seemed to care only for folk tunes, or patriotic songs, or ballads that had dramatic significance. Frequently, when his children were at the piano, he would ask them to sing "Bonnie Dundee," "Caller Herrin," or "The King's Highway," with Weatherly's words

> ... Lord of a thousand acres wide,
> While I the beggar must stand aside,
> Go thy way! Let me go mine—
> I to beg and thou to dine!

When he was deep in thought he had a trick of gazing out a window and tapping a tattoo on the glass while he whistled over and over a few bars of "The Battle Hymn of the Republic," "Yankee Doodle," or one of his other favorites. In both pitch and rhythm his performance left something to be desired, but usually his knotted brow would relax. One day, in the sitting-room, he drummed away for a particularly long time—oblivious, of course, to the others present, who all kept silent—until a small

---

* Both my mother and her mother before her were artists in embroidery. My mother had an eye for color like a rug-weaver and loved to cover table cloths with shaded flowers of enchanting delicacy. Her mother stitched the details of their dresses—my mother's evening dresses and wedding-gown—with the expertness of a Parisian seamstress. These garments were made, Annie George used to say, "with the red blood of time."—Agnes de Mille

niece, Alice George, remarked in a stage whisper, "My, Uncle Henry's thinking *awful* hard today!"

Only on rare occasions could he be inveigled into singing one of the sailor chanties he had learned in his days before the mast. But the first and only time he tried to dictate into a dictograph, for his daughter Jennie, then acting as his secretary, to transcribe, he broke loose with:

> Up jumped the shark with his crooked teeth,
> Saying "I'll cook the duff, if you'll cook the beef."
> Well done me lads all! So blow the wind wester
> How the wind blows
> Our ship she's in full sail—how steady she goes! [6]

This was followed by another sea song from his youth concerning the resentment of a certain bumboat lassie who was evidently peeved at the commander-in-chief of the fleet. "Kind admiral, you be damned!" [7] he roared into the machine with such gusto that both the apprehensive George domestics went scuttling upstairs, only to find the master of the house alone beside the speaking tube of the strange contrivance. Carney's [8] account of it was vivid:

Mary and me rushed up from the kitchen and there he was sittin' in front of a box and singin' into a chube. When he seen me, nothin' would do but I must sing 'Dublin Bay' into it (you know, the song I sing whilst I be doin' me cleanin'.) And so he turned the thing on agin', and me, with me feather duster in me hand, there I stood singin' into the horn. But the chune stuck in me throat. "Oh, Mr. George," I sez, "I can't. The machine makes me feel that queer!" "Carney," he sez, "'tis exactly the way it affects me!" An' with that he clicks off the phonygraph and goes leapin' down the stairs whistlin' 'Yankee Doodle' an' outer the house. An' that bein' done, Mary remarks "Well," sez she, "'tis a good thing he doesn't have to earn his livin' with his whistlin'!"

Carney gave a chuckle, and then snorted indignantly, "The nerve of her, speakin' like that!"

CHAPTER XXVII

CHARACTER TRAITS

"IF IT HAS been given me to help forward a great movement, Henry George once said, "it is through no merit of mine. . . . It is from the simple fact that, seeing a great truth I swore to follow it. . . . If I were to take to myself such flattering things as have been said to me tonight my usefulness would soon be ended." [1]

This little testament of modesty, so typical of George, was delivered at a place and time—in Sydney during the Australian tour—when his popularity was high and the adulation of crowds knew no bounds.

His modesty was the result of a conscious discipline that he might not become the victim of ambition. To Frances M. Milne he wrote, "Praise is the deadliest poison that can be offered to the human soul, and were I ever to accept it, my power would soon be gone. What power I have comes from the fact that I know my own weakness; and when duty lay on me have neither feared blame nor sought praise." [2]

Once, while walking with a friend, George dropped into a postoffice where he noticed a man struggling to fill out a money order. George offered to help him, and did. "It is not every day that such a man can have a philosopher to write for him," observed George's companion as their stroll was resumed. "A philosopher," was the reply, "is no better than a bootblack. Such terms are only relative to our own small affairs." [3]

When speaking of the Single Tax movement he avoided the use of the first person singular. This was not through any affectation of humility but because it was never to him a "George movement." He would refer to "our cause" or "our work." He even disliked to expound his philosophy to one person, for he felt that this was imposing his personality on another. A reporter came to him once and requested, "Mr.

George, I want you to tell me all about the Single Tax." The economist took twenty cents out of his pocket and handed the money to the surprised young man. "I've told all about it in a book; buy it—paper edition," he said, and walked away.[4]

One time a friend at the Reform Club took him to task for allowing another member apparently to down him in an argument concerning his own economic doctrines. "Let him have that pleasure," said George, evidently remembering the Biblical admonition to "suffer fools gladly," and crept away from the discussion.[5]

But there was no false modesty about him. He held in later life the same attitude he had taken when *Progress and Poverty* was first published. He had said then, in answering the Sacramento *Record Union's* criticism of the book, "If I shall seem to show any of that absence of diffidence which you deem one of the remarkable characteristics of my book, do not charge it to any want of respect or lack of proper modesty, but to the fact that when a man has so thought out and tested his opinions that they have in his mind the highest certainty, it would be but affectation for him to assume doubts that he does not feel." [6]

At one of the Sunday "at homes" a young professor [7] who was teaching his youngest daughter, Anna, at the time, explained to the author that he had not yet had time to read George's last book. "Do so, when you can," was the reply, "you will find it worth while." Next morning Anna went to her teacher apologetically. "You must think that my father is awfully conceited," she said, "but he really isn't." The man smiled. "I know what he meant," he said.

But it was not until later that the daughter understood her father in terms of the Orient: "He who knows and knows that he knows, is a wise man. Follow him!"

Nervous and high-strung, Henry George was a man of infinite patience when it came to working out tedious problems, carefully explaining to a typist any difficulties in his own manuscript and taking pains to help his children with their lessons or answer their questions. But he was impatient when he called his children to him. Then he wanted immediate response and strict obedience. If they did not hear his first summons he would raise the commanding tone in his voice. This seemed a strange contradiction in one who was ever ready to give them his time. This trace of impatience did not, however, make them fear him.* In all else he treated them as though they were adults—or at least let them think that he did, with no appearance of superiority. He never pressed his own opinions on them but gave them free choice in all things that were possible. And if all four of them came to accept his economic theories, it was by a process of reasoning which any stranger might have adopted—not because their father had "taught" them.

Politic always, though fearless, Henry George tried to concede in small matters that did not count in order to win big issues which did. Believing that "the function of the politician is to minimize resistance," he tried to bow to social usage where to do so disarmed antagonism.[8] For instance, whenever he was in doubt as to the requirements of dressing for an evening affair, he always wore full dress. Probably because he disliked the clothes he made a special effort when he put them on and so usually looked well groomed. Once, however, he was discovered toward the end of one formal reception to have been wearing his dress studs back to front—three gold screws sprouting out of his white starched bosom. His shoes were always more or less of a gamble.

"Maybe Mrs. George didn't look after him like his mother!" related Carney. "Once when she went to Philadelphia she put me in charge of his clothes and maybe I didn't have to be sharp to keep him from goin' out wearin' shoes that weren't mates! And when I caught him, he laughed, 'Shure, they'll carry me just as far,' sez he. 'Oh, but Mr. George,' sez I, 'Herself wouldn't like it!' ''Tis right ye are, Carney,' sez he. And with that he changed his boots, docile-like. But I just had to give up about his cuff links matchin'. Wasn't he the pleasant man—just!"

Cuff links gave the economist little worry but on occasion cuffs did. Before making a speech he always seemed nervous, though once launched into his subject his self-consciousness vanished. Sometimes he would pace the platform and sometimes he would pound the desk before him with his fist to emphasize a point. This last vehement gesture had a way of dislodging a cuff which in those days was made separate from the shirt. Unconsciously he would remove it. If the second cuff offended, off would come that one, too, and be laid beside its mate on stand or chair. From then on till the end of the speech Mrs.

---

* Yet one of them, my mother, clearly lived in awe of him. He never spoke to her alone that she did not tremble a little, and if he addressed her directly by her given name "Anna" instead of the pet "Babe" or "Petty," tears filled her eyes.—Agnes de Mille

George was usually in a state bordering on consternation. However, he always stopped at the cuffs.

Scrupulous as to cleanliness, for the most part he was oblivious to his dress. His small, shapely, pink-palmed hands were frequently ink-stained, his clothes carelessly worn. He had an absent-minded way of letting his cigar ash fall down his coat—to the despair of family and friends. It was generally agreed that he wore the most disreputable hat in New York. Of course, it was always a neat hat when it started; Mrs. George saw to that. But by process of exchange it usually deteriorated, for he was not a good "trader," invariably picking up the wrong hat, the shabbier the better.

One day Bolton Hall, a prominent figure in the New York Tax Reform League, had a brief talk with the younger daughter of the house to the effect that while he and she loved and understood her father, strangers might get an unfavorable impression of him, and didn't she think she could occasionally brush his clothes and keep them a bit tidier, etc., etc.?

After the street door had closed on the caller, the girl obediently seized a whisk broom from the hall table and went to work on her father's fedora. She brushed and patted and poked it until it again resembled a hat. She had hung it carefully on the rack when the owner ran, whistling, down the stairs. Dutifully, she began to wield the brush about his shoulder.

"Don't stop me, I'm in a rush," he said, and kissed her good-by. He grabbed his hat by the soft crown, squashed the wrecked thing on his head—backwards—and just as the ash from his cigar cascaded down his coat, dashed off!

Henry George took his speaking seriously. He was a cheery man with a ready laugh, but he cautioned Louis F. Post, who was an extraordinarily fine raconteur, to tell fewer funny stories in his speeches lest his audiences take him as a humorist and not heed his real message. George feared Post would have to pay the penalty Mark Twain suffered. (Possibly he remembered an afternoon when he returned home so dejected that Mrs. George had thought he was ill. "No, I'm not ill," he had replied to her anxious question, "I'm just blue. I've just come from two hours with Sam Clemens.") He explained to Post that Mark Twain, having established himself as a funny man, was now almost heartbroken because he could not get the public to take him seriously.

George usually wore an air of high optimism. But there were

times when his spirits were low. Years earlier he had written
Dr. Taylor, "It does not surprise me that you feel that despond-
ing mood sometimes, for I so often feel it myself. And I presume
that is the case with every man who really amounts to anything.
What we do is *so* little as compared with what we feel we could
do, and ought to have done." [9]

In *Progress and Poverty* he had written: "The bitterest
thought—and it sometimes comes to the best and the bravest—is
that of the hopelessness of the effort, the futility of the sacrifice.
To how few of those who sow the seed is it given to see it grow,
or even the certainty to know that it will grow." [10]

Frank Stephens recalled having gone to visit George one
afternoon before a meeting. The host did not rise to greet his
guest, as was his custom, but remained stretched out on his
couch, wearing an expression that moved Stephens to ask,
"Stage fright?"

"No," replied George slowly, "worse than that! I was wondering if it was all worth while!" [11]

Perhaps at that moment he was conscious of what Tom Johnson later observed, "Men like Henry George in all ages have had
to pay so big a price for just the chance to serve." [12]

The unevenness of George's public speaking has been mentioned before. He was not uniformly eloquent. His speeches
were inspirational and depended much upon the temper and
type of his audience. He was always grieved if he felt his effort
had fallen below par. One day, after he had delivered what he
considered a poor address, he said to Charles Frederick Adams,
who was a member of the Single Tax League of Washington,
D.C., "Come to lunch, Charley. I am so ashamed of that lecture
as an artistic performance that I want to spend the money I got
for it." [13]

Usually amiable and patient under heckling, he could on
other occasions be terse and sharp. When, for instance, someone
wrote him "for the purpose of deciding a wager" and asked,
"Can a man be a Single Taxer and not believe in free trade?" he
replied, "I do not know that I am called upon to decide wagers.
I have not hid my own opinion."

Though hardly a wit, he had a robust sense of humor which
led him into retorts that were so apropos as to be extremely
amusing. After most of his speeches he invited questions. Once,
at a meeting in Texas, he was asked, "Suppose for argument's
sake, Mr. George, that you owned all the land and I owned all

the capital. What in that case would you say?" His answer came back like a shot, "Move!"

The same question was often asked in different forms and was as differently answered. When someone inquired if industrial slavery was caused by "the aggregation of capital," George replied, "You can aggregate capital as much as you please, as long as you leave to labor the raw material."

And again, this time at a great meeting at Lambeth Baths, to the question, "What about capital?" he replied quickly, "When you've got the cow you've got the milk!"

On another occasion he was asked, "How do you explain the Savior's declaration that 'The poor ye have always with you?' "

"Because," answered George, "He was talking to the scribes and Pharisees and hypocrites!"

A gentleman in England, pained at the thought of surrendering his unearned increment, complained, "But this land has been in my family for seven hundred years!"

"Well, don't you think it has been in your family long enough?" asked George mildly.

A clergyman in Scotland, who apparently was of the same mind as his English neighbor, announced, "We read in Holy Writ that Jacob owned land. If it is right for Jacob it is right for me!"

"We read in Holy Writ," replied George, "that Solomon had five hundred wives and one thousand concubines, but I do not consider it right for me."

At an Anti-Poverty Society meeting the question was raised, "How does Mr. George propose to ascertain the value of the unearned increment?"

"I propose," George answered, "to get at the value of land by boards of assessors." His eyes began to twinkle. "A sign could be placed on every lot, saying, 'This lot measures so much, and it is assessed at so much.' If that assessment is too high, the man upon whom it was made will let you know. If it is too little, the neighbors around who are assessed higher will let you know."

While he rarely used notes when he made a speech, he usually retired to his couch beforehand, where, smoking slowly, he thought through what he had to tell his audience.

Much of the formative work on his writing was done in the same manner. A knotty problem solved, he would jump up and write the answer at his desk in longhand or type it in a code form—using single letters or punctuation marks to represent words. This would be expanded later, perhaps by his secretary—if he happened to have one at the time.

His method of work was particularly baffling to William T. Croasdale, who as managing editor of *The Standard* was always conscious of having to meet deadlines and who had a weekly tussle with the procrastinating editor to get his copy in on time. Frequently George would consult office boys or repair men, or whoever happened to be handy, about the structure of a sentence. This exasperated Croasdale but Louis F. Post understood it perfectly. "It was no idle habit though it seemed so to some of us," he wrote (in *The Prophet of San Francisco.*) "The reason that Henry George gave for it was that English should be written so as to be understood by even the least literate reader."

His rules for expression were few—"Make short sentences, avoid adjectives, use small words." But in spite of his effort to simplify his writing, he was aware that his books could not always be assimilated at first reading. To Josephine Shaw Lowell he wrote, "I ask you to read *Progress and Poverty* again. With the exception of your father and perhaps a few others, I have never known anyone who got the argument clearly in one reading. I do not think the fault is in the book—it arises from its scope and the necessary connection between the links of a logical chain." [14]

He was a prodigious reader, devouring works of history, biography, and poetry. He possessed that enviable gift of being able to quote on demand a useful phrase out of the storehouse of his memory. It was the dramatic rather than the lyric quality which he loved best in poetry. He wrote to Dr. Taylor when his friend sent George some of his verses, "It is good, but why, when the great struggle is on and history is being made, will you go off into the woods and play the flute? I should rather see you put your lips to the trumpet!" [15]

He found it difficult to approve "a piece of art without high purpose." [16] In 1881 he had written Francis George Shaw, "I have been reading again the extract you gave me from *The Light of Asia*. It rings in my memory like sweet music." A few weeks later he wrote, "I send you Arnold's translation of the *Gita Govida*, which you tell me you had not seen. It is a little the worse for wear for I have read it over and over." [17]

Early he taught his children Leigh Hunt's "Abou Ben Adhem" and Julia Ward Howe's "Battle Hymn of the Republic." If asked to read aloud he usually turned to Browning's "Rabbi Ben Ezra," "Abt Vogler," "Saul," or to the Bible.

"Maybe Mr. George didn't know the Bible—every wurrd of it," said Carney. "Sundays when I'd come home from Mass he'd say: 'An' what was the text today, Carney?' An' as sure as I'd start to tell it, an' maybe fumble in the tellin', he'd finish it. An' me only after havin' just heard it, too! An' do you know, I got the habit of goin' up front in Church where I could hear what the priest said—just so Mr. George couldn't catch me on the text!"

This little boat, for my little girl,
New York, July 19, 1886

A drawing by Henry George for his eight-year-old daughter, Anna.

CHAPTER XXVIII

TWO MORE BOOKS

FOR A succession of summers in the 1890's the Georges spent their holidays at a place in Sullivan County, New York, called Merriewold Park. It was a lovely stretch of wild woodland which Louis F. Post had discovered when the doctors had advised him to take his wife to the pine country for her health. The land was so cheap that a number of Single Taxers had joined in the purchase of a large tract. The little cabin-like homes were hardly more than camps. Life was simple and most informal.

When their clothes were too worn to give away, the Georges used to save them to wear at Merriewold. Henry George went about looking more bedraggled than ever. One time when he bicycled to a neighboring farm, a strange dog mistook him for a tramp and bit him. George said he did not mind the bite half as much as the motive back of the bite. It was a disappointment to find a dog that could be such a snob as not to recognize a friend beneath towsy garments, for he always loved dogs. Friends who owned them used to shut up their animals when Henry George was coming to call, hoping then that the guest might give undivided attention to his hosts.[1]

On their first visit to Merriewold the Georges stayed with Mr. and Mrs. Post. William Croasdale also lived there in the summers and had just completed a house. He was having difficulty in finding someone to clear away the debris left by the builders. Mrs. George learned of his dilemma and undertook the job on a "contract" basis—a dance, with ice cream and cakes for refreshment, to be the pay. Commandeering all the youngsters at Merriewold she put them to cleaning windows while she and the other women swept and dusted the house. In the meantime, Croasdale, Post, and George, working in the big room which they had turned into their summer editorial office, clicked serenely away on their typewriters.

When the night of the housewarming came, the clean, new cottage had been decorated with wild flowers and lighted gaily with candles. Everyone was invited to the party. But Mrs. Anna Post was too weak to walk even the short distance to the Croasdale home and it seemed as though she must forego the fun.

Henry George had a different notion. He swung a hammock in sailor fashion from a long pole which he and Post could balance on their shoulders. In this litter, with Mrs. George walking beside to steady it and the children marching ahead and behind carrying Japanese lanterns and singing a song Mrs. Post had written, the invalid traveled to her last party.

Never was lord of manor more full of pride, never was host more gracious, than William Croasdale. He resembled Theodore Roosevelt, though his face was much broader. Croasdale's laughter was loud and hearty, and on the night of his housewarming, frequent. He was particularly amused at the country fiddler who kept interrupting his own music to instruct the city dancers in the way they should turn. As his young guests consumed ice cream and cake, he regaled them with tales of his own youth. "I found that I could save most of my lunch money by just buying dried apples, eating them dry and then drinking lots of water," he said. "M'ium, m'ium—you'd be surprised how nice and full I used to feel afterwards—and all for two cents!"

A few weeks after this sweet and simple Merriewold evening —this was in 1891—William Croasdale was taken ill and died in the little house he loved so well. And a few weeks later Mrs. Anna Post died.

For George, Merriewold became hallowed by memories of these dear friends. He came to the place whenever he could. He worked in the quiet of the woods, stopping for an occasional swim in the lake or for a row on its surface or to watch the children play. He used to call for a game called "Trades," the object of the game being for one group of children to guess what occupation the other group was acting out in pantomime. Forgetting that he was supposed to be merely an onlooker, George would cry out gleefully "carpenters!" or "shoemakers!" This often spoiled the game for the youngsters. But they liked him, and any chagrin they might feel was overcome by pride in his enjoyment of their acting.

One of the cottagers had brought along a city boy to do the

chores. His flame-colored hair was cut in such a way that it stood on end. He had a bright mind and George liked to engage him in conversation. After one of these little talks and the boy had gone away, the man stood silently gazing after him. He suddenly turned to his youngest daughter and said, "Do you think if I gave Morris five cents he'd let me run my fingers through his bristles?"

The little girl squealed in horror. "Oh, please don't ask him," she said. It would embarrass him terribly!"

George sighed resignedly. A few days later, however, he called her back into consultation. "Do you think," he asked her, "if I gave him *ten cents* he'd let me?" Her horrified "NO" was emphatic. But he brought up the question again—"Do you think if I gave him fifteen cents?" She grew panicky, for fifteen cents was enough to make almost anyone feel he could endure anything—even having his head rubbed. In dismay she looked pleadingly into her father's eyes. And there, at the corners, the little crinkles had come out! Of course, he was only fooling.

After William Croasdale's death in August of that year Louis F. Post took over the management of *The Standard*. He and George spent all the time they could in Merriewold. They acquired an old, dilapidated woodsman's cottage which they furnished, mostly with soapboxes, for their workshop. Much of the writing on his new book George did in these surroundings.

His new enterprise was an open letter in answer to Pope Leo XIII's encyclical letter of May, 1891. Many persons, including Cardinal Manning, had felt that while this message from the Vatican confused socialism and anarchy with the Georgist philosophy, it was aimed specifically at the latter. Certainly Archbishop Corrigan welcomed it as a vindication of his own attitude toward Father McGlynn.

George wrote to Father Dawson, "It is very sad to see the general tendency on the part of clergymen to avoid the simple principles of justice. As Tolstoy put it, they are willing to do anything for the poor but get off their backs. This is leading them into the advocacy of principles which will tend ultimately to atheism. . . . You see the result in Ireland of ignoring principle." [2]

And seven months later he wrote to the same friend, "I wish that the spirituality of the Church could in some way be separated from its political and corrupt machine, which turns into merchandise the efforts and sacrifices of the men and women who are really God's servants." [3]

His answer to the papal encyclical, which he called *The Condition of Labor*, grew under his pen to a book of 25,000 words. In it he explained carefully, and in what has been called some of his best writing, how and why he differed from the Anarchists and Socialists and what he advocated in the hope of economic reform.

The book was published simultaneously in New York and London, and, translated into Italian,[4] was brought out in Rome by the same firm which had recently published the Italian edition of *Progress and Poverty*.[5] A specially bound copy was presented to the Pope through the medium of Monsignor Caprini, Prefect of the Vatican Library. But George never received a word of acknowledgment.

One of the most understanding reviews of the work, thought George, appeared in the Swedenborgian periodical, *The New Church Messenger*, from the brilliant pen of Alice Thacher, who was to become the second wife of Louis F. Post. She contended in this criticism that George "has never written anything that more clearly, briefly and logically presents his conception of economics. . . . Its author applies spiritual principles to the solution of natural problems in reply to a supreme Church dignitary who has applied in these problems principles that are only natural. . . . That the science of economics should be placed on this spiritual level is much. That spiritual doctrine should be brought down to the level of economics is much more. There is a summing-up value in the fact that the Pope, speaking for the old economics, says: 'Nature'; George, speaking for the new, says, 'By Nature you mean God.'"

Friends who had been alarmed at the author's recent physical breakdown were relieved when they saw the power and strength of his latest writing. "I have just finished the 'Letter,'" wrote John Russell Young. "I envy you the vigor and truth and splendor of your style which has not been surpassed in any political writing since Burke. However, that is with me an old opinion. Only I am more than pleased to find that your illness has not dulled the temper of the sword, as I was afraid might come." [6]

The book had been written specifically "for such men as Cardinal Manning, General Booth, and religious-minded men of all creeds." [7] It deeply touched some of them. Father Richard

L. Burtsell [8] of the Epiphany Church, New York, who was Father McGlynn's adviser, wrote, "Accept my hearty congratulations for your cogent and most satisfying and wonderfully written reply to the Pope." And Father J.O.S. Huntington of the Order of the Holy Cross quoted his own father, Bishop Huntington, who said, "I wish there were money to circulate ten thousand copies of Mr. George's 'Letter'—not only as an economic argument but as a religious tract." [9]

Although the "Letter"—*The Condition of Labor*—had four printings in England and was widely circulated in the United States, it did not attract the attention for which the author had hoped. But in December of the following year (1892) George reported to Father Dawson:

Something wonderful has happened on this side of the water. The Pope has quietly but effectively sat down on the ultramontane toryism of prelates like Archbishop Corrigan. Their fighting the public school has been stopped. Dr. McGlynn is to be restored, and the fighting of the Single Tax as opposed to Catholicism effectually ended. I have for some time believed Leo XIII to be a very great man, but this transcends my anticipations. Whether he ever read my "Letter" I cannot tell, but he has been acting as though he had not only read it, but had recognized its force. [10]

The hierarchy of the Roman Catholic church apparently had come to the realization that Father McGlynn's excommunication had been unjust. Whether this was due to the exemplary and dedicated life which the priest lived after the censure had fallen upon him, or whether it was owing to the deep evidence of Henry George's spirituality which came to the surface in *The Condition of Labor*, or whether, finally, it was out of fear of public reaction, Father McGlynn's reinstatement did come about. When Archbishop Satolli visited the United States he listened, as a representative of the Pope, to Father Burtsell's arguments for a reversal of the act of excommunication. Written and oral examinations of McGlynn followed. These were found to contain nothing contrary to the teachings of the church. Accordingly, the priest was reinstated. Moreover, he was given permission to continue to teach the Georgist philosophy at the Anti-Poverty Society, Cooper Union, or anywhere else he chose.

Henry George sent a telegram of congratulation to his friend, and their estrangement seemed ended. On December 30, 1892, George wrote to Father Dawson:

Of course you have heard the news of Dr. McGlynn's restoration to his faculties, which seems to have been without anything like any public promise or apology. It took place on Christmas Eve, was announced directly from the Ablegate in Washington, and on Christmas Day the Doctor said Mass three times and spoke at the Anti-Poverty Society in the evening. It has completely "flabbergasted" the Archbishop and his party, some of whom have been actually talking of getting up a meeting in protest, but the cooler among them have prevailed.[11]

Next spring Father McGlynn made the trip to Rome which he had always consented to do—provided that he could go as a priest, in full communion. He had twenty-five minutes alone with the Pope, who had already received the report of the McGlynn case from Monsignor Satolli. In fluent Italian Father McGlynn stated his case. "But surely you admit the right of property?" asked Leo XIII. The American replied, "Why of course I do, and we would make absolutely sacred the right of property in the products in individual industry." The Pope conferred his blessing.[12]

A year after *The Condition of Labor,* George wrote and published another book, *A Perplexed Philosopher.* This was an answer to Herbert Spencer's recent repudiation of his beliefs on the land question in his book *Justice,* published in 1891. George, who had acclaimed *Social Statics* far and wide, felt compelled to refute what he considered Spencer's changed viewpoint and shift toward materialism. In *The Standard* George wrote that Spencer's position would be "a shock to many Single Tax men," but he recalled, "I got that shock over seven years ago when, in a London salon crowded with men distinguished in literature, science and politics, I for the first and only time, met Herbert Spencer and heard him declare with the utmost vehemence that he was in favor of any amount of coercion in Ireland that was necessary to give the tenants freedom to pay their rents." [13]

George explained the motive for *A Perplexed Philosopher* in the introduction. After paying his respects to Spencer's great intellect, he wrote:

Since philosophy is the search for truth, the philosopher who in his teachings is swerved by favor or by fear forfeits all esteem as a philosopher....

The philosopher whose authority is now invoked to deny to the masses any right to the physical basis of life in this world is also the philosopher whose authority darkens to many the hope of life hereafter. . . .

What gives additional interest to the matter is that Mr. Spencer makes no change in his premises, but only in his conclusion, and now, in sustaining private property in land, asserts the same principle of equal liberty from which he originally deduced his condemnation. . . .

Not only do I hold the opinion which Mr. Spencer now controverts, but I have been directly and indirectly instrumental in giving to his earlier conclusions a much greater circulation than his own books would have given them. It is due, therefore, that I should make his rejections of those conclusions as widely known as I can, and thus correct the mistake of those who couple us together as holding views he now opposes.

One day while George was sitting in his shirtsleeves laboring over the proofs of this book, Peter Burt arrived unexpectedly from Glasgow at *The Standard* office. Burt was a young Scotsman who had traveled about Scotland with George and regarded himself as a devoted follower of the American economist. Completely forgetful of time and space, George greeted him as though he were a daily visitor, "Hello, Burt!" he exclaimed. "I've fairly flayed this fellow [Spencer] alive!"

George himself had had many critics in his controversial lifetime. Obviously, he could not reply to them all. But in answer to an attack in the September, 1890, issue of *Nineteenth Century*, he hit back at Professor Thomas F. Huxley, his critic, through the character of "Professor Bullhead" in the satire entitled "Principal Brown" at the end of the book.

He also devoted a long chapter to the injustice of "compensation of landowners if their exclusive ownership be abolished." He had touched on this subject in *Progress and Poverty* but here he treated it at greater length.

A Perplexed Philosopher was widely read. But it was not as widely read nor was it translated into as many languages as George's other books. Incidentally, it brought no response of any kind from Herbert Spencer.

Shortly before the publication of *A Perplexed Philosopher* George reached the conclusion that *The Standard* had become too much of a burden, financially and otherwise. He preferred, in any case, to devote his energies to other projects. And so he suspended publication of the paper, stating in the last issue: "The work that *The Standard* was intended to do has been done, and in the larger field into which our movement has passed there is no longer need for it. . . . I did not start *The Standard* for the purpose of establishing a paper, but for the purpose of advancing a cause. . . . Let us say good-by to it; not as those who mourn, but as those who rejoice. Times change, men pass, but that which is built on truth endures." [14]

George had felt for some time that he would like to direct his pen to a full treatment of the subject of political economy, destroying the confusions, establishing the terminology and clearing the whole field irrefutably. "Something about interest and currency is badly needed," he thought. He had wanted to write on Immortality. He had wanted to republish *Robinson Crusoe* with copious notes of his own on the economics of the story. He had wanted to devise a primer of political economy.

But now that he had made his answer to Leo XIII in *The Condition of Labor* and to Herbert Spencer in *A Perplexed Philosopher,* and now that he was free from the strain of editing a weekly newspaper—now, at last, he turned to the full treatment of the science of political economy which had been his ambition for long.

CHAPTER XXIX

GEORGIST PROGRESS

HENRY GEORGE'S doctrines meanwhile were reaching a widening audience. Tom L. Johnson, who was representing his Ohio district in the House of Representatives, conceived the idea of reading *Protection or Free Trade* into the *Congressional Record*.

The book had already enjoyed a large circulation, first by a newspaper syndicate, then in regular book form, and later in a cheap paper edition of 200,000 copies issued through the extraordinary efforts of William Justus Atkinson and John G. Carlisle, son of the Senator from Kentucky. It was (and still is) the custom in Congress for members to have their own remarks or remarks which they had inserted reprinted, paying for the printing but using their franking privilege to send such matter free through the mails. Tom Johnson rallied some of his colleagues, Jerry Simpson of Kansas, William J. Stone of Kentucky, Joseph E. Washington of Tennessee, John W. Fithian of Illinois, and Thomas Bowman of Iowa. The six congressmen divided *Protection or Free Trade* into six parts and read it into the *Record* as "remarks" during the tariff debate, which was then in progress.[1]

The six sections of the book were then reassembled and brought out in an edition so large that its unit cost was only about five-eighths of a cent a copy. It retailed at one cent.

Needless to say, the whole affair annoyed the high-tariff Republicans in the House. In retaliation they inserted in the *Record* a book by George Gunton which defended monopolies. When the Republicans attacked the Democrats for putting over "St. George," as the edition of *Protection or Free Trade* was called in the House, even those Democrats who had not been out-and-out free traders struck back in defense. The matter was discussed in the press and in clubs all over the country. Tom

Johnson sent 200,000 copies of the book back to Ohio; the Democratic National Committee distributed 70,000 copies in Indiana, and the Reform Club of New York circulated 100,000 copies in the Northwest.

Altogether, 1,200,000 copies of the one-cent, "St. George," edition of *Protection or Free Trade* were distributed, as well as 200,000 copies of a two-cent edition. It is safe to estimate that almost 2,000,000 copies of the book in English and foreign languages were circulated in the first eight years after its original publication. No other work in economics, save only *Progress and Poverty*, has such a record.

There followed for George the hard-fought Cleveland campaign of 1892 and the bitter disappointment when the newly re-elected President subordinated the tariff question to the money question. But when the tariff did come up in Congress, George was present in the gallery to hear Tom L. Johnson, manufacturer of steel rails, urge that his own product be put on the free list. Indeed, Johnson made a strong plea to abolish the tariff in its entirety.

During the House debate a member noticed George in the gallery and pointed with derision to "the master" listening to his "pupil" (Johnson) on the floor. Probably to the surprise of this member, a group of independent Democrats promptly left their seats and climbed the stairs to shake hands with the small, tawny-bearded man who had been sitting there quietly. In spite of Johnson's impassioned plea the duty on steel rails was not lowered.

Disappointed as George was over Cleveland's attitude on the tariff, he was even more chagrined when the President set aside the state authority of Governor John Peter Altgeld of Illinois and sent Federal troops to quell the Chicago railroad strike. None of the New York newspapers criticized Cleveland, but some 10,000 men gathered in and about Cooper Union at a protest mass meeting.[2] Among the speakers were the Reverend Thomas A. Ducey, of St. Leo's Catholic Church; Charles Frederick Adams, the attorney; James A. Herne, the actor; and Henry George. Priest, lawyer, actor, and economist raised their voices loud in protest at what they considered a gross injustice. George said, in part:

The action of Grover Cleveland in throwing the standing army, without call from local authority, into the struggle between the railroads and their workmen, was in violation of the fundamental principles of our Government and dangerous to the Republic. . . . . I yield to nobody in my respect for law and order and my hatred of disorder; but there is something more important even than law and order, and that is the principle of liberty. I yield to nobody in my respect for the rights of property; yet I would rather see every locomotive in the land ditched, every car and every depot burned and every rail torn up, than to have them preserved by means of a Federal standing army. That is the order that reigned in Warsaw. That is the order in the keeping of which every democratic republic before ours has fallen. I love the American Republic better than I love such order.[3]

Cleveland aroused George to biting criticism a third time when the President, in a message to Congress, threatened war with England in the Venezuelan boundary dispute. The mere suggestion of war between these two great English-speaking nations made George writhe. He spoke in vigorous denunciation of the President's message at a mass meeting in Cooper Union.

News from other parts of the world was more cheering. The cause of the Single Tax was gaining in Australia and New Zealand, and in the British House of Commons James Stuart came within twenty-seven votes of winning a motion which read: "In the opinion of this House, the free-holders and owners of ground values in the metropolis ought to contribute directly a substantial share of local taxation." [4] Also in England, the Land Restoration League under the management of the indefatigable Frederick Verinder had been conducting an educational campaign, traveling in big vans from town to town.

At home, in Congress, Representative James G. Maguire and Tom Johnson had introduced (in 1894) a Single Tax amendment to the income tax bill. For the first time the Georgist fiscal reform was debated on Capitol Hill. It got only six votes—three more than expected—but the "sympathy is such among radical Democrats," wrote George, "that the House cheered when the six men stood up." [5]

Nearly a year later a meeting was held in Cooper Union to discuss the report of the Tenement House Commission. George was present. According to the *New York Herald*, "in one of the most forcible addresses he had delivered in the city in years. . . . [he] threw what proved to be a bomb." Perhaps—to quote from George's remarks on that occasion—this was the "bomb":

Of the 21 recommendations in the report, some are good and some are bad.... Some are indifferent but all are alike in that they go nowhere toward the settlement of the question the committee has brought up.... You can turn the East Side with its tenements into the most beautiful part of the city and the results will be that our millionaires will soon be living there.... You want to tear down those tenements and let no one live there unless he has 600 feet of cubic air. Where are the people turned out from those houses to go? Into the streets, into the police stations, that this very night are crowded, or into the almshouses? It seems to me that when we talk of quackery, the greatest quack of all is he who tells you to go slow; is the quack who would substitute charity for justice; is the quack who tells you that in instituting reform no one need be hurt.

"As Mr. George took his seat," reported the *Herald*, "the audience rose at him and cheered him for some minutes." [6]

Doubtless it seemed strange to many at this meeting that Henry George, who had dedicated himself to improving the condition of the poor, should denounce proposals for tenement house reform and vehemently oppose the plan to use public money to *buy* condemned tenements and build better ones. He had made it so clear that taxing land according to its value would make it too expensive to use it for slums and that un-taxing "improvements" would automatically produce good buildings instead of human rookeries. He had proved definitely that these were the quickest, the most just, and the most fundamental means of slum clearance, so it was now difficult for him to be patient.

"Those inviting him [George had been invited to speak by the Social Reform Club] knew what he stood for: that he had a contempt for trying to head off the real, radical reform by milk-and-water methods," recalls Whidden Graham, one of the sponsors of the Cooper Union meeting. "They knew that living conditions would not be substantially improved so long as the existing system of land holding and taxation was maintained. Yet they invited him to speak, and he spoke truths that threw them into consternation."

In the early summer of 1896, a group of enthusiastic Single Taxers from Philadelphia, and Richard George and Bolton Hall from New York, decided to "invade" the state of Delaware and introduce their reform in practical affairs through a speaking campaign. They promptly ran afoul of one of Delaware's "blue laws"—the one against public speaking. Frank Stephens was arrested after delivering a brilliant oration. The zealots saw in this incident a chance for publicity which might attract sympathy to their cause. Accordingly, they planned to be arrested one after another, and wired an invitation to Henry George: "Do you wish to personally test the law? Sentence for 30 days certain."

George's answer and reaction may have been surprising, but they were characteristic of his stand on such matters. He replied:

I do not shirk unpleasantness in the discharge of duty but I do not want to put myself, or have the Single Tax put in a false position, and it seems to me that the committee is taking a false position. The point where issue is being joined does not involve the right of free speech, but the right to disregard local ordinances and the action of local authorities, as to the use of streets. It is doubtless true that the authorities are moved by a spirit opposed to the Single Tax; but so far as they have *acted*, their right to act does not seem to be questionable.

Our work in the Single Tax is to arouse the intellect and conscience of men. This cannot be done by irritating prejudice, still less by arousing adversely a proper state respect.... I admire the zeal of these men, but not their discretion; and I fear to trust great matters to zeal untempered by discretion.[7]

The "Delaware Campaign"—as such—gradually petered out.

In the spring of 1895, Mr. and Mrs. George gave up the 19th Street House and went alone into the peace of Merriewold woods. This sylvan retreat was one of the sweetest of their experiences. Mrs. George did all the cooking (she knew how to concoct other things than black fruitcake now) and the housework. George did literally hew the wood and draw the water.

When the autumn came the family went to live at Fort Hamilton in one of the oldest houses in New York State. It was the Stanton Cottage, overlooking the Narrows and opposite Fort Wadsworth. Across the road was the home of Tom Johnson's father, Col. Albert W. Johnson.

Here "Tom L." came often to rest. The cares of the steel magnate-congressman were laid aside while he played like a boy. When the tide was high he joined the swimmers at the Johnson pier, and in twenty feet of water would gleefully float about on a huge, submerged cork-filled ring so that only his rosy face, with its permanent smile, could be seen. In the evenings he danced in spite of his great weight—with extraordinary lightness, Mrs. George testified. And his fabulous store of sleight-of-hand tricks amused adults as well as Fort Hamilton's considerable population of children.

George never indulged in what he considered—with perfect tolerance—aquatic "stunts." Because his father had become deafened in diving, he never took the risk or permitted his children to do so. He swam with a firm, steady breast stroke. Frequently he could be seen in the shallow water teaching some youngster to swim.

Indeed, George was devoted to children. At one of the Cooper Union meetings a child began to cry during his speech. "Put it out," called someone in the audience. "Take it home where it belongs," shouted another. Henry George paused for a moment and then said, "Let the baby stay. And let him cry if he wants to; all babies have to cry sometimes." He then proceeded to speak above the obbligato of wailing. After the meeting, he took the offender in his arms.

The panorama from the George home at Fort Hamilton was a never-ending delight: Sandy Hook, a dim line on the horizon to the south; the sweep of the great lower bay; the grey masonry and grassed breastworks of Fort Wadsworth; the stretch of low Staten Island hills; the dimly silhouetted buildings of Manhattan massed to the north; the dome of ever-changing sky; the circling gulls. But to the man who still remembered how to box the compass and how to spot the rigging of any ship afloat, the parade of boats of varying types and sizes, of yachts and yawls, of ocean greyhounds, tramp steamers, pleasure sloops or tug-escorted scows—all this was the greatest joy in view.

Henry George's book-lined study on the top floor looked south and west and was flooded with light, since he would have no curtains on the windows and kept the shades up. The customary couch was present. A huge wicker clothes hamper served as a waste basket, and it was infrequently emptied in case he might wish to retrieve some paper he had discarded. Magazines, papers, and books were strewn about the great flat top desk and on tables of varying dimensions in what, to the uninitiated, seemed utmost confusion. But of course George knew where everything was, for his memory had catalogued its whereabouts even as he had distributed each paper and magazine.

A poor business man when it came to his own affairs, George was nevertheless able to give clear practical advice to others—he who had been called a "dreamer!"

"I have consulted him repeatedly," Arthur McEwen reported a financier as having said, "and never found his judgment unsound. When I have placed a business problem of many factors before him, he has given his mind to it with the same ability to detect the seeming and get at the real that he shows in resolving into plainness the complexities of political economy. Voltaire went to the Bourse and made a fortune to prove that a man of genius was as clever as common men on their own ground, and George could have done the same, but, like Agassiz, he has had no time to make money."

George had happened to visit Arthur J. Moxham, president of the Johnson Steel Rail Company, in Johnstown, Pennsylvania, during the financial panic of 1893 when the very existence of the company was in jeopardy. Although the company was receiving large orders, payment was slow. George suggested this solution:

The bonds of the street railway companies ordering rails from the Johnson company should be taken in lieu of money for payment, and certificates should be issued against these bonds and be given in payment to the Johnson company's employees.

Moxham, who was a highly regarded man in the community—having been chosen dictator with powers of life and death during the Johnstown flood [8]—was able to put this plan into effect with the cooperation of his workmen and the townspeople with whom they traded. The company was saved from failure.[9]

This business stroke convinced George more firmly than ever that the United States should issue a paper currency, based upon its credit and interchangeable with its bonds, and so diminish its currency difficulties. He stood clear in his understanding of the money question, although to the dismay and grief of some of his dearest friends and staunchest supporters he placed himself behind Bryan in his 1896 Presidential campaign against McKinley, the arch-protectionist. "Bryan certainly did not represent my views," George said in a letter to his ever faithful correspondent, Dr. Taylor, "but I had to take the best offered, and he came nearest it." [10]

George studied both candidates and their platforms carefully. He went to both Democratic and Republican conventions and wrote articles all through the campaign for the *New York*

Journal. The free silver plank in the Democratic platform mattered little to him compared to the menace of McKinley's high protective tariff. On the day before the election he wrote in the *Journal:*

Gold and silver are merely the banners under which the rival contestants in this election have ranged themselves. The banks are not really concerned about their legitimate business under any currency. They are struggling for the power of profiting by the issuance of paper money, a function properly and constitutionally belonging to the nation. The railroads are not really concerned about the "fifty-cent dollar," either for themselves or for their employees. They are concerned about their power of running the government and making and administering the laws. The trusts and pools and rings are not really concerned with any reduction in the wages of their workmen, but for their own power of robbing the people. The larger business interests have frightened each other, as children do when one says, "Ghost!" Let them frighten no thinking man.[11]

But George's cause lost again. McKinley was elected. "This result makes our fight the harder," he said. And he who had been so buoyant began to show signs of discouragement and weariness—a sort of world sorrow.

Leo Tolstoy [12] had become an enthusiastic follower of the economics of George, although it was not until several years later that he expressed his enthusiasm in fiction form in his novel—*Resurrection.* The messages of the economist and the novelist were the same—the brotherhood of man, although their methods of preachment were different. They were so much in sympathy, George felt, that he resolved to visit the great Russian on his next trip to Europe. In the meantime they exchanged letters. Tolstoy wrote on April 8, 1896:

The reception of your letter gave me a great joy for it is a long time that I know you and love you. Though the paths we go by are different, I do not think that we differ in the foundation of our thoughts.

I was very glad to see you mention twice in your letter the life to come.

There is nothing that widens so much the horizon, that gives such firm support or such a clear view of things as the consciousness that although it is but in this life that we have the possibility and the duty to act, nevertheless this is not the whole of life but that bit of it only which is open to our understanding.

I shall wait with great impatience for the appearance of your new book which will contain the so much needed criticism of the orthodox political economy. The reading of every one of your books makes clear to me more and more the truth and practicability of your system. Still more do I rejoice at the thought that I may possibly see you.

Tolstoy had touched upon one of George's convictions. Henry George very definitely believed in a life after death. Yet his religious attitudes were not fixed in any pattern. Having for his personal friends clergymen of many Christian as well as non-Christian denominations, he nevertheless had little liking for dogmatic forms.

To him the label made no matter; one could live and preach the message of "not I but thou" outside the church as well as in it. "Although I do not sympathize with any of these orders from St. Anthony down," as he had written to his sister-in-law back in the days when he first knew her, "I am glad your lot is among the Sisters of Charity, for they do not run away from human nature, they seem to ennoble it.[13]

Twenty-five years later he wrote her, "Though you and I do not think alike on all the little details, my faith is as firm as yours that there is another life beyond this and I can think of growing old and passing away without repining or wishing to change the order of the Creator."[14]

Loving liberty, he left his children to make their own choice of religious expression, and for himself chose no creed on which to hang his belief. He worshipped in any church, or, as was more often the case, in none.

Also, he had no feeling for hard and fast nationalism any more than he had for religious antagonism. "I am not concerned with anyone's religious belief," he wrote at the end of A Perplexed Philosopher. "But I would have men think for themselves. . . . There are things which it is given to all possessing reason to know, if they will but use that reason. And some things it may be there are that—as was said by One whom the learning of the time sneered at, and the high priests persecuted, and polite society, speaking through the voice of those who know not what they did, crucified—are hidden from the wise and prudent and revealed unto babes."[15]

WHAT HENRY GEORGE WILL DO
AS MAYOR
OF GREATER NEW YORK.

PUT YOUR X IN THE CIRCLE UNDER THE ROOSTER.

THE DEMOCRACY OF THOMAS JEFFERSON.

FOR MAYOR,

HENRY GEORGE

FOR COMPTROLLER,

CHARLES W. DAYTON

FOR PRESIDENT OF THE COUNCIL,

JEROME O'NEILL.

Election poster, second mayoralty campaign.

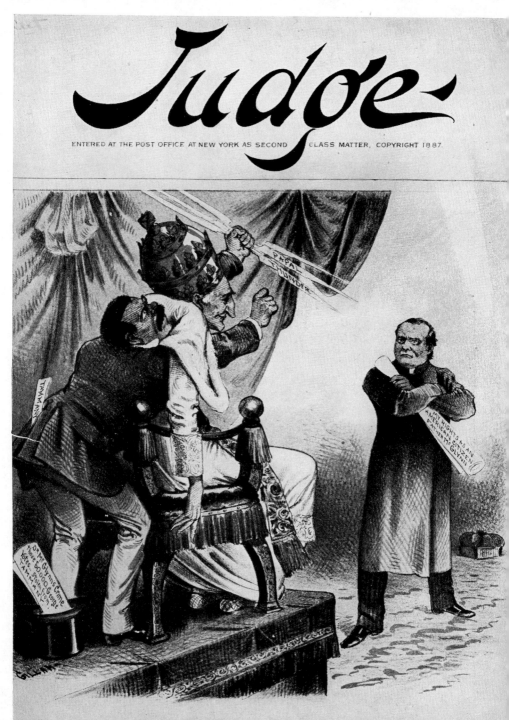

THE POWER BEHIND THE POPE.
"The voice is Jacob's voice, but the hands are the hands of Esau."

A pro-McGlynn cartoon in *Judge*, February, 1887.

EPPLER & SCHWARZMANN, Herausgeber   COPYRIGHT, 1888, BY KEPPLER & SCHWARZMANN.   PUCK BUILDING, Ecke Houston & Mulberry St.

ENTERED AT THE POST OFFICE AT NEW YORK, AND ADMITTED FOR TRANSMISSION THROUGH THE MAILS AT SECOND CLASS RATES.

"Cold, bitter cold!" An anti-McGlynn cartoon in *Puck*, January, 1888.

An anti-George cartoon in *Puck*, November 3, 1886.

BY GEORGE!

Cartoon in the *World*, October 5, 1897.

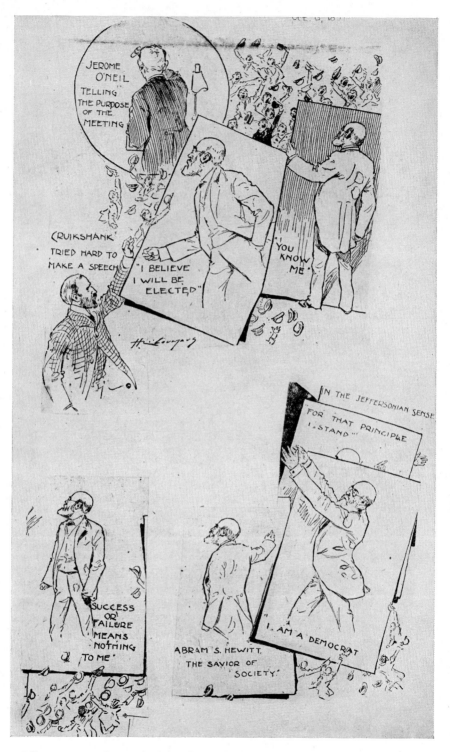

Cartoons on George's second mayoralty campaign appearing in the
Telegram, October 6, 1897.

HENRY GEORGE SAYS HE WILL NOT WITHDRAW, BUT WILL STAY IN THE FIGHT TILL THE VOTES ARE COUNTED.

CHARACTER STUDIES OF HENRY GEORGE.

CERTAINLY shall not withdraw. Our fight is against Bossism. Our platform is against Bossism. To overthrow Bossism, Crokerism, Plattism is to fight—not retire. I am in the field to stay while a man remains to war on Bossism.

If Mr. Low or his supporters desire the overthrow of Bossism, let them join our movement. Let them support the only Jeffersonian ticket in the field. Its triumph will end Bossism. Its triumph will give Greater New York true reform. I shall never desert the men with me in our Great Cause.—HENRY GEORGE to the Journal.

Character studies of Henry George from the *New York Journal*
of October 30, 1897.

THE BODY OF HENRY GEORGE BORNE AT THE HEAD OF THE NIGHT PAGEAN

ALL DAY LONG A MULTITUDE LOOKED ON THE DEAD FACE OF HENRY GEORGE.

The funeral cortege of Henry George, from the *New York Journal*, November 1, 1897.

CHAPTER XXX

'NINETY-SEVEN

R ICHARD GEORGE, the family's second son, had developed into a sculptor of ability. Early in 1897, he modeled a head of his father which proved to be the best likeness ever made of the economist—better, even, than the busts done by John Scott Hartley (son-in-law of George Inness) or Carl Roel-Smith, the Dane.[1]

Because he was a restless man, Henry George proved to be a difficult sitter. Fortunately, however, the position of a subject is not as trying for a sculptor as for a painter, and Richard George had an easier time of it than George deForest Brush who, at the behest of August Lewis, had painted a portrait of Henry George. During those sittings Lewis had read Schopenhauer aloud to hold the interest of the model; but the German philosopher's work usually made George either sleepy or angry—neither mood being what the artist desired to set on canvas. The picture was therefore long in the making.

Physicians had warned George's family that although there was nothing organically wrong with him, he was far from strong. They had detected a failing of his usually high spirits and a waning of his vigor. Every effort was made to keep him cheerful and interested in what was going on about him. During the sessions of sitting for the bust, some member of the family almost invariably read aloud to him from Defoe, Stevenson, Conan Doyle, Macaulay, Jefferson, or the Scriptures.

One day, when the one son was working on the bust and the other was reading aloud, the father said, musingly, "When I am dead you boys will have this bust to carry in my funeral possession, as was the custom with the Romans." [2]

His mind was occupied with the thought of death, more so perhaps because an apparent bilious attack had left him for long weeks devoid of his old strength. A physical weariness seemed to be overtaking him. Arthur McEwen described him in this period:

Under five and a half feet and of less weight and smaller girth than many a boy of sixteen ... the fine head, the greying-reddish beard, the blue eyes looking absently out from under the thicket of brows and through large spectacles, the soft hat set on any way— when these have appeared at the door of the editorial room to inquire for a friend or bring an article, the stranger-journalist, unaware of the visitor's identity, has mistaken him for a colporteur, a retired schoolmaster, an unrecognized, or anything meek or unworldly.... It is proof of his quality that fame has made him simpler.

Although nearly fifty-eight, Henry George had enjoyed little rest or relaxation in a life crowded with adventure and toil. Not only had he borne more personal worry than comes to most men but he had launched a world movement which had survived very largely because of his own unswerving faith and indomitable will. Almost, it seemed, his work was done.

Once he told Mrs. George that he was confident the "great advancement of our ideas" would be disclosed more after his death than during his life. "Neither of us can tell," he said, pacing the floor vigorously after springing from his couch, "which of us will die first. But I shall be greatly disappointed if you precede me, for I have set my heart on having you hear what men will say of me and our cause when I am gone." [3]

Next to the Stanton Cottage was a plot of land which Tom Johnson had given him. With money left him for personal use in the will of Silas M. Burroughs, of Burroughs, Welcome & Company, who had died but a short time before, George began building his own home. "The money," he wrote Mrs. Burroughs, "enables me to put my wife for the first time in a house of her own and gives her a security preferable to life insurance."

Work on the house absorbed his whole interest, and this gratified his family and friends who sought to keep him away from his desk as much as possible. The house grew rapidly—the house with its wide, hospitable hall, George's own study on the top floor, and "Jen's room" that was to be always waiting for a visit from the beloved daughter who, married, now lived in Baltimore.

But one night, before Jen's room in the new house was finished, and while she and her seven-months-old son were visiting the Georges in the old house, death came suddenly and with faint warning to Jennie George.* The blow was a crushing one for the adoring father. But he concealed the pain of it and gave his strength to comforting others. As dawn came on the early May day of Jennie's death, he sat alone with his broken-hearted Harry. Between Harry and Jen there had been such a bond as existed between Henry George and his own sister Jennie.

The funeral took place in the sun-flooded, flower-decked house where Father McGlynn, who had performed Jennie's wedding ceremony only two years before, now read the last rites. Henry George himself stood at the door and greeted the many friends who came. The death of this beloved daughter was a test of his philosophy and his faith. With characteristic courage he wrote to his cousin, George Latimer, "We are not of those who sorrow without hope. . . . What is left of life will be solemn, but I trust better and it may be—sweeter." [4]

In the meantime the generosity of August Lewis and Tom L. Johnson had freed him from the strain of having to lecture for pay and write magazine articles. With all the persistence which his waning strength permitted, he set about to finish *The Science of Political Economy.*

"It would be a fit title for my last work," he wrote a friend. [5] And in a lighter mood, "The book still swells and I will be lucky if I get through this year. But Adam Smith took twelve years to write *The Wealth of Nations* and the subject has been greatly bedeviled since then." [6] He had doubts that he might be able to finish the work and he feared also that it might not be up to his standard.

To prevent a loss such as he had sustained with *Protection or Free Trade,* this manuscript was set up by linotype. A copy was sent to Dr. Taylor for "criticism." On receipt of that criticism he wrote to his friend in San Francisco, "You may understand now how much I have treasured what you said of that first volume—that it showed there was no loss of power from *Progress and Poverty.* That is what I wanted to hear." [7]

He had also hoped sometime to write an autobiography, not through any sense of vanity but rather because he wanted to throw light and understanding on certain essential facts of his own career. But there had been no time for such a book, just as

* She died of a sudden heart attack—Editor.

there had been no time for the book on Immortality, or the "Primer," or the notes on Robinson Crusoe.

Into the manuscript of the new work, however, he slipped autobiographical references. He talked of his past and of his experiences to family and friends, and he let his friend Ralph Meeker bring a stenographer and take long notes. As though he felt compelled to leave a record of the history of *Progress and Poverty,* he wrote Chapter VIII, Book Two, ahead of the chapters leading up to it. His son Richard, who copied these nine and a half pages, was the only one who saw this portion of the book until after the author's death. He wrote the dedication to "August Lewis and Tom L. Johnson who of their own motion and without suggestion or thought of mine, have helped me to the leisure needed to write it, I affectionately dedicate what in this sense is their work."

As was afterward revealed, he was quietly "setting his house in order." But there was nothing gloomy about his manner during this time. Put to the test, now that he believed he was facing death, he seemed to live what he had preached—free from fear, and with "grace and guidance and strength to the end." He was cheerful, he maintained his interest in world affairs, and he saw many friends, old and new, including the young lawyer Samuel Seabury. Gently teasing the youngsters and swimming sometimes with a crowd of merrymakers from the Johnson dock, outwardly he maintained much of the routine which he had established at Fort Hamilton. But those who knew him best detected a growing detachment and a weariness that was not merely of the body.

During that summer of 1897, there were frequent reports that Henry George would be asked to run for mayor of what was now Greater New York, on an independent ticket. When the rumor reached Dr. James E. Kelly, his personal physician whom he had known first in Ireland, Kelly hastened to warn George that his physical condition would not permit the strain of another political campaign. Dr. John H. Girdner corroborated Dr. Kelly's statement. And Dr. M. R. Leverson, an old friend of San Francisco days, recalled a conversation he had with George.

I, as well as many others, endeavored to dissuade him from accepting the nomination as likely to injure his health. Speaking on the subject one day, he asked me what was likely to be the result. Seeing that he wished to know, I said: "It may be fatal." "Do you mean," he said, "that it may kill me?" I answered, "Yes." "Well," said he, "I've got to die, and what can be better than to die fighting for the people. Besides, this will do more for the cause of their emancipation than anything I'm likely to be able to do during the rest of my life."

I dreaded lest any moment his body may collapse.

Dr. Walter Mendelson, brother-in-law of August Lewis, wrote to Henry George:

. . . I take the liberty of a friend, who is at the same time a doctor, of warning you most earnestly not to accept the nomination. Knowing your physical condition as I do I feel quite certain that both Dr. Kelly and Dr. [Frederick] Peterson will agree with me, when I say that the bodily fatigues and nervous strains which a political campaign would involve might—nay, in all probability, would—be accompanied by the greatest dangers, not to your health alone, but to your life. . . . It is not flattery, I am sure, to tell you that you have better work to do than to be Mayor even of Greater New York. . . . I believe you ready to make any sacrifice for that which you think right. But I urge you to save yourself for the sake of others. . . . There have been thousands of mayors of cities, but so far but one *Progress and Poverty*. . . .[8]

The response was brief: "I thank you for your friendly counsel. I shall take it, unless as I can see it duty calls. In that case I must obey." [9]

The pressure from radical Democrats to have George accept the nomination increased steadily. Pressure from intimate friends to refuse it mounted proportionately. George leaned toward acceptance. Failing to convince him that poor health was an insurmountable barrier, his friends tried to dissuade him on the ground that machine politics would thwart an honest administration of the city's affairs and that he might better serve his cause by writing about it. He answered that although this might well be true, he believed that democratic government required the choice of men not necessarily the best equipped for office but men who first of all typified the popular sentiment. If he were elected he might not be the ideal executive but he would represent the principles of those who elected him.

The Democratic party, under the thumb of Tammany Hall, chose Judge Robert Van Wyck as candidate for mayor. Seth Low, twice mayor of Brooklyn (which had now been absorbed in

Greater New York) and at this time president of Columbia University, was nominated by the independent Republicans in protest against the "regulars" who had chosen General Benjamin F. Tracy, a prominent attorney and Secretary of the Navy in the cabinet of President Harrison.

The pressure grew as George was importuned to enter the contest against the Republican and Democratic machines and uphold the principles of Jeffersonian democracy. He called a meeting of about thirty of his friends at the New York office of the Johnson Company in October. All of them knew that he did not desire political place. They knew that he preferred his private study to an office in City Hall. Did they know that now he was probably measuring his own waning strength? Had he time to finish his book? Or only time to make one more appeal to the people—the people who would listen to that appeal if he made it himself, but who would not accept a deputy?

At any rate, one by one he heard his friends' advice for and against accepting the nomination. He quickly silenced every reference to his physical condition. When they had all spoken, he made a summary of their opinions. Everyone, he concluded, had admitted that his candidacy would mean publicity for the Single Tax cause. It would bring before the voters the very ideals for which this group stood. Plainly, therefore, it was his duty to accept the nomination.

"Not a man there who did not feel at the beginning perfectly competent to guide Mr. George," said Arthur McEwen, "and at the end there was not a man there who mentally did not stand hat in hand before his superior practical sense.... In the presence of simplicity and unselfishness the wisdom of the shrewd became as foolishness to them.... The 30 who had met divided in opinion went away as one, and that one on fire with devotion to Henry George and lifted to his plane for the hour."

Henry George attached one condition to his acceptance—his wife must be consulted. Certainly, however, the decision had been reached in his own mind. His old vitality reappeared and he left the meeting whistling—passing and, quite unconsciously, almost bumping into Richard Croker, "boss" of Tammany, with whom he would soon be in mortal conflict.

Arriving home at Fort Hamilton, he told Mrs. George of the conference with his friends. Then he reminded her of what she had said in Dublin to Michael Davitt at the time of the Phoenix

Park murders—that Davitt should go to his people even though it cost him his life.

"I told you then," said Henry George, "that I might some day ask you to remember those words. I ask you now."

Annie George's answer was brief. "You should do your duty at whatever cost," she replied quietly.

CHAPTER XXXI

LAST STAND

HENRY GEORGE accepted the nomination of "The Party of Thomas Jefferson" on the night of October 5 at an overflow meeting in Cooper Union.

The new party was a combination of several independent political groups, mostly Democratic, and its name had been suggested by George himself. Mrs. George had tickets for herself and her daughter entitling them to sit on the crowded platform. But it was only by using her name that they were able to enter the hall—pushed in through the mob by enthusiastic policemen who led them to places on the stage.

The girl knew nothing of the fears which George's doctors had expressed. She did not know the weight on her mother's heart. But in her own heart there grew a nameless fear when she saw her father (who had nearly fainted on the way to the meeting) advance to the speaker's stand. Now he stood before that sea of faces, his own face ashen, his once strong body now so frail. He stood there—looking as though he must drop, while the huge audience thundered applause and cheers.

("Dear God," prayed the girl, "support him. Do not let him fail. Give him strength.")

At last the tumult ceased. Presently he spoke, his voice small, weak, almost inaudible, difficult to recognize as the voice of Henry George, the "orator," the "prodigy of platform eloquence." The girl muttered her prayer again.

Gradually a change came in the short, slight, weary man on the platform. He braced his shoulders, threw back his head in the old way, and almost in the old voice with almost the old ring, spoke staunchly:

I hold with Thomas Jefferson that no man can ignore the will of those with whom he stands when they have asked him to come to the front and represent a principle.

The office for which you name me gives me no power to carry out in full my views, but I can represent those who think with me—men who think that all men are created free and equal. . . . To make the fight is honor, whether it be for success or failure. To do the deed is its own reward. . . .

I believe, I have always believed, that . . . there was a power, the power that Jefferson invoked in 1800, that would cast aside like chaff all that encumbered and held it down; that unto the common people, the honest democracy, would come a power that would revivify, not merely this imperial city, not merely the state, not merely the country, but the world.

No greater honor can be given to any man than to stand for all that. No greater service can he render to his day and generation than to lay at its feet whatever he has. I would not refuse it if I died for it.

What counts a few years? What can a man do better or nobler than something for his country, for his nation, for his age?

Gentlemen, fellow Democrats, I accept your nomination without wavering or turning, whether those who stand with me be few or many. From henceforward I am your candidate for the Mayoralty of Greater New York.

After the meeting was over, mother and daughter tried in vain to get through the crowd that swarmed about Henry George and shut him off from them. They made their way at last to the street, but he was far ahead in the crowd, flanked by Tom Johnson and his brother Albert, borne along in a mass of excited, cheering men, who chanted as they marched:

George! George! Hen-ry George!
George! George! Hen-ry George!

The next morning Mrs. George asked her daughter, "What-ever were you doing last night while your father was making his speech? He says he could hardly think of what he wanted to say because he was so conscious of your eyes, staring at him."

Even to her mother, the daughter felt too shy to say that she had been praying. And so she replied, questioningly, "How could he have seen me across that jam of people? I wasn't doing anything—just sitting there beside you."

The new party chose the Union Square Hotel as headquarters because of its central location. Mr. and Mrs. George took rooms there, which the newspapers dutifully described in their ac-

counts of the campaign, in order to avoid the hour-and-a-half
trip between the city and Fort Hamilton.

"Mr. George is now in his fifty-ninth year [he had just passed
his fifty-eighth anniversary, on September 2]," wrote Arthur
McEwen, "and those whose personal contact with him has been
recent are most struck by his gentleness, and next by the abstraction of his manner. On his social side he is the least self-
assertive of men now. 'As a neighbor, a friend, and the head of a
family,' said one who is near him, 'Henry George is the justest,
the most considerate, the sweetest, and most lovable of men!'
For some years he has been living in retirement, giving the
leisure and the matured thought of his ripened life to the
composition of an elaborate work on his *Science of Political
Economy*. It is to be his *magnum opus*. It shows no decline in
power, but there is in it what there is in George himself—a
milder tone. He had sat in his evening to tell before night came
all he thought of the world in which he found himself—to face
its problems and offer his solutions. His absorption in this vast
task was complete until the call to the Mayoralty contest came.
Then he woke up as a pasturing war-horse might at the bugle's
blast, and he is the old Henry George again as I knew him in San
Francisco when he was in his thirties."

Three weeks of intensive work followed, for this four-cornered
fight for mayor of New York was one of the fiercest ever waged.
They were weeks of excitement and boundless enthusiasm for
the Jeffersonian Democrats, whose attack on Tammany was
fearless and merciless. Campaign funds, however, were meager.
The largest contributions came from August Lewis, Tom Johnson, and John R. Waters. Small contributions made up the rest—
and greater part—of the fund. George put some of the money
from the Burroughs bequest into the campaign against the
advice of his friends. Willis J. Abbot, author of several histories
and later editor of *The Christian Science Monitor,* was chairman
of the campaign committee. August Lewis served as treasurer.
The committee was composed of men seasoned in politics.
Arthur McEwen wrote:

Men laugh at themselves for his power over them. They go to
him to advise, to expostulate, to argue, and come from him wroth
with their own past littleness. For they find in him not only the
capacity to think largely and clearly, but utter honesty in speaking
his thought. He appalls the strategists who enlist under him. One

of these politically experienced said "Every move we have made in
politics against George's advice we have been wrong, and every
time we have followed his advice we have come out right. We all
think we know more about the ins and outs of the game than he
does, but he has a sort of instinct that guides him straight." "Perhaps," suggested another, "it's because of the old fact that a man
placed high can see further than the man down below him. Isn't
it just possible that a large mind can think better about anything
than a small one can?"

Among George's intimate friends, Louis F. Post was forced by
his work to remain in Ohio. But Tom Johnson, Frank Stephens,
and Dr. S. Solis-Cohen of Philadelphia and James G. Maguire of
San Francisco were among those who came to New York to help
in the fight.

Among the New Yorkers, Frederick C. Leubuscher, Lawson
Purdy, Samuel Seabury, Oscar Geiger, Charles O'Connor Hennessy, Joseph Dana Miller, and Hamlin Garland were active in
George's behalf. The tenderness, the devotion of the many men
of varying backgrounds and interests who put aside their personal affairs and rallied to Henry George, was a thing so beautiful to Mrs. George that she could never speak of it without a
quaver in her voice.

The candidate was happy and cheerful in his fight. But he had
little of the old enthusiasm. The committee saved him as best it
could but on some days he insisted upon making as many as five
speeches. In fact, he seemed to thrive under the pressure of the
fight—to be keener, stronger, than he had been for months.

Each noonday during the campaign he went to lunch with
the Lewises at their charming home on East Sixteenth Street.
After lunch, usually, he rested. Late one night he stole off with
a friend to view the heart-breaking sight of the long line of poor
but decent-looking men waiting in front of Fleishman's Bakery
at Broadway and Eleventh Street for their midnight handout of
stale bread. He left no record of this event. Anyway, what was
there to be said that he had not iterated and reiterated all down
his life? A companion said that suffering was written on his face
as he walked away in silence.

The Thursday night before the Tuesday election embraced a
hectic schedule. With Father Thomas Ducey as the main figure
at the big Jeffersonian Democrat rally at Cooper Union, Henry

George had started out to speak at five meetings. His wife was always with him, at his request, and of late his brother Val had been going along as a sort of self-appointed bodyguard. On this night Samuel Seabury and Lawson Purdy traveled ahead to hold the meetings for the candidate. The first appearance was at Whitestone, Long Island.

This was the night of his death. The *New York Journal* reported the next day:

. . . The figure of Mr. George on his last night on earth was one of remarkable pathos. The crowd at Whitestone noticed it and did not know what to make of it. The people seemed afraid to make a noise. They did not know what it was, this indefinable something in Mr. George's manner and voice.

His manner can best be conveyed by imagining a martyr, racked with wounds for conscience's sake, speaking to the people, while his soul was far away looking on other scenes. To one who never saw Mr. George, and upon whom this air had not grown gradually, the effect was startling, for he seemed more like a racked and wounded saint than a man stumping for political office.

The second speech was at College Point. To the large audience composed for the most part of working men, he was introduced as "the great friend of labor and democracy." George at once disclaimed any special or exclusive friendship for labor. He said, "Labor does not want special privileges. I have never advocated nor asked for special rights or sympathy for working men! What I stand for is the equal rights of all men!"

From College Point the party went to Flushing. Daniel Carter Beard presided over the meeting. The *Sun* reported that Beard and Mrs. George, alarmed at George's now obvious fatigue, urged him to return home without speaking. But he was adamant. "I shall speak!" he said. "These people have come because I promised to speak to them. So long as I can speak I shall speak!"

Beard introduced George, and as he related, "Mr. George took a few steps, faced the side of the stage, looked upward for a moment, and raising his right hand as if addressing someone overhead, said: 'Time and tide wait for no man.' His arm fell to his side, his head fell forward, the chin on the breast, and he stood as if lost in thought. Presently he roused, turned to the audience, and said: 'I have only time to come, take a look at you, and go away.' "

In his brief speech he touched on the various candidates: "I shall not attempt to dictate to you. I do entertain the hope, however, that you will rebuke the one-man power by not voting for the candidate of the bosses. I am not with Low. He is a Republican and is fighting the machine, which is all very good as far as it goes. But he is an aristocratic reformer; I am a democratic reformer. He would help the people; I would help the people help themselves."

After the meeting in Flushing the party sped to the Central Opera House in Manhattan. On that frantic last night they seemed to be racing against time. It was nearly eleven o'clock when Mr. and Mrs. George and Val George reached the auditorium. Most of the audience had left the hall, believing that George was not coming. But now the crowd surged back.

As Henry George walked to the platform, someone cried out, "Hail, Henry George, friend of the laboring man!"

"I am for *men!*" he corrected.

George was so weak and so weary from his exertions that his brother almost lifted him up the stairs of the hall. His speech was short. But unlike the other speeches that night it was disconnected and rambling. With agony of heart, his wife and brother noted the difference. Outside again, and in the fresh air, he seemed to revive. However, it was too late for the fifth speech, and the party drove back to the Union Square Hotel.

Six friends who were lingering about headquarters joined them in the dining room for a light supper. Lawson Purdy, who was present, drew a diagram of the table and the seating arrangements on a letterhead of the campaign committee. In addition to the Georges and Purdy, who is the sole survivor of the campaign committee, there were present: Dr. John H. Girdner, Willis J. Abbot, Charles F. Adams, Arthur McEwen, Dr. R. S. Law, and Jerome O'Neill. "There was friendly talk," he recalls, "and the party broke up at one A.M."

Some of his dinner companions remarked that George looked tired and that he seemed to have an unhealthy pallor, but he did not act as though ill and appeared to enjoy his after-dinner cigar.

Before going to bed he complained of indigestion. Toward morning, Mrs. George awoke and became conscious at once that he had left the room. She called out and he answered that he was all right. But he did not return. She arose and found him in the sitting room of their suite.

"He was standing," so his son, Henry, Jr., wrote, "one hand on a chair, as if to support himself. His face was white; his body rigid like a statue; his shoulders thrown back, his head up, his eyes wide open and penetrating, as if they saw something; and one word came—'Yes'—many times repeated, at first with quiet emphasis, then with the vigor of his heart's force, sinking to softness as Mrs. George gently drew him back to his couch. He moved mechanically and awkwardly, as though his mind was intensely engaged, and little conscious of things about him." [1]

Mrs. George called her son Henry. Someone ran for August Lewis, while Frank Stephens rushed for Dr. Kelly and then to the Waldorf Hotel for Tom Johnson.

When Johnson saw Stephens in his room at that time of night, he knew his errand without being told. "My God!" he murmured in a grief-drowned voice, "My God!" and writhed, says Stephens, "as one writhes who has been pierced by a sword." [2]

In spite of all his skill, in spite of all his knowledge of the human body, Dr. Kelly could do nothing to raise his stricken friend from unconsciousness. The cord had parted. Dr. Kelly tried to comfort Mrs. George, but overcome by his own helplessness, this often cynical but always tender-hearted Irishman threw himself face downward on the floor and wept.

Henry George was dead.

CHAPTER XXXII

'IF NEED BE, DIE FOR IT'

The truth that I have tried to make clear will not find easy accept-
ance. If that could be, it would have been accepted long ago. If that
could be, it would never have been obscured. But it will find friends
—those who will toil for it: suffer for it; if need be, die for it. This
is the power of truth.[1]

—Progress and Poverty

HENRY GEORGE died in the arms of his life partner, his
first-born and namesake beside him, his beloved friends
close by, his army of devoted followers at hand, his work done,
his life crowned.

A glorious death!

But in that hotel room in New York in that grey dawn, they
could not see the glory of it. It was the men who broke; it was
the woman who gave them courage.

By the time Frank Stephens, the courier of this shocking
event, had reached Fort Hamilton with the message and Richard George and his sister had hastened back to the Union
Square Hotel, the cry of "Extra! Extra!" was already ringing in
the ears of early risers.

"Henry George is dead!" was the cry that went up and down
the city's streets.

The effect of his death on his followers is poignantly described by James R. Brown, the chairman of the campaign
speakers committee. " . . . in the morning, when on my way back
to headquarters, I reached the newsstand at the corner of our
block, I picked up an early paper with a full front page announcement of this great man's death. It staggered me, and I
took counsel with hope, that it could not be, that it was perhaps
a mistake. I climbed the elevated railway stairs slowly and painfully; took a train, and, still refusing to believe although the
crowd in the car all accepted the announcement of the death as

a fact and were almost to a man visibly affected by the sad news, I got out of the train at Fourteenth Street and walked west toward Fourth Avenue.

"When directly in front of Tammany Hall I met Richard Croker in a group of his political henchmen. They were laughing and joking and making merry over something. Again I thought, Henry George cannot be dead; these men would at least be serious and thoughtful if he were. In a minute or two I had turned the corner of Fourth Avenue and entered the Union Square Hotel. . . .

"Everywhere in the building men and women were weeping their hearts out. As I went up the stairs I passed Edward Mc-Hugh, seated about one-third of the way up, convulsed with sobs; two or three men just above him were in like condition of grief; and at the top, poor Tom L. Johnson walked through the corridor, tears streaming down his face."

The general public was almost equally moved.

"Since the stirring times of the Civil War," said the *New York Sun*, "few announcements have been more startling to New York than that of the sudden death of Henry George, candidate of the Democracy of Thomas Jefferson for Mayor of Greater New York." The press of the world, friendly to his doctrines or antagonistic to them, now united in speaking of his uprightness, his integrity of purpose. "Today the earth loses an honest man" . . . "A tribune of the people, poor for their sake, when he might have been rich by mere compromising" . . . "Fearless, honest, unsullied, uncompromising Henry George."

The *New York Journal* said in an editorial:

There was nothing of the pompous consciousness of greatness about Henry George. His mind was of such pellucid clearness that no false modesty could obscure it. But while he felt a serene confidence that he had possession of a truth of vast importance to mankind, that consciousness never betrayed him into the faintest touch of vanity. He retained throughout a simplicity, a modest, almost diffident bearing and an approachability that knew no distinction of persons. . . . He was undoubtedly the most popular economic writer that ever lived. New York mourns her great citizen.[2]

In its obituary editorial the *New York Times* declared:

Profoundly tragic as is the death of Henry George at this moment, it can truly be said that his life closed in the noblest services to his ideals, fitly rounding a career that from the start has been singularly worthy. . . . Whatever we may think of the theory he worked out, no one can dispute its benevolent spirit. . . . He was the most unselfish of men. He coveted neither wealth nor the leisure so dear to the thinker. Ambition in the ordinary sense did not move him and though he dearly loved the sympathy of his fellow-men the usual rewards of popularity left him indifferent. His courage, moral and intellectual, was unwavering, unquestioning, prompt and stead-fast.

One of the candidates was out of the race for the mayoralty. But Henry George's supporters, wishing his name to remain on the ballot, urged that his son, Henry George, Jr., carry on by allowing his own name to appear on the ticket.

The *New York Sun* reported: "Young Mr. George was informed of his nomination by Tom Johnson, in the corridor of the [Union Square] hotel. Mr. Johnson was so full of emotion that he could hardly speak. He took hold of Mr. George by the two shoulders and blurted out: 'They have nominated you for your father's place.'

"Young George had not expected it, and he turned pale at the announcement. For a moment or two he was silent, then he said:

"'I will accept the nomination and I promise if elected to carry out all the promises my father made. I stand for the principles for which he stood. I pledge myself to carry them out.'"

The vote which the son received on election day was only a tribute of loving sentiment. To George's party and followers it seemed in no way an indication of the number of votes which his father would have received.

This campaign of the son was, of course, only a nominal one. Indeed, issues in the election were almost forgotten in the sorrow, and with the sorrow a dedication, which filled the thoughts of the economist's friends. Grief-stricken visitors poured into the Jeffersonian Democracy headquarters. Mrs. George received many of them, perfectly poised and tearless. It was not until four months later that she was able to write of her husband's last campaign to the faithful Edward Robeson Taylor in San Francisco:

In the face of such a loss I can only say that for him I have nothing to wish—the end was a fitting one to life—a glorious one. Oh, Doctor, you should have been here to see "politics" as they were conducted in the Union Square Hotel for those three weeks. It was a beautiful experience to see him surrounded by his friends and neighbors, all ready to sacrifice anything for principles laid down by their beloved leader.

He grew Christ-like within the last year (everyone spoke of it) and like the Master he lashed the wrongdoers when he got before an audience—and what audiences he had, marvelous in size and earnestness! Strength seemed given to him. Even the last night his speeches, though short, were clear, connected and strong.

He had felt as if his work was ended, so it is best that it should have closed in this way, painlessly and quickly. I try to find comfort and do, in the fact that I was useful to him. But he was my companion and teacher for thirty-six years and I wonder how to live without him.[3]

Early Sunday morning his body was borne from the Union Square Hotel by the two sons and the daughter and several of the close friends. They drove through the deserted streets of the still sleeping city as the rising sun gilded the tops of the grey buildings.

Into the great building on Lexington Avenue at 44th Street, the Grand Central Palace, they carried their dead, banking about him the flowers that came from countless friends. They placed beside him the elaborate offerings sent by his three Mayoralty opponents. And closer still they laid the roses that had come from Carney.

Unknown to the family, someone had brought from the Fort Hamilton home the newly cast bronze bust of Henry George made by his son Richard. This was placed close to the coffin. (He had prophesied: "When I am dead you will have this bust to carry in the funeral procession.")

From seven o'clock in the morning till two in the afternoon, when the doors were closed in preparation for the funeral service, thousands of persons moved past the bier in double lines to pay tribute to the man who had said, "I am for men." In the first hour there were fifteen hundred; in the next, from eight to nine, four thousand; the numbers growing hourly, until in the seventh hour there were nine thousand. When the doors closed, police estimated that as many as ten thousand more were gathered in the street seeking admission.

In the afternoon the funeral services were held in the

thronged building. The Reverend Heber Newton, the life-long friend, read the beautiful Episcopal service and offered a prayer. Dr. Lyman Abbott spoke, followed by Rabbi Gustav Gottheil.

When Father McGlynn spoke it was with a depth of feeling and sincerity which electrified the throng of seven thousand gathered before the simple, low, black-draped bier. After a few sentences the priest and friend said of George, "He was not merely a philosopher and sage; he was a seer, a forerunner, a prophet; a teacher sent from God. And we can say of him as the Scriptures say: 'There was a man sent of God whose name was John.' And I believe I mock not those Scriptures when I say: There was a man sent from God whose name was Henry George!'"

At these words the slowly gathering tension in the vast auditorium suddenly broke. A thunder of applause burst forth. At first it seemed a desecration, in that place which had become a church. Father McGlynn waited a moment, and then went on:

He had a lion's heart, the heart of a hero. . . . It was that loving heart of his that grieved over the sin and misery that he saw. . . . In the concluding chapters of that immortal work of his he makes a confession and a profession, and says that the faith that was dead in him revived. . . . That book is not merely political philosophy. It is a poem; it is a prophecy; it is a prayer. . . . When the names of the mayors of New York and the presidents of the United States will be but little more than catalogues of names or called to memory only by an allusion in history, in a niche in one of the walls of the hall or that parliament of nations, there shall be found honored, loved and revered the name of Henry George.

Applause had punctured the remainder of Father McGlynn's funeral address and it burst out anew at his conclusion. It came again as Judge John Sherwin Crosby, the last speaker, alluded to the bitter criticism which George had endured because "he threatened established institutions." "Threatened?" asked the speaker, who was then unknown to most of the crowd. "He has not only threatened them; he has shaken them to their foundations. Threatened your institutions, has he? To whom have you built statues in your cities but to men who threatened your institutions? Your Garrisons and Phillipses, your Lincolns, Sumners and Sewards, all threatened institutions defended in their time by pulpit and press. Yes, Henry George has threatened established institutions, and they are now tottering to their fall, because not founded on the eternal rock of justice, but built upon the shifting sands of expediency."

The applause at a funeral service had shocked many of George's intimate friends, especially the clergymen. And yet, before the end, it became infectious, and most of the crowd joined. The Reverend Heber Newton said later to Alice Thacher Post, "When the applause first broke out, I was amazed and shocked. When it was repeated, I felt righteously indignant. But as it was again and again renewed, and I myself felt the thrill of the Christian sentiments it so unconventionally approved, the gratifying thought came to me that this was not a funeral, but a resurrection."

The services concluded, the coffin was placed on a high draped catafalque, drawn by sixteen horses shrouded in black nets. It was escorted by hundreds on foot through the canyons of the city in the gathering dusk. A single band played Chopin's "Funeral March" and the "Marseillaise," moving at the head of the column. From the window of a great house on Madison Avenue someone dropped a white rose which clung to the casket as it passed.

"I am for men," Henry George had said. And now, despite the soft rain that was falling, an unbroken line of people stood—sometimes five deep—uncovered, silent, sorrowful, along the way of march. The procession passed through City Hall Park, close to the steps of the beautiful old building where this man might have governed. It was dark and empty. No sound came from it save the deep-toned tolling of the bell. To the slow rhythm of the dirge the cortege moved across the Brooklyn Bridge. There all other traffic had been stopped; the span was deserted and silent except for the muffled sounds of wheels and tramping feet.

The two great cities stretched vague and mysterious in the Sunday calm. In the grey hush, boats passed dimly on the leaden colored waters beneath. Across they went, the followers with their leader, to Brooklyn—newly made part of Greater New York—and to Borough Hall. There, every window alight and with bells tolling, they lifted his coffin from the catafalque and delivered it to his family.

And now, no longer the public servant, Henry George became again just the beloved friend, the husband, the father, and those closest to him took their dead home for one last night.

"He lived nobly, he died grandly, and those who knew him best loved him the most. What more could be said of any man?" wrote Dr. Taylor.[4]

Next day in the morning sunshine, after services conducted by the two Episcopal ministers, John W. Kramer and George Latimer, and the Catholic Edward McGlynn, they laid his tired body to rest on the hillside in Greenwood, near the beloved daughter Jennie—out under the broad sky and looking toward the far ocean.

On the edge of the crowd stood Carney, the faithful servant, too.

"In all the years I lived in his house," she said to the girl at her side, "he was as kind to me as me own father. Glory be to God! He was a lovely man! Everythin' he used to do was nice and pleasant. He was the innocentest man that ever I knew!"

And long later came another eulogy—a quiet, time-tested judgment from Father Dawson of Dublin:

"He was one of the really great—pure of heart, loving his fellow-men—a citizen of the world!"

NOTES

CHAPTER II

1. "A Guide to the Lions of Philadelphia" (Philadelphia, 1837), p. 71.

2. The house is now the property of the Henry George Foundation of America (809 Keystone Building, Pittsburgh, Pa.) which acquired it in December, 1926, with the intention ultimately of establishing a museum in it.

3. The edifice was built in 1762 on Third Street between Walnut and Spruce. See *A Handbook for the Stranger in Philadelphia* (Philadelphia: Appleton, 1849). Since 1904, St. Paul's has been the headquarters for the Protestant Episcopal City Mission in Philadelphia.

4. Henry George Collection hereafter referred to as "HGC"), Box VIII, New York Public Library.

5. Mantle Fielding, *Dictionary of American Painters* (Philadelphia, 1926).

6. *Ibid.*

7. *Ibid.*, p. 380.

8. Henry George, *Progress and Poverty* (New York: Robert Schalkenbach Foundation, 1940), p. 562.

9. See letter from the Rt. Rev. Ignatius F. Horstmann, Bishop of Cleveland, in the *National Single Taxer*, Aug. 31, 1898. The clipping, with a personal letter to Henry George, Jr., is in HGC, Box IX. The original Horstmann letter, which was addressed to the late Joseph Dana Miller, is in the private collection of the writer.

10. Related by John Vallance George to the writer.

11. "A Guide to the Lions of Philadelphia," p. 61, cf. also "The Chain of Colonial Houses" (Philadelphia: Associate Committee of Women of the Museum of Art, 1932).

12. Letter of reminiscences written for his children by R.S.H. George, Oct. 15, 1875, HGC.

13. Henry George, Jr., *The Life of Henry George* (New York: Doubleday and McClure Co., 1900), pp. 7-8.

14. He accepted a call to All Souls Church, New York, in 1870.

15. Protestant Episcopal clergyman, author of many widely circulated religious writings and several novels.

16. Henry George, Jr., *op. cit.*, p. 9 ff.

17. Incorporated in 1824.

18. Henry George, Jr., *op. cit.*, p. 9 ff.

19. See Henry George, Diary I, Jan., Feb., and March, 1855, HGC. (There are five diaries for 1855 but no one of them is complete. The writer has numbered them in an effort to eliminate confusion. Diary I, on folded paper and written in both pencil and ink, begins on January 6 and continues to March 31. The second diary, composed of two small hand-stitched books, is marked "Sea Journal," as it starts on the *Hindoo* as a ship's log. This is the most complete of all the diaries; it covers most of the period between May 27, 1855, and March 12, 1856. Sea Journals II, III, and IV are, for the most part, "fair copies," carefully written in Spencerian penmanship. These three cover many of the same months and are evidently different interpretations, made later and on shore, of the roughly written and now almost faded Sea Journal I. Sea Journal III peters out as a diary after Aug. 29, 1855; it contains lists of the kings of England and the presidents of the United States and quotations from Emerson, Carlyle, etc. Sea Journal IV records a few weeks of 1855, of 1856, and of 1857, sketches of ships and sailors and penciled impressions of Calcutta and of the beauty of a storm.)

20. Henry George, Jr., *op. cit.*, p. 18.

CHAPTER III

1. See the Rev. George A. Latimer's diary notes. April, 1855, HGC, Box VIII.

2. *The Anxious Enquirer After Salvation*, by the Rev. John Angill of Birmingham, England. (It was published by the American Tract Society in the 1840's.) Copy in the New York Public Library.

3. Married to Chloe Vallance, youngest of the sisters of Mrs. R. S. H. George.

4. The Rev. George A. Latimer's diary notes, *op. cit.*

5. Letter to his parents written on board the *Hindoo*, April 6, 1855, HGC. Cited by Henry George, Jr., *op. cit.*, p. 20.

6. *Ibid.*

7. *Ibid.*, addition dated April 7, 1855.

8. Henry George, *The Science of Political Economy* (New York: Robert Schalkenbach Foundation, 1941), p. 352 (Henry George, Jr., *op. cit.*, p. 27n.)

9. *Ibid.*, p. 353.

10. See Journal III, Aug. 25-29, 1855, Hobson's Bay, HGC.

11. *Ibid.*

12. Captain Miller's account of the voyage: "Dec. 10, 1855. We were this day delighted by receiving all our letters." HGC, Box I, Miscellanies.

13. May 9, 1855, HGC.

14. Charles Walton, May 10, 1855, HGC.

15. "March 31, 1855. Staid [*sic*] at home in the morning finishing my original, painted her. After my last dinner at home, went with father and mother to get our daguerreotypes taken...." George, Diary I, HGC. The daguerreotype of George is reproduced in Henry George, Jr., *op. cit.*, facing p. 24.

16. May 10, 1855, HGC.

17. Letter from Calcutta, Dec. 12, 1855, HGC.

18. Calcutta, Dec. 3, 1855. Sea Journal IV, HGC. Henry George, Jr., *op. cit.*, pp. 34-35.

19. Letter to parents, Hooghly River, Jan. 28, 1856, HGC.

20. George, *The Science of Political Economy*, p. 30. Cited by Henry George, Jr., *op. cit.*, p. 37.

21. Letter from Jo Jeffreys to Henry George dated Nov. 1, 1858. See p. 7, dated Nov. 20, HGC. Quoted by Henry George, Jr., *op. cit.*, p. 40.

22. Henry George, Jr., *op. cit.*, p. 42.

23. *Ibid.*, p. 43.

24. *Ibid.*, pp. 43-44.

25. Originals in HGC, Box VI, "Articles and Miscellaneous Writings." Henry George, Jr., *op. cit.*, p. 49.

26. Letter from Charles Walton to Henry George, July 29, 1863, HGC. Quoted by Henry George, Jr., *op. cit.*, p. 49.

27. *New York Journal*, Oct. 10, 1897. "Sailor and Printer and Editor and World-Famous Economist," unsigned but part of the Ralph Meeker notes. Clipping in Scrap Book 29, Miscellany, TIQB, HGC. Henry George, Jr., *op. cit.*, p. 50.

28. Letter to B.F. Ely, Sept. 30, 1857, HGC. Quoted in part by Henry George, Jr., *op. cit.*, pp. 50-51.

29. Arthur Charles Cole, *The Irrepressible Conflict, 1850-1865*, "A History of American Life" Series (New York: Macmillan, 1934), VII, 32.

30. *Ibid.*, p. 33.

31. *Ibid.*, p. 153.

32. Record of *Shubrick* from U.S. Lighthouse Board at Washington. Typed notes signed by C. H. Thompson, Clerk, Twelfth Lighthouse District, San Francisco, Oct. 21, 1898. HGC, Box IX, Oct. 1898, folder.

33. Ralph Meeker notes in Harrisburg paper, Nov. 18, 1897, entitled "Henry George's Own Story of His Career." Clipping in Lerop Book 29, "Miscellany," TIQB, George. Econ. Div. NYPL. Quoted in part by Henry George, Jr., *op. cit.*, p. 57.

34. This page can be found with *Shubrick* typed notes, HGC, Box IX.

35. Letter from Henry George to Charles Walton, Feb. 18, 1858, HGC. Compare Henry George, Jr., *op. cit.*, pp. 62-63.

36. Ralph Meeker notes, *op. cit.*

Chapter IV

1. Letter to Mrs. Curry in Oregon (quoting Emma Curry) May 29, 1858, HGC. Henry George, Jr., *op. cit.*, p. 70.

2. Jan. 1, 1858, HGC.

3. *Ibid.*

4. Henry George, address, "Justice the Object, Taxation the Means," San Francisco (Metropolitan Hall), Feb. 4, 1890. *Henry George's Works,* IX, 299; cf. Henry George, Jr., *op cit.*, p. 80.

5. Jan. 4, 1859, HGC.

6. Henry George, Jr., *op. cit.*, p. 78.

7. "Golden Jubilee Recalls Pioneer Days." News story of the fifth wedding anniversary of Mr. and Mrs. George B. Wilbur. *Evening Post* (San Francisco), July 1, 1911. (Typed copy in the writer's private collection.)

8. Henry George, Jr., *op. cit.*, p. 81.

9. Dec. 6, 1858, HGC. Henry George, Jr., *op. cit.*, p. 84.

10. Dec. 18, 1858, HGC.

11. *Evening Post, loc. cit.*

12. *Ibid.*

13. Feb. 3, 1859, HGC. Henry George, Jr., *op. cit.*, pp. 87-88.

Chapter V

1. April 18, 1860, HGC. Passage quoted by Henry George, Jr., *op. cit.*, p. 102.

2. July 2, 1860, HGC.

3. The writer's mother related this to her.

4. Brought from the Sandwich Islands.

5. Oct. 12, 1843.

6. In 1851.

7. Ten acres bought for $8,000 by the Sisters from B. D. Wilson (for whom Mt. Wilson was named). It was at the corner of what was later Alameda and Tracy streets. The site is now the property of the Southern Pacific Railway.

CHAPTER VI

1. May 20, 1861, HGC. Henry George, Jr., *op. cit.*, p. 112.

2. Sept. 25, 1861, HGC.

3. Sept. 15, 1861, HGC. Quoted in part by Henry George, Jr., *op. cit.*, pp. 115-19.

4. Among the books was a copy of *The Household Book of Poetry*, edited by Charles A. Dana (New York: Appleton, 1860), now in the private collection of the writer.

5. Undated. Probably written in Nov., 1861. HGC.

6. March 3, 1862, HGC.

7. Sacramento, June 5, 1862, HGC. Henry George, Jr., *op. cit.*, p. 131.

8. *Ibid.*, pp. 130-31.

CHAPTER VII

1. Nov. 30, 1861, HGC.

2. Letter from Henry George to his sister, Caroline, July 5, 1862, HGC.

3. Related to the writer by her mother, Feb. 2, 1879. In the private collection of the author.

4. "Out of this inquiry has come to me something I did not think to find, and a faith that was dead revives."—*Progress and Poverty*, 50th Anniversary edition, p. 557.

5. George Wilbur had married Annie George's friend, Mary Kerrigan.

6. A. A. Stickney, a printer George had met in Sacramento. He and Mrs. Stickney also came to live in San Francisco.

7. Jan. 27, 1865.

8. Incident related by Henry George to Dr. James E. Kelly, in Dublin, 1882. See Henry George, Jr., *op. cit.*, p. 148.

9. These are now part of the Henry George Collection in the New York Public Library.

10. Feb. 17, 1865, HGC.

11. Feb. 18, 1865, *ibid.*

12. Feb. 19, 1865, *ibid.*

13. For the complete essay see Henry George, Jr., *op. cit.*, 157-59. (The original manuscript is in HGC, Box VI.)

14. The *Californian,* founded in 1864, lasted for three years.

15. It was published in the issue of April 8, 1865.

Chapter VIII

1. April 17, 1865.

2. Henry George, Jr., *op. cit.*, pp. 162-63.

3. "Abraham Lincoln," *Daily Alta California,* Sunday, April 23, 1865, in Library of Congress, Washington. Typed copy, HGC, Box VI. Quoted in part by Henry George, Jr., *op cit.*, pp. 161-65.

4. Henry George, Jr., *op. cit.*, pp. 166-67. In October, 1897, Henry George dictated autobiographical notes to Ralph Meeker on this as well as other incidents. This particular incident is in the *New York Sunday Journal,* Oct. 10, 1897, HGC, Scrapbook 29, Miscellany.

5. The *New York Sunday Journal, loc. cit.* Quoted by Henry George, Jr., *op. cit.*, p. 169.

6. Called "Dust to Dust," it was published in June, 1866, in the *Philadelphia Saturday Night.* (Henry George's boyhood friend, Edmund Wallazz, was foreman and part owner.) It was reprinted July 4, 1866, in the *Californian,* San Francisco.

7. A short story, subtitled "A Tradition of the Northwest," written for the *Californian.*

8. Henry George, Jr., *op. cit.*, p. 174. See copy of interview made by him Feb. 14, 1898, in HGC, Box VIII, and the confirmation of this by Noah Brooks, Jan. 3, 1899, in the same box.

9. *Ibid.*

10. The letters are in the writer's private collection.

11. Related to the writer by her mother.

12. *The Overland Monthly,* October, 1868 (files in the New York Public Library). Part of this article is quoted by Henry George, Jr., *op. cit.*, pp. 177-79.

13. Related by Alexander D. Bell to his son, William Lewis Bell, who recounted it in a letter to the writer dated Dec. 14, 1939. (Letter in the writer's private collection.)

14. Related to the writer by her mother.

15. Sept. 15, 1868. In the writer's private collection.

16. Oct. 1, 1868. *Ibid.*

17. *Ibid.*

18. Nov. 30, 1868. In the writer's private collection.

19. June 20, 1869, HGC.

CHAPTER IX

1. This news agency was a forerunner of the present Associated Press.

2. Oscar Lewis, *The Big Four* (New York: Knopf, 1938), p. 72.

3. Gustavus Myers, *History of the Great American Fortunes* (1910) (New York: Modern Library, 1938), p. 440.

4. *Ibid.,* p. 667.

5. John A. Kouwenkoven, *Adventures of America* (New York: Harper, 1938), Section 3, p. 134.

6. A. T. Stewart, a drygoods merchant. The structure was built of white marble at 34th Street and 5th Avenue, across the street from the present site of the Empire State Building.

7. Printed March 5, 1869.

8. Henry George, Jr., *op. cit.,* p. 182.

9. *Ibid.,* pp. 181, 183-86.

10. Lewis, *op. cit.;* Myers, *op. cit.*

11. Myers, *op. cit.*

12. Letter by Henry George to the Rev. Thomas Dawson, O.M.I., of Dublin, Ireland; New York, Feb. 1, 1883. The holograph MS was presented to the Brotherton Library, Leeds, England. A photographic copy is in the private collection of the writer.

13. Tenth Governor of California, 1868-72.

14. Leland Stanford held that "more prudent and economical, they are content with less wages." Lewis, *op. cit.,* p. 72.

15. "The Chinese on the Pacific Coast," *New York Tribune,* May 1, 1869. Copy in Scrapbook 21, HGC. Quoted in part by Henry George, Jr., *op. cit.,* pp. 194-95.

16. George, *The Science of Political Economy,* p. 200.

17. Meeker notes, *New York Journal,* Oct. 10, 1897. Scrapbook 29, HGC. Quoted by Henry George, Jr., *op. cit.,* p. 210.

18. *The Science of Political Economy,* p. 160.

CHAPTER X

1. Lewis, *op. cit.,* p. 160.

2. *Ibid.,* p. 36.

3. Related to the writer by her mother.

4. This apt characterization, the origin of which is obscure, was, of course, made popular by the late Frank Norris. His novel of that title, a useful contribution to the record of this period, is one of the American classics of social criticism. *The Octopus* (New York: Doubleday, Page, 1901).

5. Copy in Scrapbook TIQB, V. 3, HGC. Quoted in part by Henry George, Jr., *op. cit.*, pp. 211-17.

6. *Ibid.*, p. 218.

7. "Our Land and Land Policy," Henry George's Works, Memorial Edition (New York: Doubleday, Page, 1904), pp. 71-72.

8. *Ibid.*, p. 106.

9. *Ibid.*, p. 112.

10. *Ibid.*, p. 113.

11. It was new, of course, only to dominant thought in Western civilization. George's followers have found many anticipations of his ideas, not only in times recent to his, but, in a number of instances, in earlier times. His own efforts to credit the French Physiocrats as his forerunners was based on inadequate second- or third-hand information about their theory; the Physiocrats were only partial anticipators, several of which were almost perfect parallelisms. George's conception actually was as original as any contribution in his field; on this see Dr. George Geiger's thorough study of the problem, *The Theory of the Land Question* (New York: Macmillan, 1936).

12. Broadus Mitchell, "Single Tax," *Encyclopaedia of the Social Sciences* (New York: Macmillan, 1934), XIV, 65.

Chapter XI

1. Published February, 1871.

2. Published December, 1871.

3. See Eldon Cobb Evand, *History of Australian Ballot System in the United States* (Chicago: University of Chicago Press, 1917), a Ph. D. thesis. "At first this new reform in Australia and England does not appear to have created much of an impression in this country. According to Mr. John S. Wigmore, it was first advocated by a member of the Philadelphia Civil Reform Association in 1882, in a pamphlet called 'English Elections.' The following year Henry George in the *North American Review* advocated the adoption of the English system as a cure for the vice arising from the use of money in elections."—P. 18.

4. Henry George, Jr., *op. cit.*, pp. 237-38.

5. Ralph Meeker notes, typed pages in private collection of the writer. Henry George, Jr., *op. cit.*, pp. 238-39.

6. For these descriptions and anecdotes pertaining to the *Post* and its editor the writer is indebted to Mr. Stephen Potter; his typed "Reminiscences" and personal letters concerning these data are in the writer's private collection

7. Files of the *San Francisco Evening Post,* HGC.

8. *Ibid.*, June 24, 1872.

9. *Ibid.*, Oct. 26, 1872.

10. *Ibid.*, Feb. 1, 1873.

11. *Ibid.*, April 21, 1873.

12. *Ibid.*, March 11, 1873.

13. *Ibid.*, Oct. 1, 1873.

14. *Ibid.*, July 2, 1872.

15. Told by Mrs. George to Mrs. Edith M. Hibbard, who recounted it to the writer.

16. Son of Mrs. George's uncle, Matthew McCloskey. Letter, dated May 14, 1927, to the writer.

17. Told to the writer by her mother.

18. *San Francisco Evening Post,* Feb. 22, 1876.

19. *Ibid.*, Jan. 7, 1876.

20. Henry George, Jr., *op. cit.*, p. 241, who quotes former Judge Robert Ferral. Mr. Ferral, as a reporter on the *Post*, had attended the investigation with George.

21. Meeker notes. *New York Journal,* Oct. 10, 1897, HGC. Also Stephen Potter's "Reminiscences" and letters (Dec. 29, 1935) to the writer.

22. Stephen Potter, *op. cit.*

23. File in HGC.

24. Announcement in the issue of Aug. 21, 1875.

25. According to Louis H. Fox, director of the Newspaper Division of the New York Public Library, no predecessor to this illustrated Sunday newspaper can be found.

26. Letter from Stephen Potter, April 5, 1938, to the writer.

27. Told by George B. Wilbur to his daughter, Mrs. Wilbur Barr, who related it to the writer in San Francisco, April 5, 1935.

28. Henry George dictated an account of his withdrawal from the *Post* to Ralph Meeker in the autumn of 1897. This was quoted in part only in the *New York Sunday Journal* of Oct. 10, 1897, cited by Henry George, Jr., *op. cit.*, pp. 247-49. For the source of Henry

George, Jr.'s, quotations see the typed pages of the Meeker notes in the collection of the present writer.

Chapter XII

1. Nov. 28, 1875, HGC.
2. Dec. 2, 1875, HGC.
3. From Western House, Marysville, Calif., May 26, 1876. In the private collection of the writer.
4. The Philadelphia Centennial Exposition of 1876.
5. *Loc. cit.*
6. "The Question Before the People," delivered Aug. 15, 1876, before the Tilden-Hendricks Central Club. See Scrapbook TIQB, p.v. 3, no. 6., HGC. Quoted in part by Henry George, Jr., *op. cit.*, 266-68.
7. *Ibid.*
8. *Ibid.*
9. Nov. 13, 1876, HGC. Quoted in part by Henry George, Jr., *op. cit.*, p. 271.
10. Delivered March 9, 1877, the lecture was first published in the *Popular Science Monthly*, March, 1880. It has since been reprinted many times in pamphlet form. Cf. *The Writings of Henry George* (New York: Doubleday and McClure Co., 1901), IX, 135.
11. "The University of California missed the chance to have what would have been its most famous professor." Miriam Allen de Ford, *They Were San Franciscans* (Caldwell, Idaho: Caxton Printers, 1941), p. 129.
12. *The Study of Political Economy, loc. cit.*
13. "The American Republic, Its Dangers and Possibilities," in *The Writings of Henry George*, IX, 157.
14. Henry George, Jr., *op. cit.*, p. 288.

Chapter XIII

1. March 26, 1878.
2. HGC, Scrapbook TIQB, p.v. 3; Henry George, Jr., *op. cit.*, p. 296.
3. San Francisco, June 2, 1878, HGC.
4. "Moses, or Leader of the Exodus," an address delivered early in June, 1878. The manuscript and galley proofs, and a printed copy, cut and corrected, are in HGC, Box V. In pamphlet form the essay has gone through many editions in various parts of the world, and is

found in several collections. For the definitive edition, currently, see that published by the Robert Schalkenbach Foundation of Great Britain, London; or the Henry George Foundation of Australia, Melbourne.

5. The law providing for such libraries was passed in 1878; see Stephen Potter's "Reminiscences" in the private collection of the writer.

6. San Francisco, May 3, 1879, HGC.

7. Henry George, Jr., *op. cit.*, p. 301, and letter to the writer from William Cleveland McCloskey, San Francisco, May 14, 1927.

8. Letter to Charles Nordhoff, Dec. 21, 1879, HGC; quoted by Henry George, Jr., *op. cit.*, pp. 327-29.

9. *Ibid.*

10. Preface to *The Science of Political Economy* (London: Henry George Foundation), p. viii.

11. May 8, 1879, HGC.

12. File in N.Y.P.L., Econ. Div.

13. Henry George, Jr., *op. cit.*, p. 315.

14. See Diaries, HGC.

15. Editor of the *San Francisco Star,* head of a large publishing house and, during the First World War, Chief Naval Inspector of the Port of San Francisco.

16. Told to the writer by William C. McCloskey.

17. HGC and Henry George, Jr., *op. cit.*, p. 321.

CHAPTER XIV

1. Letter to Frank Norton, June 29, 1880. Copy in the collection of the writer.

2. George C. Perkins, succeeding William S. Irwin.

3. *New York Herald,* Oct. 30, 1897. Quoted by Henry George, Jr., *op. cit.*, pp. 327, 329, and 330.

4. Birmingham, England, Jan. 5, 1880. In the collection of the writer.

5. Letter to Henry George from D. Appleton and Co., New York, Dec. 1, 1897, HGC.

6. *Ibid.*

7. From 317 First St., Jan. 31, 1880. In the writer's collection.

8. Henry George quoted this in a letter to Dr. Taylor, Feb. 17, 1880, HGC. See Henry George, Jr., *op. cit.*, p. 331.

9. April 4, 1880, HGC. Henry George, Jr., *op. cit.*, pp. 333-34.

10. April 27, 1880, HGC.

11. Letter to Dr. Taylor, Dec. 12, 1880, HGC.

12. From Port Winnemacca, Aug. 13, 1880, HGC.

13. Brooklyn, Sept. 27, 1880, HGC.

14. In the private collection of the writer.

15. Oct. 12, 1880, HGC. Quoted in part by Henry George, Jr., *op. cit.*, p. 338.

16. Dec. 18, 1880, HGC.

17. *Ibid.*

18. March 6, 1881, HGC.

19. March 14, 1881, HGC.

20. Letter to Dr. Taylor, March 6, 1881 (quoting James Mc-Clatchy, editor of the *Sacramento Bee.*) Quoted by Henry George, Jr., *op. cit.*, p. 349.

21. "The Taxation of Land Values," *Appleton's Journal* (June, 1881).

22. "Common Sense in Taxation," *North American Review* (July, 1881).

23. May 12, 1881, HGC. Henry George, Jr., *op. cit.*, p. 349.

24. Letter to Dr. Taylor, May 25, 1881, HGC. Henry George, Jr., *op. cit.*, p. 349.

25. *New York Herald*, Oct. 30, 1897, *loc. cit.*, Henry George, Jr., *op. cit.*, pp. 344-45.

CHAPTER XV

1. March 16, 1881, HGC.

2. March 23, 1881, HGC.

3. Poultney Bigelow, son of John Bigelow, former United States Minister to France and Germany. The younger Bigelow had been a fellow student and intimate friend of Wilhelm Hohenzollern, Crown Prince of Germany and afterward Emperor.

4. May 15, 1881, HGC. See Henry George, Jr., *op. cit.*, p. 351.

5. The lecture was entitled "Why Work Is Scarce, Wages Low and Labor Restless," March 26, 1878. See A. G. de Mille., "Henry George: The *Progress and Poverty* Period," *American Journal of Economics and Sociology*, Vol. 2, No. 4 (July, 1943), p. 549.

6. "The Coming Contest," Henry George's lecture on the next great struggle, *Examiner* (San Francisco), Aug. 12, 1881.

7. Henry George, Jr., *op. cit.*, p. 352 n.

8. Louis F. Post, *The Prophet of San Francisco* (New York: Vanguard, 1930), p. 25. See also Chapters III, IV, V.

9. Post, *op. cit.*, p. 33.

10. *Ibid.*, p. 34.

11. Quoted by Henry George in letter to Dr. Taylor, Sept. 7, 1881, HGC. See Henry George, Jr., *op. cit.*, pp. 353-54.

12. *Ibid.*

13. Aug. 20, 1881.

CHAPTER XVI

1. Quoted by Henry George, Jr., *op. cit.*, p. 360, from letter to Patrick Ford, written from 37 Gardiner St., Dublin, Nov. 10, 1881, HGC, Book No. 1, p. 5. (Private letters of Ford are recorded in four small red duplicate copybooks in HGC.)

2. *The Irish World*, Dec. 10, 1881, HGC.

3. *Ibid.*, Dec. 24, 1881, HGC.

4. Nov. 20, 1881, HGC.

5. Dublin, Nov. 10, 1881, HGC. Ford letter book No. 1, p. 11.

6. *The Irish World*, Feb. 21, 1882, HGC.

7. *Ibid.*, Feb. 21, 1882, HGC.

8. Letter to Ford, Dec. 28, 1882, HGC, letter book No. 1, p. 74.

9. *Ibid.*, p. 75.

10. *Ibid.*, p. 80.

11. To Francis G. Shaw, Feb. 11, 1882, HGC.

12. *Ibid.*

13. Letter to Thomas F. Walker of Birmingham, England, June 2, 1884, HGC. See George R. Geiger, *The Philosophy of Henry George* (New York: Macmillan, 1933), p. 230.

14. Henry Myers Hyndman, *The Record of an Adventurous Life* (New York: Macmillan, 1911), p. 154.

15. *Ibid.*, p. 265.

16. *Ibid.*, p. 267.

17. Sept. 7, 1882 (from J. C. Durant's office), in the private collection of the writer.

18. Related to the writer by her mother.

19. Dublin, Nov. 22, 1881, HGC. Ford letter book, No. 1, p. 52.

20. Related to the writer by her mother.

21. Letter from his daughter, Mrs. Hildegarde Wren Whittaker, Jan. 19, 1935, to the writer (in the writer's collection). Crippled by illness in his youth, Walter Wren, a brilliant scholar, had taught, sometimes from his couch, many who became distinguished men of their time—royalty, statesmen, writers, and soldiers, among the latter Field Marshal Viscount Allenby.

22. Letter in the collection of the writer.

23. Henry George, *A Perplexed Philosopher* (New York: Robert Schalkenbach Foundation, 1940), p. 80.

24. Henry George, Jr., *op. cit.*, p. 370.

25. James Louis Garvin, *Life of Joseph Chamberlain* (New York: Macmillan), I, 385.

26. London, April 22, 1882, HGC. Ford letter book, No. III, p. 18. Quoted by Henry George, Jr., *op. cit.*, p. 371.

27. *Fall of Feudalism in Ireland,* p. 357.

28. *The Irish World,* May 9, 1882, HGC. Quoted by Henry George, Jr., *op. cit.*, p. 373.

29. The Rev. Thomas Dawson, O.M.I., of the House of Retreat, Inchicore, Dublin, Ireland, has disputed George's statement, "The manifesto was written by Davitt." Father Dawson wrote (Sept. 2, 1933): "My recollection [is] that Henry George, as he must have told me himself, was the inspirer and *writer* of the manifesto. He *had* to write it. The Irishmen were so broken that terrible night and day that they could do nothing.... The expression 'nobler vision' is evidently George's." Told that the writer was unable to confirm his belief, Father Dawson on May 20, 1939, replied: "... It is not surprising... [Henry George] could not in honor make the fact (if it be a fact) known.... And the Irish politicians themselves, however grateful, could *never* wish to reveal (if so it were) that in doing all they could they had only signed."

30. Davitt, *op. cit.*, p. 359.

31. May 9, 1882, HGC.

32. Henry George, Jr., *op. cit.*, p. 375.

CHAPTER XVII

1. "Phoenix Park," in *The Standard* (New York), Vol. I, No. 16, April 23, 1887, p. 4, HGC.

2. From Dublin, May 30, 1882, HGC. Quoted in part by Henry George, Jr., *op. cit.*, pp. 380-81.

3. London, April 28, 1882, HGC.

4. Dublin, May 26, 1882, HGC.

5. The donor was subsequently found to be Francis G. Shaw's brother.

6. London, June 29, 1882, HGC.

7. Related by Frederick Verinder to the present writer.

8. July 1, 1882, to F. G. Shaw, HGC.

9. Private collection of the writer.

10. *Ibid.*

11. *The Irish World,* Aug. 22, 1882, HGC.

12. Meeker notes, Scrapbook 29, Miscellany TIQB, HGC.

13. *The Irish World,* Aug. 22, 1882, HGC.

14. *Ibid.*

15. *Ibid.*

16. Collection of the writer.

17. Department of State, Washington, Oct. 17, 1882.

18. Sept. 24, 1882.

19. Archibald Henderson, *Life of George Bernard Shaw* (Cincinnati: Stewart and Kidd, 1911), p. 4.

20. *Ibid.,* pp. 56, 155. Payment was made in full April 11, 1933, when Shaw stopped twenty-six hours in New York to deliver a 16,000-word lecture at the Metropolitan Opera House (as Prof. George R. Geiger has reported in *The Philosophy of Henry George,* pp. 233-34). Shaw also made the same statement to Hamlin Garland in reply to an invitation to attend a dinner in honor of George's anniversary in New York in 1905; cf. the original in HGC. He repeated it in his New York lecture; cf. the text in the *New York Times,* April 12, 1933.

Chapter XVIII

1. On Oct. 21, 1882.

2. *The Irish World,* July 1, 1882.

3. *Ibid.,* July 8, 1882.

4. *Ibid.,* July 15, 1882. See Henry George, Jr., *op. cit.,* p. 385. Cf. also, Stephen Bell, *Rebel, Priest and Prophet* (New York: The Devin-Adair Co., 1937), pp. 26-27.

5. To Patrick Ford, Aug. 3, 1882. Letter book No. 4, p. 83, HGC.

6. Letter written by McGlynn to Archbishop Corrigan, Sept. 9, 1886, and printed in *The Standard* (New York), Vol. I, No. 1, Jan. 8, 1887, p. 1.

7. On Nov. 7, 1882.

8. Letter to Dr. Taylor, Jan. 17, 1883, HGC. See Henry George, Jr., *op. cit.,* p. 403.

9. *Op. cit.,* March, 1883.

10. New York, April 28, 1883, HGC.

11. *Loc. cit.,* p. 282.

12. See Henry George, Jr., *op. cit.,* pp. 408 ff.

13. May 12, 1883.

14. HGC, Box II

15. *Loc. cit.*

16. From London, Jan. 5, 1884, HGC.

17. From Inverness, Scotland, Feb. 22, 1884, HGC.

18. Letter from Brooklyn, July 27, 1883, HGC.

19. Aug., 1883, HGC. Quoted by Henry George, Jr., *op. cit.*, p. 411.

20. London, 1884, undated. In the private collection of the writer.

21. Oct. 17, 1883, HGC. Henry George, Jr., *op. cit*, p. 416.

CHAPTER XIX

1. Henry George, Jr. *op. cit.*, p. 417.

2. Dec. 31, 1883.

3. See Henry George, Jr., *op. cit.*, pp. 422-23.

4. *Progress and Poverty* (1944 edition), p. 321. The best analysis of the differences between Georgism and Marxism is in George R. Geiger, "George and Socialism," in *The Philosophy of Henry George,* pp. 227 ff.

5. *Loc. cit.*, p. 365.

6. Jan. 9, 1884.

7. London, Jan. 10, 1884. Appeared in the *New York Tribune,* Jan. 24, 1884.

8. Meeker notes, typed; in the private collection of the writer.

9. Skye, Jan. 4, 1884, HGC.

10. New York, Robert Schalkenbach Foundation, 1944. Also, London, Henry George Foundation of Great Britain.

11. *Ibid.*, pp. 4-5.

12. Richard McGhee, from Lurgan, North Ireland, was one of George's first and staunchest adherents in Europe. He was Member of Parliament for a constituency in Glasgow, Scotland, for many years.

13. Henry George, Jr., *op. cit.*, p. 430.

14. March 6, 1884. In the private collection of the writer.

15. See George's lecture, "Justice the Object, Taxation the Means," printed in Henry George Complete Works, "Our Land and Land Policy" (New York: Doubleday Page and Co., 1904), p. 297.

16. Lucy Masterman, editor, *Mary Gladstone, Her Diaries and Letters* (London: Methuen and Co., Ltd., 1930), p. 293, "August 17, 1883."

17. *Ibid.*, p. 293, "Sept. 6, 1883."

18. *Ibid.*, p. 306, "March 9, 1884."

19. *Ibid.*, p. 307, "March 10, 1884."

20. *Ibid.*, pp. 307-8. Letter dated, "Selwyn College, Cambridge, March 12, 1884."

21. *Ibid.*, p. 310, "March 28, 1884.

22. March 29, 1884. Letter in collection of present writer.

23. Henry George, Jr., *op. cit.*, p. 441.

24. *Ibid.*, p. 440.

25. February, 1884, HGC.

26. *The Daily Chronicle*, Oct. 30, 1897. Quoted by Henry George, Jr., *op. cit.*, p. 438.

Chapter XX

1. Founder and head of the Central News Agency, London. For eleven years the treasurer of the Land Reform League, active follower and devoted friend of George.

2. Recounted by Frederick Verinder, General Secretary of the English League for the Taxation of Land Values, in *Land and Liberty* (London), November, 1921.

3. Louis F. Post, *op. cit.*, p. 62.

4. *Ibid.*, p. 63.

5. April 30, 1884.

6. Published by the Robert Schalkenbach Foundation, New York, 1944, in same volume with "The Land Question" and "The Condition of Labor."

7. Jamaica, Long Island, June 13, 1884, HGC.

8. Nov. 21, 1884.

9. Jan. 17, 1885.

10. *Life of Joseph Chamberlain* (London: Macmillan, 1932-34), I, 385.

11. Compare Henry George, Jr., *op. cit.*, p. 453.

12. Feb. 9, 1885.

13. Syndicated in weekly installments in 1885-86 in the *Brooklyn Eagle, New York Star, Chicago Times, San Francisco Examiner, Louisville Courier-Journal, Toronto Globe, Charleston News and Courier.*

14. At 16 Astor Place, New York.

15. Four articles appearing between August, 1886, and January, 1887.

16. May 16, 1886, HGC.

Chapter XXI

1. For a detailed account of the 1886 campaign see *The George-Hewitt Campaign*, compiled by Louis F. Post and Frederick C. Lenbuscher (New York: John W. Lovell Co., 1886).

2. New York, Aug. 26, 1886; see *The George-Hewitt Campaign*, pp. 7-11, 13-15.

3. Sept. 6, 1886.

4. The episode was recounted by George in a reply to a statement made in the newspapers by Abram S. Hewitt in Oct., 1897; quoted by Henry George, Jr., *op. cit.*, p. 463.

5. Written from 16 Astor Place, New York, Sept. 10, 1886, HGC.

6. At Thirteenth Street, between Third and Fourth avenues, on Sept. 23. One hundred and seventy-five labor organizations were represented by 409 delegates. See *The George-Hewitt Campaign*, p. 12.

7. Chickering Hall was then at Fifth Avenue and Eighteenth Street.

8. Oct. 2, 1886. See *The George-Hewitt Campaign*, p. 16, and Henry George, Jr., *op. cit.*, p. 465.

9. *The Standard* (New York), Vol. I, No. 1, Jan. 8, 1887, p. 1. For wider study of the McGlynn affair see *The Standard*, Vol. I, HGC; Henry George, Jr., *op. cit.* (see index); and *Rebel, Priest and Prophet*.

10. Told to the writer by her mother.

11. On Oct. 5, 1886.

12. *The George-Hewitt Campaign*, p. 19.

13. *Ibid.*, p. 22.

14. *Ibid.*, pp. 25-29.

15. *Ibid.*, p. 34.

16. *Ibid.*, p. 41.

17. Brooklyn, Oct. 28, 1883, HGC.

18. From 120 Ave. des Champs Elysees, Paris, Nov. 17, 1884, quoted by Poultney Bigelow in *Seventy Summers*.

19. From 16 Astor Place, New York, Oct. 19, 1886, HGC.

20. *The George-Hewitt Campaign*, pp. 41-42.

21. *The Standard*, Vol. II, No. 15, Oct. 15, 1887.

22. From Rome, July 20, 1890; in the private collection of the writer.

23. *The George-Hewitt Campaign*, p. 129.

24. *Ibid.*, p. 133.

25. *Ibid.*, p. 154.

26. Oct. 31, 1886.

27. Gustavus Myers, *History of Great American Fortunes* (1910) (New York: The Modern Library, Inc., 1946), p. 358.

28. Charles Edward Russell, *Bare Hands and Stone Walls* (New York: Charles Scribners Sons, 1933), p. 47.

29. Henry George, Jr., *op. cit.*, p. 482.
30. Nov. 6, 1886.
31. Nov. 4, 1886.
32. Quoted in the *New York Herald,* Nov. 6, 1886.
33. Nov. 3, 1886.
34. *The George-Hewitt Campaign,* pp. 169-70. Quoted in part by Henry George, Jr., *op. cit.,* p. 481.

CHAPTER XXII

1. Catherine Booth, 4 Rookwood Road, Stamford Hill, London, Jan. 2, 1887, HGC.
2. Vol. I, No. 1, Jan. 8, 1887.
3. Dated Oct. 25, 1886.
4. *The George-Hewitt Campaign,* p. 135.
5. Nov. 21, 1886.
6. *The George-Hewitt Campaign,* p. 134.
7. *Ibid.,* p. 131.
8. Nov. 4, 1886.
9. Nov. 26, 1886.
10. Letter to Corrigan, Dec. 20, 1886. See *The Standard,* Vol. I, No. 4, Jan. 29, 1887. Also, Henry George, Jr., *op. cit.,* p. 486.
11. Dec. 7, 1886. See *The George-Hewitt Campaign,* p. 139.
12. *The Standard,* Vol. I, No. 1, Jan. 8, 1887.
13. *Ibid.*
14. *Ibid.,* Vol. I, No. 2, Jan. 15, 1887.
15. *Ibid.,* Vol. I, No. 14, April 9, 1887.
16. *Ibid.,* Vol. I, No. 3, Jan. 22, 1887, editorial.
17. Jan. 16, 1887.
18. Jan. 23, 1887. See *The Standard,* Vol. I, No. 1, Jan. 29, 1887.
19. *Ibid.,* Vol. I, No. 18, May 7, 1887.
20. *Ibid.,* Vol. I, No. 18, May 7, 1887, "The New Crusade."
21. Saturday night, June 18, 1887.
22. Aug. 21, 1887, at the Anti-Poverty Society.
23. *The Standard,* Vol. II, No. 8, Aug. 27, 1887.
24. On Jan. 12, 1887. See *The Standard,* May 28, 1887.
25. Henry F. Pringle, *Theodore Roosevelt—A Biography* (New York: Harcourt Brace and Co., 1931), p. 113.
26. As he designated Henry George in a letter to Brander Matthews written on Nov. 2, 1892, and quoted in Pringle, *op. cit.,* p. 112.
27. *Ibid.,* p. 116.

Chapter XXIII

1. Louis Post, *The Prophet of San Francisco* (New York: Vanguard, 1930), p. 113.

2. The meeting, held on Nov. 13, was reported in *The Standard*, Vol. II, No. 20, Nov. 19, 1887.

3. Henry David, *The History of the Haymarket Affair* (New York: Farrar and Rinehart, 1936), p. 206.

4. *Ibid.*, p. 194.

5. Sigmund Zeisler, "Reminiscences of the Anarchist Case," *The Illinois Law Review*, Vol. 21, No. 3 (November, 1926).

6. Sunday afternoon, Oct. 2.

7. Vol. II, No. 20, Nov. 19, 1887.

8. Vol. II, No. 14, Oct. 8, 1887.

9. Letter to von Gütschow quoted by Henry George, Jr., *op. cit.*, p. 501n.

10. *Loc. cit.*

11. David, *op. cit.*, p. 402.

12. Henry George, Jr., *op. cit.*, p. 502 n.

13. *The Standard*, Vol. III, No. 3, Feb. 18, 1888.

14. *Ibid.*, Vol. III, No. 7.

15. Written on *The Standard* notepaper, 12 Union Square, Oct. 22, 1888, to von Gütschow. In the writer's private collection.

16. From notes sent to the writer by Mrs. Crane in 1938. See *Land and Freedom*, Jan.-Feb., 1940.

17. *Loc. cit.*

18. Oct. 22, 1888, from 12 Union Square. In the private collection of the writer.

19. *Ibid.*

20. April 28, 1889. Printed in tract form by the Robert Schalkenbach Foundation, New York. The speech is still in demand.

21. From 27 Keppel Street, Russell Square, London, March 8, 1889, HGC.

22. July 2, 1889.

23. Baden-Baden, Oct. 19, 1888, HGC.

24. Here given as it appeared in *Land and Liberty* (London) in September, 1934 and again in January, 1946. This is a translation from the German translation from the original French, published in *Der Jahrbuch der Bodenreform*, Berlin, August, 1934.

25. An abridged edition, omitting Dove's quaint attack on "Papistry," is published by the Robert Schalkenbach Foundation, New York.

26. Vol. VI, No. 16, Oct. 19, 1889, p. 4. See Henry George, Jr., *op. cit.*, p. 521.

Chapter XXIV

1. The meetings were as follows: St. Louis, Jan. 25; Kansas City, Jan. 26; Denver, Jan. 27; Los Angeles, Feb. 1 and 2. See *The Standard*, Vol. VII, No. 5, Jan. 29, 1890.

2. Plankerton House, Milwaukee, April 7, 1887. (In the private collection of the writer.) See Henry George, Jr., *op. cit.*, p. 509 n.

3. Jan. 25, 1890, HGC. Henry George, Jr., *op. cit.*, p. 523.

4. Monday, Feb. 3, 1890.

5. In a letter to the writer, from San Francisco, dated May 14, 1927.

6. See *The Standard*, Vol. VII, No. 9, Feb. 26, 1890. Afterwards published under the title, "Justice the Object, Taxation the Means," in the Memorial Edition of George's writings, Vol. XI (New York: Doubleday and McClure, 1901), now kept in print by the Robert Schalkenbach Foundation, New York, and the Henry George Foundation, London, in a pamphlet edition.

7. San Francisco, Feb. 7, 1890, HGC.

8. Elting E. Morison, *Admiral Sims and the Modern American Navy* (Boston: Houghton, Mifflin & Co., 1942), p. 28.

9. Vol. VII, No. 17, April 23, 1890. Quoted in part by Henry George, Jr., *op. cit.*, p. 528.

10. *The Standard*, Vol. VII, No. 17, April 23, 1890.

11. *Ibid.*

12. *The Standard*, Vol. VII, No. 18, April 30, 1890.

13. *The Standard*, Vol. VII, No. 19, May 7, 1890.

14. Frank Cotton in the Australian *Standard*. See Henry George, Jr., *op. cit.*, p. 532.

15. Philadelphia, Nov. 24, 1868. In the private collection of the writer.

16. Henry George, Jr., *op. cit.*, p. 535.

17. *The Standard*, Vol. VII, No. 22, May 28, 1890.

18. *Ibid.*

19. *Ibid.*

20. *The Standard*, Vol. VIII, No. 5, July 30, 1890. Cf. Henry George, Jr., *op. cit.*, p. 537.

21. Henry George, Jr., *op. cit.*, p. 537.

22. Undated quotation in *The Standard*, Vol. VII, No. 26, June 25, 1890.

23. *Loc. cit.*

Chapter XXV

1. Son of Simon Mendelson and brother-in-law of August Lewis and himself a devoted follower of Henry George.
2. Letter to his wife in the private collection of the writer.
3. *Arabian Nights* by Alfred Tennyson.
4. Bidwell's on 59th St. at Eighth Ave.
5. March 22, 1892. In the private collection of the writer.
6. Diary, December, 1883.
7. By Eben M. Flagg, D.D.S.
8. See Henry George, Jr., *op. cit.*, pp. 509-11, for fuller account.
9. 207 Sansome St., San Francisco, April 14, 1891.
10. *Hardly a Man Is Now Alive* (New York: Doubleday, Doran & Co., 1939).
11. *Ibid.*, p. 550.
12. *The Standard.*
13. July, 1892, Pompton, N.J. Original in possession of his son, William C. de Mille.
14. Letter to Henry George, Jr., on April 7, 1898. See *op. cit.*, p. 305. Original in HGC, Box IX.

Chapter XXVI

1. *Masterman Ready*, by Captain Marryat.
2. St. James Hotel, April 2, 1887.
3. From S.S. *Alaska*, Jan. 25, 1885, HGC.
4. Jan. 29, 1885.
5. Henry George, Jr., *op. cit.*, p. 527.
6. "Blow the Wind Wester" from *Pulling the Capstan Chanties*, collected by Cecil B. Sharp.
7. Quoted by Henry George, Jr., *op. cit.*, p. 545. (The writer has been unsuccessful in tracing the original chanty.)
8. Carney, black-haired, blue-eyed young Irish girl who worked for the Georges for a number of years until she left to get married. She gave some of the herein quoted reminiscences to the writer in 1929.

Chapter XXVII

1. *The Standard*, Vol. VII, No. 18, April 30, 1890, cf. Henry George, Jr., *op. cit.*, p. 530.
2. March 7, 1888, HGC. See Henry George, Jr., *op. cit.*, p. 507.

3. *Ibid.*, p. 551.

4. Told to the writer by Dr. Walter Mendelson.

5. Also, Dr. Mendelson.

6. Henry George, Jr., *op. cit.*, p. 325.

7. Prof. Franklin A. Baker, later head of English Department, Teacher's College, Columbia University; then teacher at Horace Mann School, 9 University Place, New York City.

8. *Social Problems*, p. 278.

9. Sept. 24, 1881, HGC.

10. Robert Schalkenbach edition (New York, 1940), p. 554.

11. Told to the writer.

12. Tom L. Johnson, *My Story* (New York: B. W. Huebsch, 1911), p. 58.

13. Henry George, Jr., *op. cit.*, p. 443.

14. London, Nov. 18, 1884, HGC.

15. Henry George, Jr., *op. cit.*, p. 550.

16. Sept. 25, 1881, HGC. See Henry George, Jr., *op. cit.*, p. 549.

17. Oct. 9, 1881.

Chapter XXVIII

1. As told to the writer by Bolton Hall.

2. 327 East 19th St., New York, May 18, 1891. Original in Brotherton Library, England.

3. 327 East 19th St., New York, December 22, 1891, Brotherton Library.

4. *La Condizione du Lavoratori*, Translated by Ludovico Eusebio.

5. Unione Tipografico Editrice, Turine and Rome.

6. Sept. 3, 1891, HGC.

7. Aug. 21, 1891, Henry George, Jr., *op. cit.*, p. 567.

8. Oct. 31, 1891, HGC.

9. Nov. 3, 1891, HGC.

10. 327 E. 19th St., New York, Dec. 23, 1892, original in Brotherton Library.

11. *Ibid.*

12. Stephen Bell, *Rebel, Priest and Prophet*, p. 249.

13. Vol. VI, No. 21, Nov. 23, 1889.

14. Vol. XII, No. 29, Aug. 31, 1892.

Chapter XXIX

1. See Henry George, Jr., *op. cit.*, pp. 571-74, and Tom L. Johnson, *My Story,* pp. 68-70, and also *The Standard,* Vol. IX, April, 1892.
2. Nov. 12, 1894.
3. Cf., Henry George, Jr., *op. cit.*, p. 557. See *New York Journal,* Oct. 20, 1896, letter from Henry George quoting this speech.
4. See Henry George, Jr., *op. cit.*, p. 578.
5. To Richard McGhee, Feb. 13, 1894. See Henry George, Jr., *op. cit.*, p. 579.
6. *New York Herald,* Jan. 31, 1895.
7. Fort Hamilton, June 2, 1896. Letter to Frank Stephens.
8. Johnstown Flood, May 31, 1889.
9. See Henry George, Jr., *op. cit.*, p. 557, and Tom L. Johnson, *op. cit.*, p. 35.
10. Feb. 10, 1897, HGC.
11. November, 1896.
12. Letter in the private collection of the writer.
13. In the private collection of the writer.
14. Nov. 27, 1889. In the private collection of the writer.
15. Robert Schalkenbach edition, p. 276.

Chapter XXX

1. A bronze copy of this is in Denmark.
2. See Henry George, Jr., *op. cit.*, p. 586.
3. *Ibid.*, p. 587.
4. Fort Hamilton, May 5, 1897, HGC.
5. To W. D. Burbay, Sept. 9, 1897, HGC.
6. To Dr. Taylor, April 10, 1897, HGC.
7. June 18, 1897, HGC.
8. October, 1897, HGC.
9. October, 1897, HGC.

Chapter XXXI

1. Henry George, Jr., *op. cit.*, p. 607.
2. Recounted to the writer by Frank Stephens.

Chapter XXXII

1. *Progress and Poverty*, Conclusion, "The Problem of Individual Life," p. 555.

2. Saturday, Oct. 30, 1897.

3. Letter written from 38 Lexington Ave., New York, March 1, 1898, HGC.

4. Letter to Henry George, Jr., San Francisco, April 17, 1898, HGC.

INDEX